# The Weekend Homesteader

The Weekend I

# omesteader

*A Twelve-Month Guide to Self-Sufficiency*

## Anna Hess

Skyhorse Publishing

Skyhorse Publishing books may be purchased in bulk at special discounts for sales promotion, corporate gifts, fund-raising, or educational purposes. Special editions can also be created to specifications. For details, contact the Special Sales Department, Skyhorse Publishing, 307 West 36th Street, 11th Floor, New York, NY 10018 or info@skyhorsepublishing.com.

Skyhorse® and Skyhorse Publishing® are registered trademarks of Skyhorse Publishing, Inc.®, a Delaware corporation.

Visit our website at www.skyhorsepublishing.com.

10 9

Library of Congress Cataloging-in-Publication Data is available on file.

Print ISBN: 978-1-61608-882-8
Ebook ISBN: 978-1-62087-952-8

Printed in China

To Melissa, who helped make my homesteading dream a reality.

# Table of Contents

# Acknowledgments

This book—and our homestead—wouldn't exist without the help of dozens of friends, family members, and strangers. If I thanked everyone, the acknowledgments would be as long as the book, so don't think I've forgotten you if you don't see your name listed here.

My parents, Adrianne and Errol Hess, made it easy to steal their back-to-the-land dream and turn it into my own. More recently, Daddy talked me into accepting Skyhorse's kind offer to publish this book on paper, while Mom pored over every word to make the rough draft a little less rough. (Any remaining mistakes are entirely my own.)

My brother, Joey Hess, has provided technical support for my family for decades. He helped me build the blog that grew into this book, and he gave me a free website until I was able to pay my own way.

My sister, Maggie Hess, recorded our childhood so vividly in her poetry that I was able to stick to writing about plants. She kindly allowed me to reprint one of her poems in the rain barrel chapter.

Two friends gave me pro bono advice that was essential to publishing this book. Seth Johnson helped draft a contract that was in both my and Skyhorse's best interests, while Heather Weidner read the second draft and talked me into removing the preachy bits. Meanwhile, Jennifer McCartney at Skyhorse Publishing allayed my fears about print publication (and worked hard to craft a beautiful book).

My husband, Mark Hamilton, took many of the photos in this book, split an excessive amount of firewood so that I could write in front of flickering flames, and kept the farm running while I was engrossed in the manuscript. He reminds me every day that I live in paradise.

Every one of our blog readers had a hand in this book. They asked great questions, shared their experiences, and connected us to a larger homesteading community. Some contributed photos and advice that you'll see on these pages. But I have to thank two readers specifically: Everett Sizemore at www.livingasimplelife.com helped us reach a wider audience, and Darren Collins at www.green-change.com had the idea of a book for weekend homesteaders. I hope you'll join this community by visiting www.waldeneffect.org.

Finally, our farm has supported every step along our homesteading path, both literally and figuratively. Despite having been clear-cut by previous owners, she decided to take a chance on us. She has been bountiful and beautiful and has provided everything we need.

# Introduction

Do you dream of growing your own food, spending your days tending a flock of chickens and a big garden? Do you yearn for land, or perhaps for a homestead in the city? Are you concerned about how your family would make it if you were stuck without power for two weeks? Or perhaps you just want to live a bit more simply so you can spend less time at work and more time on pursuits you enjoy.

Maybe you've considered jumping on the homesteading bandwagon but don't know where to begin. You've got a full-time job and lots of commitments, so you don't have time to milk a cow, and you lack the cash to go off the grid. Is there a middle ground?

My husband and I have been homesteading since 2006, and we know how daunting the endeavor can be. We started out with the land but with very little capital, made every mistake imaginable, tore out our hair trying to balance time and money, and have finally reached an equilibrium where our projects (mostly) fit into the time and budget allotted to them. Along the way, we learned which homesteading projects are simple and cheap enough to recommend to anyone and which ones are better saved for later. Many of the easiest projects are great stepping-stones to true self-sufficiency, and those are the ones that made it into this book.

*Weekend Homesteader* is full of short projects that you can use to dip your toes into the vast ocean of homesteading without becoming overwhelmed. If you need to fit homesteading into a few hours each weekend and would like to have fun while doing it, these projects will be right up your alley. They cover the basics of growing your own food, eating the bounty, preparing for emergency power outages, and achieving financial independence. You won't be completely eliminating your reliance on the grocery store, but you will be plucking low-hanging (and delicious!) fruits out of your own garden by the time all 48 projects are complete.

The book begins in April because that's when the gardening bug strikes many of us, but you can work on most projects out of order and can start at any point in the year. You should feel free to skip projects that feel out of your league, and if you've been dabbling in homesteading for a while already, you might decide other exercises are too basic for your tastes. Remember, homesteading is all about finding the freedom to pursue your own passions, so I hope you'll consider the projects in this book a jumping-off point rather than the Gospel of Homesteading.

## What is homesteading?

"Homesteading" used to mean hacking a livelihood out of the wilderness, building a log cabin, and living off the sweat of your brow. Modern homesteading is a bit different.

Homesteaders now live in high rises and suburban neighborhoods as well as in areas where supplies have to be helicoptered in. Many homesteaders spend forty hours a week working at a desk job or are homemakers busy ferrying their kids from music lessons to soccer practice.

To folks over the age of fifty, I usually describe homesteading this way: "Remember the back-to-the-land movement of the sixties and seventies? Homesteading is the same thing . . . without the drugs and free love."

Modern homesteaders want to provide their families with a better life than they could afford if they had to pay cash for the trappings. They're willing to start where they are and use sweat equity to grow nutritious, delicious food, create sustainable heat from locally grown wood, and use free organic matter to rebuild the soil. Most of all, homesteaders want to be healthy, happy, and cheerfully self-sufficient.

# APRIL
*(October Down Under)*

# Find room to homestead

**GOAL**: Seek out growing space even if you don't own any land
**COST**: $0
**TIME**: 1 hour to 2 hours
**DIFFICULTY**: Medium
**KID-FRIENDLY**: Maybe

If you're lucky enough to own or rent a substantial acreage in the country, this exercise isn't for you. Your problems will probably consist of reining in your enthusiasm so that your homestead doesn't sprawl out over the entire back forty and drive you nuts. But many modern homesteaders have a very different dilemma—they live in the city and don't have any land to call their own. Luckily, opportunities abound for growing your own food even if you live in a high-rise or ritzy suburban neighborhood.

## Lawns

Suburbanites have one easy growing space close at hand—the lawn. Depending on whom you talk to, Americans care for somewhere between 14 million and 40 million acres of lawn. That's a twentieth to an eighth of an acre of potential garden for each man, woman, and child—plenty of space to grow all our own vegetables and a significant portion of our fruit and meat.

But what will the neighbors think if you turn your verdant lawn into a potato field? One option is to leave the street side impeccably manicured and stuff all your homesteading into the shielded backyard. Or you could build a stealth chicken tractor so cute that your neighbors can't find anything to complain about as the flock grazes (and fertilizes) your grass. (Check your zoning laws and stick to hens for best results.)

Edible landscapers consider it a challenge to grow tasty food in a beautiful fashion. Several fruits and vegetables are so aesthetically pleasing (and unusual) that most nosy neighbors won't even know you're raising food in your flower beds. In the annual garden, look for Mexican sour gherkins, Swiss chard with brilliantly multicolored stalks, scarlet runner beans, and okra with cheery, Rose-of-Sharon-like flowers. I see ornamental cabbages, sweet potatoes, sunflowers, and amaranth all the time, suggesting that if you choose a variety that is tasty as well as pretty, your garden can blend right in.

An even easier sell (but more costly to install) is a perennial planting with stunning fruits like hardy kiwis (originally brought to this country as ornamentals), blueberries (with their brilliant fall foliage), and peaches or cherries for spring blooms. In many upscale neighborhoods, edible landscapers will come and turn your lawn into a fruit paradise that pleases the eye just as much as it does the belly—for a fee, of course.

## Container gardens and house plants

Photo credit: Nellie Appleby, www.thepleasureofgardening.blogspot.com

Dwarf Meyer lemon trees are one of the most productive house plants around. Frank Hoyt Taylor's tree bore 100 fruits the year this photo was taken.

What about apartment dwellers who have no lawn? If you've got a sunny balcony or window, you can grow a considerable amount of food in pots. Those of you with very limited space should focus on herbs and perhaps a tomato, although I've known folks who potted a single sweet potato slip in the spring, watched the beautiful foliage trail down the side of their building all summer, and then enjoyed several pounds of tasty tubers for Thanksgiving.

Light is one of the most important characteristics determining whether your container garden will thrive or fail. If your growing space receives sun for only part of the day, stick to growing plants that produce edible leaves—herbs like thyme and chives, leafy greens, and lettuce are better choices than peppers and tomatoes.

Next, consider your soil. Container vegetables thrive in fluffy soil chock—full of organic matter, so start a worm bin if you don't want to spend an arm and a leg buying potting soil and fertilizer. Then you need to commit to feeding the plants at least once a month with a high nutrient amendment, like compost tea. Remember, container plants don't have the ability to reach deep into the earth looking for food and water, so you have to provide for all their needs.

## Urban homesteading

Although many of us envision large farms in the country, a growing number of people are homesteading right where they live. The urban homesteading movement brings chickens, goats, vegetable gardens, fruit trees, and much more into cities and towns.

If you're hemmed in by pavement, I recommend you check out *Urban Homesteading* by Rachel Kaplan with K. Ruby Blume. The book is full of stunning photos, personal experiences, and interviews with individuals and organizations walking the walk of self-sufficiency. You can read more on their website at urban-homesteading.org.

Even a small driveway can turn into a vibrant garden. *Urban Homesteading* gives tips on the best tools and tricks to use during pavement demolition.

Photo credit: Kitty Sharkey, www. havenscourthomestead.com

## Beyond your yard

If you've used up your handkerchief-sized lawn and one sunny window, it's time to look for more space in the local community. Many cities have community gardens where you can rent a plot of land and raise whatever you like, working beside friendly gardeners who are often willing to show you tricks of the trade. In the spring, these community gardens are often filled to the gills, but gardeners drop like flies in the summer heat, so you might be able to spread out into two or three plots for your fall planting.

Less affluent neighborhoods often have empty lots where condemned buildings have been torn down. If you talk to the owner, promising to keep the lot from growing up in a mass of brambles and weeds, he might let you turn the whole area into a garden.

An even better arrangement is to talk to neighbors just down the road about growing space that may be going to waste. Many elderly gardeners are unable to keep their large garden plot thriving—they'd probably be thrilled to share a bit of land with an enthusiastic new homesteader (especially one who leaves the occasional basket of carrots on their back porch).

Churches, schools, and other public facilities are great spots for expanding your homestead, since you'll likely serve as an ambassador for the idea of cheerful self-sufficiency. If you're civic-minded, you can include students in the project, teaching them to grow some of their own vittles. Maybe your church would be willing to sink some of the cash they use to buy canned goods for the needy into a garden that would feed the poor more wholesome, locally grown food?

Finally, don't get stuck on the notion of vegetable gardens as the only way to expand your homestead into the neighborhood. A friend of mine shares a clothesline with her neighbor—unless you're pinning up clothes for an extra large family, one clothesline can easily serve several households. You could collect food scraps from your neighbors to feed chickens or rabbits hidden away in your garage, or just to fill your compost bin. Think outside the box and you'll make friends while expanding your homestead.

## Rooftops

If you live in a high-rise with north-facing windows and no balcony, are you sunk? Nope—there's always the roof. Some intrepid gardeners are tending vegetable plots on top of skyscrapers, but I always get exhausted thinking of hauling all that compost up several flights of stairs. An easier way to bring your homestead to the roof is honeybees.

A seldom-visited rooftop in the city may well be the perfect location for a honeybee hive—yes, even better than a forty-acre farm. Most folks who garden in the city plant flowers and lots of them, and the pavement all around holds in the heat so the blooms continue for nearly every month of the year. City hives have been shown to produce even more high-quality honey than their country cousins, and it tastes just as good.

# Survey your site

**GOAL**: Figure out the assets and problems presented by your yard and
        community

**COST**: $0–$5

**TIME**: 2 hours to 5 hours

**DIFFICULTY**: Medium

**KID-FRIENDLY**: Maybe

What's the best spot in your yard to plant an apple tree or plan a chicken run? Is there free food going to waste in your neighborhood? This exercise walks you through mapping the important features of your yard and community so that your homestead will thrive.

## Map of your yard

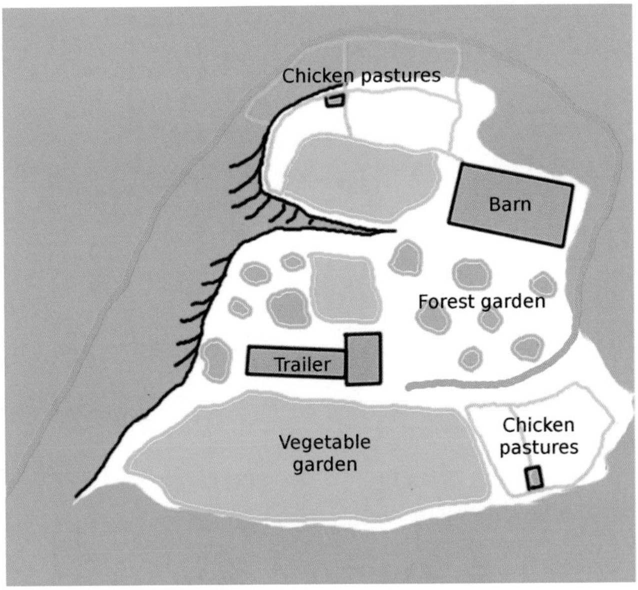

Mapping your yard allows you to keep track of current projects and to plan for the future. This diagram shows the core of my homestead, which is located on a small plateau surrounded by wooded hills.

Start out by drawing a map of your own habitat. If you live on a large parcel of land, make two maps—one that shows your whole property and then a close-up version that illustrates the most-used zones close to home. Mark the location of your house and the edges of your yard.

Add trees, shrubs, vines, your vegetable garden, the chicken coop, the doghouse, and anything else you see. If you have a septic field, include it on the map, along with any buried power, phone, or water lines. Sloped ground is important to designate, as are potential sources of water like creeks and ponds.

Some of you are probably tearing out your hair by now. "I can't draw!" you're telling me. "I failed art!" Please don't worry if you're not a prime draftsman—no one needs to see this map except you. If you're having trouble drawing to scale, you can pace off distances from your house to a tree, the length of your fence line, and so forth, then use a ruler to mark off approximate distances on your map. Graph paper makes this step easier since you can set a square to equal a foot, two feet, or ten feet and do away with the ruler. But I don't want you to think that this map has to be perfectly to scale and rendered like a blueprint—it's just a memory aid, so make it as sketchy as you like.

Once you have a somewhat accurate rendering of your yard, scan it into the computer and print out a few copies (or just photocopy the map). Put the original away somewhere safe so that you can make more copies if necessary, and move on to the next step.

## Sunlight

By combining Google SketchUp and Google Earth, you can estimate shade patterns at different times of the year. Molly Phemister at www.eatcology.com created these two images, showing early afternoon shade during the summer and winter solstices.

Every living thing is affected by the amount of sun and shade in its habitat, so you're going to devote an entire map to outlining the sunniest and shadiest spots in your yard. The first step is to mark north on your map and look for any obstructions to sunlight, like hills, trees, or buildings. Get up at dawn one morning this week and trace in the shadows when the sun is low, then repeat this endeavor in the evening just before the sun sets. If you're technologically inclined, consider using Google SketchUp to designate parts of your yard that are in full sun even during the shortest day of the year.

Next, think about areas that aren't shady now but will be soon. Draw the canopy spread your fruit trees will exhibit when fully grown (see December's"Plant a fruit tree" project for average sizes), and add on the shade line from the porch you plan to build.

You should now have a good idea of the sunniest and shadiest parts of your yard. Sun is good for your garden, your chicken coop in winter, your beehive, and your clothesline. Shade is perfect for relaxation during hot weather, for summer chicken habitats, and for planting northern species (like gooseberries) at the southern limit of their range.

## *Soil quality*

After sunlight, the most important factor influencing plant life is soil quality. An exercise in January will walk you through sending your soil off for scientific testing, but for now we're going to focus on what you can see with the naked eye.

Start with sogginess. During heavy rains, are there parts of the yard that puddle up or turn into a muddy mess? If so, mark these on your map. Even if you've never seen your yard after a rain, you can get an idea of swampy areas from the plants growing there. In mowed yards, sedges and rushes will often grow up in waterlogged spots. These plants look like grasses to the untrained observer but are easy to distinguish once you start paying attention. "Sedges have edges," meaning that their stems are triangular in cross-section rather than round (easy to tell by spinning a stem between your thumb and finger), and sedges also produce flowers and fruit that look different from grass seed heads. "Rushes are round," meaning that these plants have stems that are totally circular, a bit like grass but lacking any flat leaf blades. Rushes also tend to be darker green than other grasslike plants, while sedges tend to be more yellow green.

Next, look for soil fertility. Are there areas where grass struggles to grow and patches of bare ground show through? There's probably something wrong with the soil there (or it's just a high-traffic part of the yard, which is also good to know). Large expanses of broomsedge (a tall grass that turns red brown during dry weather) are indicators of poor soil, especially in fields that aren't mowed down into a lawn regularly. If you're living on the site of an old farm, you might also find very fertile areas where the family dumped their compost or where their outhouse once stood, often marked by lush stands of wild blackberries.

You can learn a lot about your soil by digging up a spadeful and peering inside. Earth full of worms is usually rich with organic matter.

If you want, you can go a step further and dig up a spadeful of soil from several spots in your yard. Is the soil all the same, or does the dirt look darker (more fertile) in some areas than in others? Is your earth hard to pierce with a shovel (a sign of clay), full of rocks, or sandy and easy to spade up? Are many worms present (a sign of highly organic matter)?

Each soil type provides prime conditions for some plants but will make others struggle. For example, we spent years trying to grow fruit trees in a waterlogged part of the yard before learning that we had to create mounds of raised soil before planting or the trees' roots would drown. On the other hand, this area would be a great spot to install a pond or plant cranberries. The best soil for your vegetable garden will be fertile, not too wet, and made up of a mixture of sand, clay, and organic matter. Meanwhile, a field of broomsedge might be a good location for a chicken run since these animals' high-fertility manure will naturally improve poor soil.

## Nodes and paths

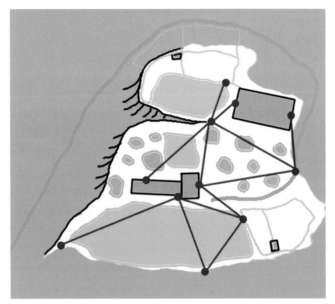

To create paths your dogs and kids will follow, design around nodes (designated by red circles on this map). Assuming there's no obstruction (like a tree) between nodes, most people and animals will follow the path of least resistance, even if that "natural path" (shown as a red line) tramples through your flowerbeds.

The next map you'll draw is a traffic diagram of your yard. We all like to believe that we start with a clean slate and can do anything we want to with our habitat, but the truth is that your dog is going to run from the house to the garage every time your spouse comes home from work, and the kids aren't going to follow that beautiful, winding path and will instead cut straight across your flower bed. It's easier to figure out where natural paths lie in advance and then work around them rather than spend your days yelling at Fido when he walks in the wrong spot.

Nodes are a good way of discovering natural paths. A node is any spot in your yard (or just outside the boundaries) that receives a lot of attention from any human or animal in your family. Every door is a natural node, and so is the spot where you park your car, the pond your dog likes to drink out of, and the tree your kids love to climb. Most of us are pretty linear, and if you draw straight lines between your yard's nodes, you've probably discovered the natural paths.

Your traffic map will give you an idea of where to create mulched or stone pathways to prevent mudholes during rainy days, and where to place gaps in raised beds so that your dog doesn't make his own hole right through your prize tomato plant. On the other hand, high-maintenance crops or herbs you use often should be planted close to a main thoroughfare so that they get attention and are cared for and harvested regularly.

## Map of your community

The final step in this weekend's exercise is to create a diagram of your community. The simplest way to start is to go to Google Maps and print out a map showing the area within a few miles of your house. Your community map will vary drastically depending on whether you live in a walkable urban area and spend most of your time within a mile or two of home or whether you live in a rural setting and have to drive twenty or thirty miles every time you head to the store.

You should tweak this map to focus on what's important to you, whether that's bagged autumn leaves to mulch your garden or discarded building supplies to turn into a shed out back. Mark down sources of free garden fertility, like the coffee shop that throws away its grounds, the mill with excess sawdust, or the stable with piles of manure. Neighborhood fruit trees are another natural fit for this map since many city dwellers have forgotten what to do with wormy apples and leave them to rot on the ground; if you know when the June apples two blocks over are ripe, it would be worth marking the event on your calendar so you can ask to harvest some found fruit. A community garden and the home of an elderly neighbor whose vegetable patch is starting to flag from lack of energy are worth noting if you have limited growing space—both could turn into supplemental garden plots for you. Consider areas you walk or drive to regularly—can you pick up out-of-date newspapers from a store on your way to work and turn them into worm-bin bedding?

You may also want to consider negative ways that your community might impact your homestead. Do you have a neighbor who's concerned with tidiness? If so, it might be a good idea to put your clothesline out of his sight. Does another neighbor spray herbicides along the property line? Best keep your vegetable garden a few feet back from the boundary so you don't end up eating poisons. Is there a polluting industrial facility within a few miles that will send windborne pollution in your direction? Perhaps a windbreak of bamboo or trees on that side of your property would capture the chemicals and keep them out of your yard.

## Weather

There's a reason farmers like to sit around and talk about the weather—temperature and precipitation have a huge effect on crops and livestock. It wouldn't hurt to get into the habit of paying attention to the weather on your homestead at the same time you're learning about its physical landscape.

I try to keep track of the amount of precipitation and of the maximum and minimum temperature every day, recording the information in a notebook or spreadsheet (or on my blog). I also note down the date of the first frost and the first killing freeze in the fall, along with the last frost in the spring.

The main piece of equipment you'll need to start your miniature weather station is a digital thermometer that keeps track of the maximum and minimum temperature. You can buy a rain gauge as well, or you can simply use a straight-sided bucket combined with a ruler to measure water depth.

Your records will be most useful during the growing season, when precipitation totals will help you decide whether to water your garden. In addition, you'll begin to learn how your homestead's microclimate differs from the local weather station that supplies your daily forecast. Our homestead sits on the north side of a hill, so we can count on spring freezes even if the forecast predicts a low of only 36°F, which helps me know when to pull out the row covers to protect strawberry flowers. After a few years on your farm, you'll know which direction the storms come from, will be able to locate an exposed spot that might someday house a windmill, and much more.

## What do I do with all these maps?

Hopefully, the simple act of making these maps has gotten your creative juices flowing. Maybe you're itching to put in an herb bed right outside the kitchen door or to approach that neighbor two houses down whose luscious peaches are attracting yellow jackets. Feel free to let the maps guide your interests.

On the other hand, even if you're sick of the project, don't throw your maps away. Rustle up a binder or folder and put the maps together in a safe spot so that you'll have them when it's time to find a spot for your beehive or currant bush. It never hurts to gather extra information when planning a homestead.

# Plan your summer garden

---

**GOAL**: Decide on the size, location, and layout of your summer garden and choose the vegetables to plant

**COST**: $0–$20

**TIME**: 1 hour

**DIFFICULTY**: Easy

**KID-FRIENDLY**: Maybe

---

This week's project is a simple thought experiment that can be completed in an hour with pen and paper and a short stroll around your yard.

## *Garden size*

The worst mistake most beginning gardeners make is to bite off more than they can chew. I've heard several reports of ambitious gardeners who put in a huge garden in May then lost the whole thing to weeds before they ate a single tomato. After five years growing most of our food, I've gained a healthy respect for the large amount of time it takes to weed the garden, harvest the produce, and process it for the winter, and yet I still tend to try to plant a bigger and bigger garden every May. I hope you'll do what I say, not what I do.

So how big is a realistic garden? If you are truly a weekend homesteader with only a couple of hours per week to throw at the vegetable garden, I recommend an initial planting area of no more than 144 square feet of growing area (excluding the aisles). If you lay out the garden in three-foot-wide beds (as I'll discuss below), that's a single row forty-eight feet long. A garden this size will keep you well occupied through the weekends of the growing season, so if you have other commitments, you might choose to halve that recommendation and start with an even smaller space. When in doubt, err on the side of caution—you can always expand next year.

Many of you may be curious about the size of my own garden. Using a tenth of an acre of growing space (4,356 square feet, not counting the aisles), my husband and I grow all our vegetables and an increasing amount of our fruit, along with staple crops that many folks don't bother with, like sweet potatoes, white potatoes, onions, and garlic. We preserve food throughout the summer so that we can eat our own vegetables all winter, and we give away about a fifth of our garden's produce. I'm telling you this because I want you to realize that your first little garden is a huge step in the right direction. If you felt confident enough to double your growing area annually, in just three years you'd be growing all the vegetables one person could eat!

## Garden location

Now that you've decided on the size of your first garden, it's time to select a spot. If you live in the city, you may have very little choice about the location (but see the April project "Find room to homestead" for great ideas on hunting down arable land in town). If you have options, it's a good idea to choose a spot that gets full sun, doesn't have standing water for long after rains, and has dark-colored soil.

Even more important than the quality of the growing space, though, is the proximity to your front door. I promise that you will eventually let that garden patch go to weeds if you plant it a quarter of a mile away at the end of your driveway, so locate your garden as close to home as possible so that you can enjoy its beauty and easily run out the front door to pick a tomato for your salad.

## Garden layout

Long beds divided by wide aisles make gardening easier. My permanent beds never get compacted by foot traffic, so they produce higher yields every year.

If you've gardened before, you might be used to tilling up a big plot of land and planting your vegetables in nice long rows. As you'll see in the next chapter, I'm going to tell you to let your rototiller rust, so I might as well go ahead and tell you to ditch the rows too.

Permanent beds and aisles have a lot of advantages for the backyard gardener. In most cases, permanent beds produce larger quantities of vegetables than row gardens do because the plants don't have to deal with compacted soil and because the gardener can concentrate her precious compost in the beds rather than wasting it in the aisles. You can often plant your vegetables closer together, too, which results in even higher yields.

What about size and shape of the beds? Most experts recommend making your permanent beds four feet wide so that you can reach the middle easily from both aisles. I'm on the short (and lazy) side, though, and have discovered that three-foot-wide beds work much better for me. These skinnier beds allow me to do many garden chores while sitting down, saving my back and increasing my enjoyment of time spent in the garden. I've also found that wide aisles—just as wide as the beds—make it easy to maneuver wheelbarrows and lawnmowers around and that long, straight beds are perfect for that purpose. If you're gardening in a very limited space, you should ignore my advice and maximize your growing area, but if you've got room to spread out, I think you'll be happier with the guidelines I've listed here.

## Record-keeping

Unless you have a stellar memory, gardening depends on keeping good notes. I recommend you start a map and spreadsheet (or notebook) to keep track of plantings at the same time you are laying out your new garden.

If you're building permanent beds, you can sketch your garden once, scan the drawing into your computer or make several photocopies, then never have to repeat the drafting work. Giving each garden bed

*(continued)*

# Record-keeping *(continued)*

a label makes it easy to refer quickly and easily to that location in your notes. I find it helpful to use a number and letter combo to distinguish a bed, so the first row of beds in my garden is labeled "A1," "A2," "A3," etc., the second row of beds is labeled "B1," "B2," "B3," and so forth.

A spreadsheet helps you keep track of where vegetables were located in years past.

| | Date | Variety planted | Seed source | Bed | Sub-bed | Notes |
|---|---|---|---|---|---|---|
| 49 | 3/16/2011 | Carrot, Nelson F1 | Johnny's | q-6 | north half | |
| 50 | 3/16/2011 | Carrot, Nelson F1 | Johnny's | q-5 | north half | |
| 51 | 3/16/2011 | Broccoli, Blue Wind F1 | Johnny's | q-4 | south half of bed, east | |
| 52 | 3/16/2011 | Cabbage, Tendersweet F1 | Johnny's | q-4 | south half of bed, north | |
| 53 | 3/17/2011 | Garbanzo, Black Karbouli Bush | saved from 2010 | p-4 | | only one car |
| 54 | 3/17/2011 | Pea, Mammoth Melting Sugar | saved from 2010 | q7 | | |
| 55 | 3/17/2011 | Pea, Sugar Snap | Johnny's | r1 | | |
| 56 | 3/17/2011 | Pea, Sugar Snap | Johnny's | r2 | | |
| 57 | 3/17/2011 | Pea, Sugar Snap | Johnny's | r2 | | |
| 58 | 3/22/2011 | Oats | feed store (2010) | CP2 | southeast third and slop | |
| 59 | 3/22/2011 | Field Peas, Maxum | Johnny's | CP2 | southwest third and a fe | |
| 60 | 3/22/2011 | Clover, Dutch White | Organic Growers ! | CP2 | slope and entrance | |
| 61 | 3/19/2011 | Clover, Crimson | feed store (2009) | CP1 | interplanted, also not su | |
| 62 | 3/22/2011 | Parsley, Plain | Ferry Morse (from | i-2 | | |
| 63 | 3/22/2011 | Radish, Oilseed | Johnny's | g-1 | | |
| 64 | 3/30/2011 | Potato, Yukon Gold | Southern States i | h0 | | |
| 65 | 3/30/2011 | Potato, Yukon Gold | Southern States i | h-1 | | |
| 66 | 4/1/2011 | Salad Blend | American Seed (V | CP3 | scattered seeds where | |
| 67 | 4/1/2011 | Mustard, Curly | Southern States ( | CP3 | scattered seeds where | |

Either way, I recommend coupling your garden map with a spreadsheet (or at least a notebook if you're technophobic). Every time I plant a bed, I note down the date, the vegetable variety, the seed source, and the bed number. In some cases, I'll also record the portion of the bed planted (if I'm combining more than one vegetable species or variety in the same bed), soil amendments I used, harvest information, and disease and insect problems. You *can* put all the same information in a notebook, but using a spreadsheet makes it much easier to search through your notes.

## *Simple vegetables and herbs*

Healthy gardens are full of beneficial insects, like this praying mantis climbing an okra pod.

Now for the really fun part—deciding what to grow! If the worst beginning gardener mistake is starting with a huge garden that completely overwhelms you, the second worst is trying to grow the trickiest plants and then throwing in the towel when they succumb to pests and diseases. Assuming that your only experience with growing things has been sprouting a sunflower seed in kindergarten, you should probably pick your first plantings from the following list of easy summer vegetables:

**Swiss chard—**This summer green is one of the most trouble-free plants in our garden. You can cook it just like spinach, but Swiss chard is much simpler to grow.

**Okra—**Okra may seem like an odd choice for your first garden, but if you live in the hot South, it is one of the easiest and most productive vegetables. The hardest part about growing okra is remembering to pick the fruits every day before they get woody, and then finding creative ways to put this nutritious vegetable on your plate. We've discovered that steaming the fruits whole (with the stem intact) prevents the sliminess that turns so many folks off okra.

**Summer squash (including zucchini)**—These squashes require space and can be somewhat problematic in the Southeast where they succumb to mildews and squash vine borers. However, if you have room and live in a hotter, drier climate, a zucchini or summer squash should have a spot in your first garden for its sheer productivity. It's inspiring to come in from the vegetable patch with an overflowing basket of vegetables . . . all from one vine.

French filet beans are picked when small, so you don't need to snap them and remove the strings. We swear by Masai, a variety that keeps plugging along from an early summer planting until the first frost.

**Green beans**—Like squash, green beans have some serious insect pests, but if the bugs don't hit your patch, you'll have a copious harvest just a few weeks after planting. Bush beans don't require trellising but will need to be planted each month after your frost-free date for a continual harvest.

**Tomatoes**—If you start with sets (seedling plants bought at the local feed store or farmer's market), tomatoes are pretty simple. Transplant the tomatoes deeper than they came in the pot, since submerged stems will grow extra roots and give your plants a better start. Tomatoes can succumb to blight if you have too much rain, so put them in the sunniest part of the garden and tie the plants up along a stake, pruning out excess growth. Actually, tomatoes are really a plant for intermediate gardeners, but they have to go on the year-one list because the taste difference between homegrown tomatoes and those blocks of wax you buy in the store is so extreme that even one fruit will make you catch the gardening bug.

**Mint**—Mint is the easiest herb you can grow, as long as you put it in a pot or sink a root barrier into the ground around your mint patch, so that the vigorous plants don't take over your whole garden. Unlike the rest of the plants listed here, mint is also a perennial in zones 3 through 11, so once you plant it, you'll have a mint patch for years.

**Basil**—Basil is one of the lowest maintenance plants in our garden—we clear away mulch, throw down the seeds, and then just snip fragrant leaves all summer. Despite that, I've heard that some folks encounter disease problems, so don't feel too bad if your patch bombs.

Although the vegetables and herbs listed above are the easiest, don't feel obliged to put in a big patch of okra if your family detests the taste. That said, I started out my gardening career as an extremely picky eater then discovered that nearly every vegetable I thought I hated tasted heavenly when picked at the peak of perfection from my own garden. Maybe it would be worth putting in a bed of those awful green beans and tasting them before giving up on the whole species?

## Vertical gardening

Photo credit: Brian Cooper

Brian began his trellises as a way of protecting his vegetables from squirrels. Now he produces beans, peas, watermelons, cucumbers, and Malabar spinach in a small space by growing them up instead of out.

*(continued)*

# Vertical gardening *(continued)*

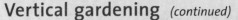

City gardeners with very limited growing area should consider getting creative with trellises. A trellis can be as simple as two lightweight metal fence posts holding up some plastic fencing material, or as complex as the beautiful wooden and metal trellises Brian Cooper designed for his suburban yard.

As an added bonus, trellises turn a plain vegetable garden into a multi-dimensional attraction. Combined with the edible ornamentals listed in the April project "Find room to homestead," vertical gardening might help you slip a stealth vegetable garden past your neighborhood association's radar.

Just be sure to take the height of trellised plants into account and locate vertical gardens on the north side of your growing space or on the south side if you're living in the southern hemisphere. Otherwise, trellises will act like trees and shade your low-growing vegetables, stunting their growth.

# Kill mulch

**GOAL**: Prepare a garden plot without tilling the soil
**COST**: $0–$100
**TIME**: 1 hour to 4 hours
**DIFFICULTY**: Medium
**KID-FRIENDLY**: Yes

Now for the fun part—getting your hands dirty preparing your garden ground! Even if you already have a big garden ready to plant, it's worth using this technique to make a new spot for a tree, bush, or herb patch just to learn the procedure. Once you know how to make kill mulches, you'll suddenly see a need for them everywhere.

## Why no-till?

If you've never grown a garden before, you're in luck—you don't have anything to unlearn. For the rest of us, it's time to revisit our deeply held belief that the only way to start the year's garden is to pull out the rototiller (or hire our neighbor to bring over his tractor) and till the earth. Tilling has three main goals:

- loosening the soil so that you can plant seeds
- killing any undesired plants
- working in compost

Unfortunately, tilling also causes problems like these:

**Erosion.** The loose soil that looks so delectable after the rototiller passes by is just waiting to blow or wash away. Erosion not only reduces your garden's fertility, it also causes problems downstream, like the 7,000-square-mile dead zone in the Gulf of Mexico.

**Death of beneficial soil microorganisms.** Bacteria and fungi in the soil help your plants grow, but they are primarily found in the top three inches. When you till the soil, you mix the layers together, and many of these useful microbes perish.

23

**Loss of organic matter.** Tilling incorporates large quantities of air into the soil and causes the remaining soil microorganisms to work double time. The job of many of these tiny critters is to break down organic matter into carbon dioxide and forms of nitrogen that plants can use. While your crops enjoy a quick burst of food, you lose the soil's long-term ability to hold water and micronutrients, and the carbon dioxide released into the air contributes to global warming.

**More weeds.** Although tilling does kill the weeds currently growing in your garden, it also moves new weed seeds to the surface where they quickly sprout and grow.

**Soil compaction.** One of the goals of tilling is to loosen up the soil, but if you can't wait until spring's rains have drained out of the ground, you'll end up compacting the ground instead. In the worst-case scenario, you can even create a layer of hardpan—a line of soil just below the reach of plow tines that is packed so thoroughly that roots and water can't penetrate it.

**Crusting.** On the other hand, if you till when the soil is too dry, you can pulverize the earth into tiny particles that form a crust on the surface after the first rain. This crust prevents subsequent water from percolating into the soil, and your seedlings die of thirst.

## Recommended reading

If you're interested in reading more about soil microorganisms and intensive gardens, I recommend the following books:

*Teaming with Microbes*, by Jeff Lowenfels and Wayne Lewis, turns what could be a boring treatise on soil biology into a text that feels like a fast-paced action novel, complete with stunning photos of the characters.

*Weedless Gardening*, by Lee Reich, gives a simple and informative description of how to manage a no–till backyard garden.

*Square Foot Gardening*, by Mel Bartholomew, suggests a method of maximizing your growing space.

## How to make a kill mulch

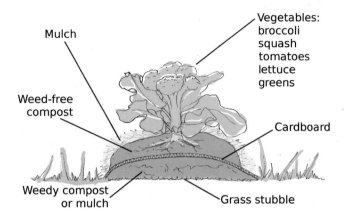

Mulch

Vegetables:
broccoli
squash
tomatoes
lettuce
greens

Weed-free
compost

Cardboard

A kill mulch creates
an instant garden
without tilling
the soil.

Weedy compost
or mulch

Grass stubble

Luckily, there is a way to prepare your garden for planting without risking any of these problems (and without swearing for hours over the rototiller as you try to get the infernal combustion engine started). No-till gardens use a thick layer of mulch on the soil surface to prevent weeds from sprouting. The extra organic matter promotes the growth of earthworms, who do the work of tilling your soil and moving compost throughout the growing zone without over-aerating and breaking down organic matter. Under a no-till system, your soil gets richer every year, and your sweat-to-tomato ratio gets lower and lower.

A kill mulch—also known as a lasagna garden or a sheet mulch—is the easy way to turn last year's vegetable plot or this year's lawn into a no-till garden. This is the no-till alternative to plowing up the ground when preparing a new garden patch: First, mow the current vegetation as close to the ground as possible, letting the plant matter lie where it falls. The goal is to make the ground flatter and easier to cover while also reducing the vibrancy of the current season's growth.

If you have any compost or mulch that contains weed seeds or living roots, you can lay it down next (although this layer is optional). The more biomass you can add to your new garden, the better, and anything put directly onto the ground at this stage won't send up weeds into your eventual garden. Spoiled hay and half-composted garden waste are two options.

Now lay down a thick coating of cardboard or newspaper—one layer of corrugated cardboard is usually sufficient, but you'll need to use at least a dozen newspaper pages to get the same effect and should double both of these thicknesses if you're reclaiming ground full of tough weeds. This is the "kill" part of the kill mulch, a layer designed to block light from reaching the weeds below, so that the plants die and rot in place. The easiest kill layer is created using large sheets of cardboard from refrigerators or other appliances, but even small boxes can be flattened out and work fine as long as you overlap the edges by at least four to six inches. Whatever you use, be sure to wet the kill layer down well, either by soaking the cardboard beforehand (I just leave mine out in the rain for a couple of weeks) or by turning on the sprinklers for a few hours before adding more organic matter.

The next layer in a lasagna garden is weed-free compost, which has gone through hot composting and, therefore, has no living seeds or roots. Your plants will keep their roots in this layer for the first month or so, until the cardboard or newspaper layer disintegrates, so be sure to add enough compost to keep your vegetables happy. One option is to plant only shallow-rooted vegetables that like high-fertility soil in your no-till garden for the first season. Good choices include the following:

- broccoli
- squash
- tomatoes
- lettuce
- greens (such as Swiss chard)

Alternatively, if you're doing these exercises out of order, a kill mulch laid down in late summer will be ready for any plants by next spring.

Finally, top the lasagna bed off with a layer of mulch. I'm assuming you're starting a vegetable garden, in which case nonwoody mulches like grass clippings and straw are your best bet, but wood chips and leaf mulches are appropriate around trees and shrubs.

The hardest part about no-till gardening is coming up with enough compost and mulch to put a kill mulch into practice—a task that is covered in later projects. For now, put on your thinking cap and see how much organic matter you can scrounge from your surrounding area. If you're going to spend money on anything homestead-related, it might be worth buying some high-quality compost to get you started. Try to purchase the best compost you can find, either from your municipality, a local horse or chicken farmer, or (in a pinch) a landscaping company. Good compost doesn't come in bags from a chain store.

# Compost pile kill mulch

Photo credit: Debbi McNeer

Finding enough compost to build a large kill mulch all at once can be a daunting undertaking. That's why Debbi McNeer turned her kill mulch project into a yearlong composting experience. After laying down cardboard, a thin layer of compost, and some straw, Debbi used the young kill mulch as a compost pile through the fall and winter months.

If creating a full kill mulch is too big a project for you, too, why not follow her lead? Start a small kill-mulch compost pile and look forward to a more vibrant garden next year.

# Hugelkultur

*Hugelkultur is a method of building rich raised beds out of rotting wood.*

*Hugelkultur* is a method pioneered by Sepp Holzer that involves creating raised beds out of rotting wood. The technique is especially appropriate for gardens with very poor soil where you don't mind waiting several years to see results.

The basic *hugelkultur* technique involves digging a hole, piling in rotting wood, then adding dirt and compost on top. This type of *hugelkultur* mound tends to be a bit high and dry the first couple of years, and the rotting wood will steal nitrogen from the soil if you don't add enough compost. Mediterranean crops like rosemary and basil will enjoy *hugelkultur* mounds their first year, and if you add plenty of compost, you can grow any vegetable you please.

I use a modified version of *hugelkultur* in the part of my orchard where past farmers allowed the topsoil to erode away, leaving waterlogged clay behind. I plant fruit trees on raised mounds of compost and soil, then, in later years, I create above-ground donuts of *hugelkultur* around each tree to expand the diameter of the raised bed. First, I lay down cardboard in a ring around the tree mound as if I was starting a kill mulch; then I layer the wood on top, toss on a bit of compost, and mulch well. By the time the fruit tree roots reach the *hugelkultur* mound, the wood has begun to break down and create fungal networks that trees love.

*(continued)*

## *Hugelkultur* (continued)

If you live in the city, waste wood may be hard to come by, but rural dwellers often have plenty of wood around them. Save the best for firewood, then set aside partially rotted logs, irregular branches, and even woody weed stems to create *hugelkultur* mounds. However you get your wood, try not to transport it more than ten miles so you don't risk expanding the range of invasive insects and diseases.

Your biggest problem with *hugelkultur* mounds will probably be small mammals. The same rich soil that feeds your plants also enhances populations of worms, grubs, and other invertebrates that moles and shrews love. I haven't had trouble with animals chewing on my plants, but I have found that my dog obsessively tears my *hugelkultur* mounds apart looking for furry snacks. You may need to lay down some sort of wire barrier to keep moles (and dogs) out.

# MAY
*(November Down Under)*

# Plant your summer garden

**GOAL**: Plant a small garden
**COST**: $0—$20
**TIME**: 1 hour to 5 hours
**DIFFICULTY**: Easy
**KID-FRIENDLY**: Yes

In April, you should have prepared the soil for your garden and decided what to plant, so now you just need to put those seeds and sets in the ground.

## When to plant

I can't tell you to plant on a certain day, because people living in different parts of the world have different climates and should plant at different times. The most important factor to consider for most of you will be your frost-free date—the calendar day after which you're unlikely to see any further weather below freezing until the fall.

In the United States, state extension agents[1] are a good source for accurate local information. These government offices often provide free classes, grants, and information about farming and home economics. At the least, they should be able to tell you your frost-free date, and those of you in the southernmost states (Texas or Florida, for example) will want to pick the extension agent's brain further since you won't be following the same spring/summer/fall planting schedule I present in this book.

Of the easy vegetables listed previously, you should plant the okra, zucchini, summer squash, green beans, tomatoes, and basil right after your frost-free date. Swiss chard can be started more than a month earlier, but there's no problem with direct-seeding it now, and mint can be planted at just about any time.

---

[1] Visit www.csrees.usda.gov/Extension/ to find an extension office near you.

## Succession planting

Many summer vegetables are planted once and then enjoyed until cold weather hits. However, some (like bush beans and sweet corn) do best for just a few weeks at a time, while yet other vegetables (like cucumbers and summer squash) may succumb to pests and diseases long before the summer is through. Succession planting allows you to enjoy short-lived crops throughout the summer rather than suffering from a glut for three weeks and then a famine for three months.

I plant new beds of succession crops biweekly starting two weeks before the frost-free date and ending in mid-to-late July. The earliest beds are a gamble—some years they escape the frost and give me the neighborhood's first sweet corn; other years my plants get nipped, and I'm out a few dollars worth of seeds. Very late plantings are also a risk since they may not have time to mature before the first fall frost. If you want to be scientific about the last day to plant a summer crop, take the days to maturity off the seed packet, add two weeks (since crops grow slower as days shorten in late summer), and count that many days back from your average first frost date in the fall.

In addition to providing a constant supply of food, succession planting can be used to make your garden match your busy schedule. For example, a school teacher who goes on vacation from mid-June to early August might plan all her cucumbers to ripen during that time period so she can pickle at her leisure. On the other hand, if you know you're going to be out of town for the entire month of September, don't plant any late beans that will just rot on the vine.

## *How to plant*

After all this preparation, planting itself is absurdly simple.

**Gently rake the mulch off the area you want to plant.** If you created a kill mulch following my instructions in a previous chapter, this step consists of raking off the top mulch layer to expose the weed-free compost. You may find it simplest to clear mulch off the entire bed and wait to replace it until your seedlings are up, or you might just push the mulch away from the rows you're currently planting. Either way, be sure that mulch can't blow on top of young seedlings and kill them.

Large seeds are planted in furrows created by dragging the corner of your hoe through the soil.

**Make a furrow in the soil of the proper depth.** Your seed packet will tell you how deep to plant your seeds, but a good rule of thumb is to put the seeds about the same depth into the soil as the diameter of the seed. Tiny seeds like those of lettuce can be scattered directly onto the soil surface, but bigger seeds like those of okra will do better a short distance underground. For very shallow furrows, lay down your hoe and gently press the handle into the soft ground to make an indentation. For slightly deeper furrows, pull the corner of your hoe's blade through the dirt to make a shallow trench.

**Place your seeds in the ground.** Again, follow the directions on the seed packet for spacing information (although you might decide to experiment with placing the plants a bit closer together in your fertile raised beds). Tomatoes and squash are so big that they take up the whole width of the bed, but you'll have room for two, three, or more rows of most crops. I tend to plant seeds precisely where I want them and fill in any gaps later with other crops rather than thinning, skipping a time-consuming and (if you're soft-hearted) emotionally difficult task.

Be sure to pack the earth down lightly with the flat side of the hoe after planting to remove air pockets.

**Fill the furrow with soil and tamp it in place.** I gently use the flat side of my hoe to compress the soil on top of the seeds.

The instructions above assume that you're starting your plants from seed, which is what I recommend for every one of the easy plants listed except for tomatoes and mint. You will see squash plants at the store when you go in to pick up your tomato sets, but resist the temptation— squashes grow so quickly from seed that you won't see much difference between seeds and sets except in your wallet. In later years, you can grow your own tomato sets, too, but for now it's worth a little extra cash to get a jump on the season.

## Maintaining the garden

Unlike many of the other exercises here, the summer garden is an ongoing affair. You'll need to weed around your new vegetables and herbs (tossing the weeds on a compost pile), add some water if they get dry, and pick the bounty. We'll cover many of these topics in later installments of this series, but keep your eye on the plants for now, making sure that they don't get overwhelmed by weeds.

# Nutrition

**GOAL**: Discover what types of food make your body healthy and happy
**COST**: $0
**TIME**: 1 hour to 10 hours
**DIFFICULTY**: Easy
**KID-FRIENDLY**: Maybe

Although nutrition can be complex, nearly everyone agrees that vegetables are good for you.

One of the over-arching themes of *Weekend Homesteader* is learning to cook simple but delicious foods using homegrown, in-season produce. But it's tough to know what to fix if you don't really understand the effects of food on your body. This exercise helps you unlearn what you thought you knew about nutrition and then guides you to help figure out what your body really craves.

## *What is good nutrition?*

Will pastured meat give you a heart attack or make your body thrive? Is soy a nutritious protein source, or is it linked to breast cancer and hypothyroidism? How about the cholesterol in eggs? Should grains and potatoes be the foundation of our diet, or do high-protein diets make us thinner? And which is better: vegetable oil or butter? For that matter, are fats necessary to our health, or are they dangerous foods to be avoided at all costs?

For a topic so integral to our quality of life, proper nutrition is surprisingly difficult to pin down. The U.S. Department of Agriculture's food pyramids (recently replaced by a food plate) have been criticized by many for being unduly affected by the interests of big agricultural companies. For example, the Harvard School of Public Health has published an alternative food plate which they argue "is based exclusively on the best available science and was not subjected to political and commercial pressures from food industry lobbyists." (You can read about Harvard's food plate at www.hsph.harvard.edu/nutritionsource. I find that the Weston Price Foundation's more controversial suggestions work better for my body—see www.westonaprice.org for more information.)

Meanwhile, nutritionists are beginning to realize that every tomato isn't created equal. In *Gardening for Maximum Nutrition*, Jerry Minnich reports that the nutritional value of fruits and vegetables sold in supermarkets in the United States declined by 10 to 20 percent between 1925 and 1971. The lower nutritional quality of modern food is probably due a combination of factors including variety selection, long periods of time between picking and eating, and a paucity of micronutrients in factory-farmed soil.

The nutrition content of animal products is also affected by how the livestock were raised. Various studies (including a well-publicized one by *Mother Earth News*) have shown that eggs from pastured chickens are much higher in healthy omega-3s and several vitamins than eggs from confined birds. Meat from pastured animals also seems to be much healthier than the grain-fed meat you're likely to find in the grocery store. These studies about the nutritional quality of fruits, vegetables, and meats suggest that dietary recommendations should differ depending on whether you're growing nutritionally dense foods or buying the watered-down versions in the supermarket.

If your head is spinning with nutritional questions, your first step for this week's project should be to clarify your understanding of proper nutrition. You might set up an appointment with a nutritionist, read a few books, or talk to your doctor. Try to steer clear of fad diets, and focus on the word *diet* in the traditional sense, coming up with a combination of foods that meet your body's nutritional needs while being tasty and easy to prepare.

## Cravings

Why do we want to eat foods that are bad for us? My informed but untested hypothesis is that every craving is a signal we're not eating something our body needs.

Take cravings for sweets as an example. Before supermarkets and restaurants, sweet foods were usually jam-packed with vitamins and minerals, so those grapes and apples were good for us as well as delicious. If we needed some vitamin C, what better way to prompt us to hunt down an orange than to crave sweets? I've got a definite sweet tooth but have noticed that if I eat a high-quality piece of fruit (not a supermarket strawberry that's been sitting on the shelf for a week), my cravings often disappear.

Unfortunately, we've outsmarted our bodies, producing food additives that taste sweet without providing any nutritional content. Studies have shown that people who eat artificial sweeteners tend to gain *more* weight, since the substances make them crave carbohydrates. One way to deal with this issue is to stick to eating real foods that our bodies understand—I've found that the less fake food I eat, the less I crave unhealthy foods. Author Michael Pollan suggests a corollary to this rule—don't eat anything if you can't pronounce all the ingredients.

Another way to reduce cravings is to maximize taste, consuming a small square of dark chocolate that boosts your serotonin levels (i.e., makes you happy) just as much as a larger square of higher sugar and lower cocoa milk chocolate would. I've enjoyed tweaking my favorite recipes to decrease the sugar content and increase the flavor, resulting in desserts that feel even more gourmet while also keeping my body healthier.

What do you crave? As part of this week's exercise, experiment with finding the causes and solutions to craving unhealthy foods.

## *Being in your body*

It's time to figure out how much of what you've discovered in your research actually works for your own body. People of different ages, ethnic backgrounds, genders, and activity levels are all going to have different optimal diets, so you have to figure it out for yourself.

I recommend spending at least a week noting down in a food journal everything you eat and how it makes you feel. Do you notice that when you stop eating a sandwich for lunch and change to tuna salad without the bun that you no longer struggle to keep your eyes open at 2 p.m.? Does your stomach feel slightly queasy or gassy after a certain meal, or does another meal make you vibrant and full of deep thoughts? Do you crave sweets if you're eating store-bought vegetables but not if you eat fresh produce from your own garden? For some of us, it's difficult to think past our taste buds, but being in touch with our bodies is a great first step toward proper nutrition.

# Mulch

**GOAL**: Mulch your garden for weed control and organic matter production
**COST**: $0–$100
**TIME**: 2 hours to 10 hours
**DIFFICULTY**: Medium
**KID-FRIENDLY**: Yes

Straw is a high quality mulch for the vegetable garden, but cheaper alternatives exist.

If you planted your vegetable garden at the beginning of May, you're probably starting to get sick of weeding by now. Luckily, there is an alternative that not only keeps the weeds down but also increases the quality of your soil over time—mulch.

## Pros and cons of mulching

Mulch replaces the hoe and rototiller in the no-till garden. By smothering the soil under a thick layer of organic matter, you block light to the soil surface, so few weeds germinate. In my own garden, I figure an hour spent mulching saves me about four to six hours of weeding over the course of the year.

Although weed control is the primary purpose of mulch, there's very little not to love about a layer of straw or other mulch on top of your garden soil. Mulch holds in moisture that would otherwise evaporate from the soil surface on a hot summer day, so your garden needs less irrigation. At the same time, when heavy rains fall, mulch helps those droplets percolate into the soil rather than run off (and carry your topsoil away with the excess water). Meanwhile, mulch slowly breaks down into compost, which will increase the organic matter levels of your soil, fertilize your plants lightly, and make your earth softer, better drained, and more capable of holding onto water.

Mulching the garden conserves water, controls weeds, and improves the quality of the soil.

In addition, there are biological benefits. Parched, bare soil in the summer sun can host very little life, but every time I peek under the mulch in my garden, I see worms, salamanders, and even toads. At the microscopic level, the effects of mulch are even more pronounced, since mulch is a paradise for the bacteria and fungi that team up with your plants to keep them healthy and well fed. However, I would be remiss if I didn't at least mention the pest animals that sometimes come along for the ride—snails, slugs, and burrowing critters like moles and voles. Personally, I've never had a problem with these mulch inhabitants, but if you're already fighting snails tooth and claw, mulch might not be a good fit for your garden.

The other problem with mulch is cost. In a later section, I'll suggest some options for finding free mulch, but the easiest way to get mulch is to buy it. Although the cost of mulch can add up quickly in a large garden, I think of that cash as an investment in my garden's fertility (and in my own health).

# Grow your own mulch

Mulch can be expensive to buy and heavy to move around, which is why smart gardeners choose to grow their own right where they need it. Cover crops are planted during fallow periods in the gardening year, then left in place to add organic matter and fertility to the soil. If you play your cards right, your cover crops can also work as a mulch that you didn't have to buy or spread.

Traditionally, cover crops are tilled into the soil as "green manure," so the no-till gardener will have to be a bit choosy and find cover crops that are easy to kill. Here in zone 6, I've found that autumn-seeded oats and oilseed radishes (planted between August 1 and mid-September) produce a lot of biomass, then die naturally during the winter. Oats create a light mulch, to which I add a bit of straw to keep the garden bed covered throughout the growing season. Oilseed radishes, on the other hand, tend to melt into the soil by planting time in the spring, so I consider them to be compost rather than mulch.

Winter is the most obvious time to add cover crops into your rotation, but I often have a couple of months of bare soil in the summer when spring crops have been harvested but winter crops have not yet been sown. Buckwheat is perfect for filling these gaps since it grows quickly, reaching maturity within about a month, then dies completely when mown down at the blooming stage. Buckwheat creates a mulch a bit lighter than oats, and most of the leaves and stems will melt into the soil within a month. You can take advantage of the short-term mulch by sprinkling the seeds of fall vegetables amid the buckwheat before cutting—the rotting buckwheat leaves will keep just enough moisture on the soil surface to allow your vegetable seeds to sprout, then will melt away before the organic matter gets in the way of young seedlings.

The best cover crops for your garden will depend on your climate, soil type, and garden conditions. For example, I'm building up poor soil, so I focus on crops that produce lots of organic matter. If your garden soil is already good and just needs annual doses of macronutrients, you may choose legumes instead, since these cover crops pull nitrogen out of the air and add it to the earth. The free publication *Managing Cover Crops Profitably* will give you a head start on choosing the best cover crops for your garden—download the ebook at www.sare.org/Learning-Center/Books/Managing-Cover-Crops-Profitably-3rd-Edition.

## C:N ratio

The most important factor to consider when looking at types of mulch is the carbon-to-nitrogen ratio (C:N), which is calculated as the pounds of carbon in the material divided by the pounds of nitrogen. For those of you who hate math, a ratio is just like a fraction turned on its side, so a higher C:N means that your mulch has a lot more carbon than nitrogen.

Nitrogen provides quick meals for plants and bacteria, while the energy in carbon can only be accessed slowly, often by fungi. Knowing the C:N ratio of a material helps you decide whether to use that organic matter as compost, mulch, or neither.

**The C:N ratio of humus, a stable form of organic matter, is 10:1.** Finished compost will usually have a C:N ratio of between 10:1 and 15:1.

**The C:N ratio of a well-built compost pile is 30:1.** At this ratio of carbon to nitrogen, microorganisms will thrive and quickly break down organic debris into humus. A C:N ratio of 30:1 is a bit too low for mulching, though, because this type of organic matter will melt into your soil and have to be reapplied in just a couple of weeks.

**Materials with a C:N ratio greater than 30:1 are most often used as mulch.** As you increase the proportion of carbon to nitrogen, microorganisms struggle to get a foothold. In fact, mixing materials with a high C:N ratio directly into the soil can result in starving plants, since microorganisms will pull nitrogen out of the earth to consume as they break down the high-carbon materials. Gardeners usually place materials with a high C:N ratio on top of the ground as mulch, relying on the limited surface area to prevent microorganisms from stealing excessive amounts of nitrogen from the growing zone. However, materials with an extremely high C:N ratio (like freshly chipped oak wood, with a C:N of around 500:1) are too high in carbon to use even as mulch.

## C:N and soil microorganisms

In addition to influencing how much nitrogen is in the soil and how long a mulch will last, the carbon-to-nitrogen ratio also has an impact on soil biology. In general, bacteria are good at breaking down organic matter with a relatively low C:N, while fungi are the only microorganisms that can handle woodier debris with a high C:N. That means you change your fungi-to-bacteria ratio at the same time you change your C:N, which will in turn impact the plants growing in your garden.

Woody plants enjoy woody mulches. In other words, trees, shrubs, and other perennials tend to team up well with fungi in the soil, so they thrive in mulches like rotted wood chips that promote the growth of these helpful microorganisms.

On the other hand, vegetables enjoy the quick nitrogen meals served up by bacteria. Carrots, lettuce, and crucifers (broccoli, kale, etc.) prefer strongly bacteria-dominated soils, while tomatoes, corn, and wheat like a more even mixture of bacteria and fungi. Either way, your garden plants aren't going to thrive under a woody mulch with a very high C:N ratio and would instead prefer a more nitrogenous mulch like straw or grass clippings.

## *Types of mulches*

Now that you understand the chemistry and biology of mulch, you can choose the right material for each part of your garden. Below, I'll run through the pros and cons of some of the most common garden mulches.

**Straw** is my favorite choice for the vegetable garden, if you can afford it. With a C:N of 50:1, straw hangs around long enough to mulch your garden for about half the year but still promotes bacterially dominated soil that your vegetables love. Other than cost, the only major downside of straw is that you can't use fresh straw around very small seedlings, because the large stems will blow on top of your crops and smother them. Short of growing your own grains, the best way to get straw is to find a local farmer who has straw bales as a waste product from his grain operation. Expect to pay $2 to $3 per bale if you time it just right and can pick the straw up out of the farmer's field, or $4 per bale if the farmer has already hauled the straw to his barn. At the feed store, straw runs about $5.50 per bale in our area.

Wood chips need to be aged before being used as mulch. Keeping the young wood chips in your chicken pasture expedites the process since the flock turns the chips and adds high nitrogen manure.

**Rotted wood chips** are my top choice for perennials but only if I produce the mulch myself. When I can flag them down, the people running the wood-chipping truck that deals with debris cleared off the power lines are willing to dump big truckloads of fresh wood chips in my yard for free. (Your local wood chippers are likely to be similarly helpful.) Fresh wood chips range in C:N from about 200:1 (for softwoods) to 600:1 (for hardwoods) and are too high in carbon to be applied directly to the soil. After two years of being ignored (or one year of being worked over by chickens), the chips are halfway decomposed, full of fungi, and ready to make my fruit trees very happy. That said, whenever I try to buy wood chip mulch from local landscaping companies, I'm very disappointed by the quality—store-bought wood chip mulch tends to lack biological activity.

**Municipal waste mulch** varies from place to place. Many cities collect grass clippings, autumn leaves, and other organic debris, grind it all up, and compost the organic matter down into a mulch. The quality of this mulch can vary dramatically depending on the city's operations and the type of waste going in, but the mulch is often very reasonably priced. Since you don't know exactly what you're getting, it will take some experience to decide whether this mulch is coarsely grained, woody, and appropriate for mulching your fruit trees or finely ground, well composted, and ready to go on the vegetable garden.

**Grass clippings** have a C:N of about 20:1 and make an excellent (though short-lived) mulch for the vegetable garden. If you have to mow your lawn anyway and use a chicken tractor to fertilize the soil, why not put a bagging attachment on the mower and use the clippings on the garden? Urban dwellers can pick up bags and bags of clippings during the summer on trash day but should be aware that clippings from someone else's lawn could have herbicides or pesticides on them. There are a few other problems with grass clippings as mulch, but you can work around them if you're prepared. First, it's best to use clippings fresh because if they sit around in a bag for a while, the grass turns slimy and develops a foul odor. You also need to pay attention and not put clippings on the garden once your grass starts to go to seed—that's a great way to defeat the purpose of mulching by introducing lots of weed seeds. Finally, grass has such a low C:N that it tends to melt into the soil in just a few weeks, so you'll need to reapply often to keep from seeing bare ground.

**Comfrey leaves** are similar to grass clippings in their effects on the soil, but this dynamic accumulator also carries a healthy dose of micronutrients. You can't buy comfrey leaves anywhere, but if you grow a few plants in an out-of-the-way location in the garden, you can cut the leaves every other week.

**Autumn tree leaves** have a C:N of around 50:1 (higher for oak, lower for maple), but the leaves tend to resist decomposition more than the C:N would suggest. As a result, uncomposted leaves promote fungi the same way more woody mulches do, making them a good choice around perennials. Like comfrey, many trees are dynamic accumulators, so you can add micronutrients to your soil by judiciously mixing the different types of tree leaves. Autumn leaves are often available for free, either when you rake them out from under your own trees or when you snag leaves off the curb in the city. However, leaves have a major downside—if not shredded, they tend to blow away. As a result, leaf mulch is best suited for the still air zones underneath established fruit trees.

**Compost** can be placed directly on the soil surface as a mulch (a process known as "top dressing"). In my experience, top-dressed compost tends to cake up and lose a lot of its goodness if left out in the sun, so I'd instead recommend laying down your compost and then putting some straw on top to keep the compost moist.

**Cardboard** is generally used as one layer in a kill mulch rather than as a garden's sole mulch, since it may blow away if not weighted down. Although corrugated cardboard looks very woody and hard to decompose, the glues that hold the layers together are high in nitrogen, so the combo has a C:N low enough to make it appropriate even for the vegetable garden. In my experience, cardboard covered with a layer of mulch or compost will break down in just a couple of months.

**Paper** can be used as a layer in a kill mulch just like cardboard or can be shredded and used as a primary mulch under woody plants. Without cardboard's glues, paper has a very high C:N (around 50:1 for newsprint and 130:1 for office paper), so it resists decomposition well but also ties up soil nitrogen. Steer clear of glossy and colored papers since the chemicals used in their production will harm your plants.

Other mulches that I haven't had personal experience with but which others recommend include peanut shells (35:1), pine needles (80:1, good around blueberries), sawdust (325:1 and should be composted before using even around trees), coffee grounds (20:1), spoiled hay (25:1 and potentially quite weedy), and seaweed (19:1). The best approach to mulching is to figure out which mulches are free or cheap in your local area, consider their C:N, and then try out each mulch in the appropriate part of your garden.

# Dynamic accumulators

Dynamic accumulators are plants that are able to suck up sparse nutrients out of the soil and concentrate those micronutrients in their leaves. Some dynamic accumulators—like comfrey—have deep roots that reach down into the subsoil, harvesting minerals that washed out of the top layers of the soil. Others are simply good at hanging onto the nutrients already present in the normal growing zone.

Gardeners can use dynamic accumulators as a source of mulch that boosts the micronutrient levels of the soil (and of the vegetables grown there). To use a dynamic accumulator as mulch, simply let the plant grow until just before it flowers; then cut the leaves to use on your garden. The table below lists some of the common dynamic accumulators you might already have around your homestead.

|  | Na | I | F | Si | S | N | Mg | Ca | K | P | Mn | Fe | Cu | Co |
|---|---|---|---|---|---|---|---|---|---|---|---|---|---|---|
| Alfalfa |  |  |  |  |  | x |  |  |  |  |  | x |  |  |
| Borage |  |  |  | x |  |  |  |  | x |  |  |  |  |  |
| Carrot leaves |  |  |  |  |  |  | x |  | x |  |  |  |  |  |
| Chamomile |  |  |  |  |  |  |  | x | x | x |  |  |  |  |
| Chickweed, common |  |  |  |  |  |  |  | x | x | x |  |  |  |  |
| Chicory |  |  |  |  |  |  |  | x | x |  |  |  |  |  |
| Chives | x |  |  |  |  |  |  |  | x |  |  |  |  |  |
| Clovers |  |  |  |  |  | x |  |  |  | x |  |  |  |  |
| Comfrey |  |  |  | x |  | x | x | x | x |  |  | x |  |  |
| Dandelions | x |  |  | x |  |  | x | x | x | x |  | x | x |  |
| Dock |  |  |  |  |  |  |  | x | x | x |  | x |  |  |
| Fennel | x |  |  |  | x |  |  |  | x |  |  |  |  |  |
| Garlic |  |  | x |  | x |  |  |  | x |  |  |  |  |  |
| Horsetails |  |  |  | x |  |  | x | x |  |  |  | x |  | x |
| Kelp | x | x |  |  |  | x | x | x |  |  |  | x |  |  |
| Lamb's quarter |  |  |  |  |  | x |  | x | x | x | x |  |  |  |
| Mullein, common |  |  |  | x |  |  | x |  | x |  |  | x |  |  |
| Mustards |  |  |  | x |  |  |  |  |  | x |  |  |  |  |

*(continued)*

# Dynamic accumulators *(continued)*

| | Na | I | F | Si | S | N | Mg | Ca | K | P | Mn | Fe | Cu | Co |
|---|---|---|---|---|---|---|---|---|---|---|---|---|---|---|
| Nettles, stinging | x | | | | x | x | | x | x | | | x | x | |
| Oats | | | | x | | | | | | | | | | |
| Parsley | | | | | | | x | x | x | | | x | | |
| Peppermint | | | | | | | x | | x | | | | | |
| Plantain | | | | x | x | | | x | x | | | x | x | |
| Purslane | | | | | | | | x | | x | | x | | |
| Sorrel | x | | | | | | | x | | x | | | | |
| Sow thistle | | | | | | | x | | x | | | | x | |
| Tansy | | | | | | | | | x | | | | | |
| Vetch | | | | x | | | | x | x | | | | x | x |
| Watercress | x | | x | | x | | x | x | x | x | | | x | |
| Yarrow | | | | x | | | | | x | x | | | x | |

*How to mulch*

A modified kill mulch is a quick way to deal with weedy garden beds that got out of hand.

Now it's finally time for the hands-on part of this weekend's project—mulching the garden. Assuming you've chosen the right mulch and hauled it home (or had it delivered), the first step is to weed your garden well. If you're in a hurry and your crops are at least six inches tall, you can take a shortcut by weeding just around the base of each plant and then laying damp cardboard over the other weeds before applying your mulch. Either way, you want to make sure that you won't have established weeds growing up through your mulch, and you do want to pay particular attention to removing roots of perennial weeds.

When you lay down mulch in the garden, there are a few things to think about. First, make sure the mulch is thick enough that weed seeds won't be able to germinate in the soil below. At the same time, you don't want to make the mulch so thick that it swallows up your crops—it might be necessary to lay down a thin mulch around seedlings and add to it as the vegetables become heftier. Another option is to use a finely ground mulch around small plants and then layer on straw later as the plants grow.

Very little maintenance is required to keep your mulch in shape. If you start to see weeds poking through your mulch, pull them out and then add another layer. On the other hand, if you notice that your vegetable leaves are yellowing, you probably used a mulch with too high a C:N and your crops are experiencing a nitrogen deficiency. In that case, add diluted urine, compost tea, or a layer of compost to get the plants back on track. (See the "Worm bin" chapter for more information on compost tea, and refer to the "Compost" chapter to learn how to collect and use urine.)

The last step is: Try not to feel lazy as your neighbors are frantically weeding their gardens over and over. A cardinal rule of homesteading is "work smart, not hard," and your well-mulched garden is a stellar example.

# Teamwork

**GOAL**: Find a person or group of people whose homesteading skills complement your own

**COST**: $0

**TIME**: A lot or a little

**DIFFICULTY**: Medium to difficult

**KID-FRIENDLY**: Maybe

Working as a team speeds up the task and makes it more fun.

Many of us are drawn to homesteading because of the illusion of complete self-sufficiency. But the truth is that none of us can do it all by ourselves, nor would we want to. This exercise helps you narrow down the skills you'd like to find in a homesteading partner and points you in the right direction to begin your search.

## How lack of teamwork almost felled the farm

I dreamed of buying a farm ever since my parents dragged me out of the country and into suburbia when I was eight. It took seventeen years to make that dream a reality, and a single winter to nearly snuff the flame of my desire.

My 58-acre farm was a tough nut to crack. A tumbling-down house stood half a mile from the road ... with a creek, swamp, and no driveway in between. I was determined to tear down the house with tools I could carry in by hand (and using no electricity), then build a new domicile by myself, all on a shoestring budget. Halfway through a winter of crow-barring interspersed with camping out in weather so cold my drinking water froze, my wrists became inflamed with carpal tunnel syndrome, and I knew I was physically unable to complete the task.

Luckily, my husband-to-be slipped into my life and taught me the value of teamwork. His strong back and ability to think outside the box complemented my book-learning and gardening skills, and we were soon happily homesteading with no problem too difficult to overcome. I even discovered that it was more fun working with a like-minded partner than doing it all myself.

I don't want you to think the moral of the story is, "You must find your true love before starting to homestead." A single person of either gender can make a homesteading dream a reality . . . as long as he or she has help. You might form a team with a spouse, a family member, a friend, or a whole community, but wherever you find it, teamwork is key to homestead longevity.

## Useful homesteading traits and skills

The successful homesteader (or homesteading team) is a jack-of-all-trades who can milk a cow, fix a broken lawn mower, and deal with the tedium of a full day of hand-weeding. Each person's homesteading dream looks a little different, but the traits below are extremely helpful on the average farm.

**Strength and stamina.** It's always best to work smart rather than hard, but sometimes there's no way around pushing that lawn mower through weeds over your head, carrying fifty-pound sacks of chicken feed half a mile down the driveway, or whacking logs into kindling with the force of a hand tool. While your gut reaction might be that you need a man in your life for strength (and, yes, I do let my husband do a good deal of the heavy lifting), the average man and woman actually have complementary traits in this arena. Men tend to have the upper body strength that makes splitting wood a breeze, while the fit woman has the lower body strength to shovel for hours.

**Emotional stability.** Serenity may seem like an odd trait to list so near the top of the homesteading necessities, but let me tell you that when you've labored for weeks over your garden and then wake up to find the whole thing demolished by a herd of deer, a partner who can talk you down off the ledge is very helpful.

**Patience.** The homesteading life is full of joys . . . and endless repetitive tasks. There's a reason average Americans have replaced farm chores with modern conveniences like dishwashers and grocery stores, and if you don't have a modicum of patience, you might just join them. Having a friend help out with tedious tasks can also turn cutting up wormy apples into a party, even if neither of you counts patience among your strong suits.

**Common sense.** I'll be the first to admit that during our first year on the farm, we came home with two halfway-trained "working" mules despite having the tiniest pasture known to man and no way to bring our livestock hay except hauling it home on our backs. The homesteading lifestyle gives you a lot of opportunity to make truly stupid mistakes, so common sense is especially important.

**Ability to think outside the box.** Some weeks, it seems like we spend every working hour trying to figure out how to solve problems. Unless you have a lot of money to throw at homesteading, you'll need to be able to cobble solutions together out of thin air, turning those window screens you found by the side of the road into drying racks for sweet potatoes and constructing a chicken coop out of used pallets. My husband is a pro at cogitating for half an hour and then coming up with a solution I never would have considered—a perfect trait for a homesteader.

**Frugality.** A wise woman once told me that a farm is the biggest money drain you'll ever encounter. At the same time, homesteading requires hours of your undivided attention, so it's tough to combine the endeavor with a full-time job. The successful homesteader usually finds a way to keep her bills as low as possible so that she can sink her heart and soul into the farm.

**Rest.** I think that the number one reason that homesteaders give up and move to town is that they don't figure out how to rest. When you live on a farm, there are an endless array of chores and projects right at your fingertips, and it's tough to stop until you keel over from exhaustion. If my husband hadn't held firm by requiring weekends off and regular quitting times each day, I'm pretty sure I would have burnt out by now.

**Record-keeping.** The best farmers keep careful records of everything under the sun, from the varieties of tomatoes they planted this year to how many pounds of grain they bought for their chickens, along with a journal of their daily thoughts and projects. They map their gardens and orchards, measure the square footage of their pastures, and note down the date when insect infestations begin. It doesn't hurt to also be good at budgeting and using spreadsheets. If you don't remember what you did, how can you improve?

**Math.** You'd be surprised at how much relatively high-level math is involved in homesteading. As soon as you start building a shed, you'll be dredging up high school geometry. Algebra is always helpful, and it's great to be able to do arithmetic in your head.

**Building skills.** I wish I'd taken a shop class, because I've had to pick up basic tool use on the fly. Even if you aren't building your own home, you'll need to know carpentry, plumbing, and some electric wiring just to get by.

Picking Mexican sour gherkins is an excuse to hang out with family.

**Green thumb.** An understanding of the biology of plants is helpful, but what a gardener truly needs is that ephemeral trait commonly known as a "green thumb." I can look at a plant and know if it's happy or ailing, get a gut feeling for whether my garden needs water long before plants wilt, and rarely miss the optimal harvest date for my crops.

**Animal whispering.** Similar to the above, some people just have a knack for animals. They know when to stand their ground and get a thousand-pound cow moving in a new direction and when to run out of its way. They can round up a flock of twenty chickens scattered across their garden, and they never forget to check on the livestock regularly.

Chances are you can think of half a dozen other traits and aptitudes, but that should be enough to get you started.

## *Building a team*

Unless you're unbelievably talented, you won't be good at all the skills I've listed in the last section. Luckily, someone or multiple someones can round out your skill set to make up a perfect homesteading team.

Start the search process by listing your homesteading strengths and weaknesses. My primary failings are emotional instability, inability to think outside the box or to take breaks, and lack of shop knowledge. On the other hand, I'm a pro at record-keeping and growing things.

Now take a look at your immediate support network—your significant other, children, parents, close friends, and anyone else you see on a weekly or monthly basis. Do any of them share your homesteading dream and fill in the gaps in your ability level? The traits that still haven't been checked off your list mark a deficit that requires an additional team member.

There are many traditional and not-so-traditional ways to form a homesteading team. The classic approach (which I was surprised to fall into) is to locate a romantic match who also dreams of a self-sufficient life and whose weaknesses line up with your strengths. But who wants to wait until Prince Charming Farmer comes along to start homesteading? If you find someone you can work well with and who meshes with your homesteading dream, there's no reason you can't have a platonic homesteading partner instead.

Another route is to turn your whole community into an interrelated homesteading organism. You really don't have to grow all your own fruits and vegetables, raise a cow for milk, cut your firewood, and build your house all by your lonesome. One farmer might find that she's in love with the concept of dairy animals and has a barn and several pastures, so she trades her fresh milk for a neighbor's pastured eggs, another neighbor's organic apples, and a third neighbor's cord of sustainably grown firewood. If you didn't grow up in the region you eventually settle in, building a homesteading community can be tough, but by constantly being on the lookout for the right partners, you'll eventually get there.

The real trick to building the perfect homesteading team is to understand yourself well enough to know what traits you're looking for. If you can visualize the ideal partner, chances are he or she will walk into your life in short order.

## Team-building resources

If you're drawing a blank on potential teammates, why not use the power of the Internet?

**Meetup.com** is the most localized social networking site around. If you live close to a major metropolitan area, you'll have good luck finding like-minded souls through their website.

**Craigslist.com** is a better choice for those of us in rural areas. You'll have to post want ads rather than joining an existing community, but you'll also connect with a wider spectrum of people in your area.

**WWOOF.org** is an international organization that hooks up people interested in working on organic farms with folks who have farms and need helpers. But be cautious: since no money changes hands, our WWOOFers seemed to think it was okay to change their plans without notice at the last minute. However, you might have better luck.

And don't forget old-fashioned bulletin boards at your local church, library, grocery store, post office, or other gathering place.

# JUNE
## (December Down Under)

# Compost

**GOAL**: Build a compost pile
**COST**: $0–$50
**TIME**: 1 hour to 3 hours
**DIFFICULTY**: Medium
**KID-FRIENDLY**: Yes

Gardeners salivate over the rich humus in a mature compost pile.

Although most organic gardeners would consider this heresy, I have to admit that I barely compost. On the permaculture homestead, it's faster and easier to process succulent kitchen scraps by passing them through chickens or compost worms; then I use woody debris in *hugelkultur* mounds and kill mulches. I feed my garden with well-composted horse manure from a nearby stable, with chicken manure and worm compost, and with cover crops of oats, buckwheat, and oilseed radishes grown directly on the garden beds to be nourished.

That said, making compost is a skill that every gardener should have, and those of you with small urban homesteads will probably need to build a special bin to keep the neighbors happy. This week's exercise walks you through the science and art of making compost.

## What is permaculture?

Did you ever notice that plants and animals in natural ecosystems feed and maintain themselves with no help from pesky humans? Permaculture practitioners attempt to mimic these natural relationships to create healthy and self-sustaining farm ecosystems.

Joel Salatin's pasturing system is a good example. This Virginia farmer noticed that birds follow large grazing animals around, eating insects attracted to the grazers' manure. Salatin copied that natural system by combining chickens and cows to create a high-yielding pasture situation that keeps both species healthier.

The cows come through first, eating the tall grass they prefer and leaving behind cow pies that soon writhe with fly maggots. Good thing chickens live for bugs! After the cows are moved to the next paddock, poultry enjoy the young, juicy grass and grubs created by the cattle's passing. While they hunt down maggots, the chickens also break apart cow pies, helping the manure work into the soil rapidly and reducing pathogens (disease-causing organisms) that might otherwise infect cows the next time they graze the land.

Although you probably don't have room for a herd of cows and chickens, you can use permaculture on a small scale to produce higher yields than you could expect using traditional agriculture. We'll cover some of the techniques—such as using chicken tractors and creating forest gardens—in later chapters. Meanwhile, check out *Gaia's Garden* by Toby Hemenway for more information on homestead-scale permaculture.

## *Compost science*

Making compost is like baking a cake . . . but more forgiving. For the fastest, best compost, you'll want to mix just the right ingredients together, keep them moist but not wet, and turn the compost frequently so that the pile heats up inside. After a while, you'll start to get an eye (and nose) for spotting problems in the compost pile and will be able to whip up compost without a recipe. If you're new to the process, though, it's worth understanding all the "ingredients."

**Temperature.** If you want to make sure that all weed seeds and pathogens perish, you should raise the temperature of your compost pile to at least 104°F for five days, with the temperature reaching at least 131°F for five hours during that period. On the other hand, temperatures above 160°F kill off the microorganisms that make compost happen, so you don't want to overheat the pile. Well-built compost piles heat up naturally because microorganisms (bacteria and fungi) give off warmth as they decompose the plant materials in the pile. Many of the factors listed below make life more conducive for decomposing microorganisms, thus heating up the pile. You probably won't need to cool the pile down, but just in case your pile starts smoking, the easiest method is to pour on some water and then mix in high-carbon ingredients like autumn leaves.

**Browns and greens.** The previous chapter explained the concept of the C:N ratio, which most composters think of in simpler terms as browns and greens. Browns are high-carbon materials that are often brown, dry, and woody—autumn leaves, wood chips, sawdust, and shredded paper are some of the most common examples. Greens are moist and often colorful, including compostables such as grass clippings, fruit and vegetable scraps, coffee grounds, and manure. If you start with too many greens, your pile will lose nitrogen into the air and will smell like ammonia, while if you use too many browns, your pile will compost very slowly.

The compost calculator at www.klickitatcounty.org/solidwaste/fileshtml/organics/compostCalc.htm makes it easy to mix the right proportions of browns and greens. For example, if you were making a compost pile using shredded office paper and food waste, you'd want to mix up about four parts paper to one part food waste to achieve a C:N ratio of 31:1.

**Aim for a TOTAL C:N RATIO of 30.** (25-30 is good. 20-40 is OK.)

| Material | | CuFt | LbWet | %H2O | available %C | %N | available Lb C | Lb N | available C:N |
|---|---|---|---|---|---|---|---|---|---|
| Office Paper 129:1 | ⇕ | 4 | 44.44 | 20 | 25.76 | 0.2 | 9.16 | 0.07 | 128.82 |
| Food Waste 15:1 | ⇕ | 1 | 55.56 | 69 | 37.1 | 2.5 | 6.39 | 0.43 | 14.84 |
| None 0:1 | ⇕ | 0 | | | | | | | |
| None 0:1 | ⇕ | 0 | | | | | | | |
| | | | | | | TOTALS: | 15.55 | 0.5 | 31 |

For a total C:N Ratio of 31:1 mix
4 part(s) Office Paper
1 part(s) Food Waste

Your goal is to mix up browns and greens to create a pile with a combined C:N ratio of 30:1, which will work its way down to about 10:1 or 15:1 as the microorganisms in the compost pile breathe out carbon dioxide into the air.

**Particle size and shape.** Particle size affects how quickly the compostables decompose. In general, the smaller the chunks, the faster microorganisms can work, so you might choose to shred paper and put kitchen scraps through your food processor for fastest results. On the other hand, particle shape is just as important as size—if you're able to shred your compostables into such tiny pieces that they pack together and keep air and water out, they won't compost well. Flat sheets of paper also tend to mat together and rot very slowly.

**Aeration.** Composting microorganisms are a lot like people—they breathe in oxygen and exude carbon dioxide as a waste product. If your compost pile is cut off from the outside world (for example, if you put the compostables in a trash can with no aeration holes), the aerobic microorganisms will eventually smother and will be replaced by anaerobic microorganisms that can live in the absence of oxygen. Your goal is to prevent anaerobic microorganisms from taking over, since they smell bad and don't decompose your compost very well. The solution is simple—make sure your pile is open to the air and turn it regularly. You can turn a compost pile by hand with a pitchfork, or you can make a tumbler (see the next section), which will let you mix up the contents of your bin with a flick of your wrist.

**Moisture.** The same microorganisms that use up oxygen have a second requirement—moisture. Most of them live in a very thin film of water that coats all the materials being composted, and if there's too little water, they'll die. At the other extreme, excess water leaches nutrients out of your compost, slows down decomposition, and promotes anaerobic conditions by drowning the aerobic microorganisms. Perfect compost is made up of about 50 to 60 percent water and will feel like a wrung-out sponge if you squeeze a handful. In many climates, the greens and rainfall will provide just the right amount of water for composting action, but if you live in an arid climate, you might need to water your pile. At the other extreme, if your compost pile is too wet, you may need to cover it with a tarp to keep rain off or add more browns to sop up water.

**Turning.** If you want your compost pile to heat up, it needs to be large enough to hold in the microorganisms' heat—the minimum is a pile about three feet on each side. However, the center will always heat up faster than the outside layers, so you'll need to turn your compost at least once to ensure thorough composting. To turn a pile, use a pitchfork to peel off the outer layers and stack them to the side, forming what will be the center of the new pile. Then fork the center of the old pile on top of and around the less decomposed material to insulate it, forming a new pile. Turning isn't 100 percent necessary if you don't mind waiting a year or longer for complete compost action and if you're okay with a few weeds sprouting out of your compost when you apply it to the garden. On the other hand, turning is very useful since it improves aeration within the pile and breaks up large clumps that might shed water and resist decomposition, resulting in faster, better-quality compost.

**Store-bought additives.** You can buy various substances that are supposed to make your compost pile work faster and better, but in most cases they're unnecessary. Compost starters contain populations of beneficial microorganisms—these come in handy if you're composting out of reach of the soil in a new bin. After your first round of composting, throwing a shovelful of finished compost in with raw materials will have the same effect, and if your compost materials touch the ground, microorganisms will naturally colonize the pile. Other composters buy mixtures of minerals to add to their pile, but unless your soil test tells you otherwise, it's best not to add random mixtures of minerals that may already have high concentrations in your soil.

## Inside the compost pile

A healthy compost pile is full of creepy-crawlies, from microscopic bacteria to centipedes big enough to scare the skittish homesteader. They're all working together to eat up organic matter and create high-quality humus.

The tiniest compost critters are bacteria, fungi, and actinomycetes. (Actinomycetes are the microorganisms that give leaf mold its distinctive odor.) You can't usually see them with your naked eye, but these tiny organisms are essential to the compost food web. They start out the composting process, breaking down compostables into their constituent chemicals, and they also act as food for larger organisms.

*(continued)*

## Inside the compost pile *(continued)*

Meanwhile, invertebrates like nematodes, mites, snails, slugs, earthworms, millipedes, sow bugs, and whiteworms are shredding the debris. Bacteria and other microorganisms are too small to reach inside chunks of organic matter, so left to their own devices, they'd slowly nibble around the outside like you eat an apple. After a millipede chews up leaves and excretes what it can't use, though, bacteria have much more surface area to work with—in essence, the shredders have turned that hard-to-eat apple into applesauce that slides right down the gullet.

The most visible organisms in the compost pile are predators that eat smaller inhabitants. For example, centipedes, ants, and beetles are busy hunting down worms, insects, and spiders, while also consuming easier-to-digest bits of compost. While you might think that centipedes are bad since they're eating the worms that shred your organic matter, a compost pile with lots of predators is healthy because it has plenty of smaller critters for those centipedes to feed on.

When we talk about organic matter "rotting," we're really looking forward to the effects of millions of organisms living, eating, reproducing, and dying amid our kitchen scraps. So give those bugs a break the next time you see them, and try to figure out if your creepy-crawly is a millipede or a centipede before running in terror.

## *Compost bins*

Now that you understand the science behind making quality compost, you're ready to think about the right bin for your yard. Factors to consider include whether you have neighbors who will complain if your bin is less than beautiful, whether you need to keep out dogs and rats, and how quickly you want your compost to mature.

At its simplest, a compost pile can be a heap of organic matter in the corner of your garden or chicken run. If you're in no hurry, you don't have to turn the pile or make sure that it has the right proportion of greens and browns—just wait and humus will eventually form.

It's easy to turn free pallets into a double compost bin.

For a tidier appearance and quicker compost, screw or wire together pallets to make a double compost bin. Once the first bin is full, use a pitchfork to move the compost into the second bin—this turns the materials and adds air. By the time you've filled the first bin back up with new materials, the older compost in the second bin should be ready to put on your garden.

The downside of open bins and piles is that they can be invaded by dogs and rodents. Unless you're composting on a large scale, you can deal with the pest problem by putting only plant materials in your compost pile, saving food scraps like meat and dairy for your chickens. However, piles also require a lot of effort to turn, so you tend to mix piles only once or twice, meaning they cook slowly. In contrast, compost tumblers generally keep out pest animals and create compost more quickly.

Brian Cooper's compost tumbler consists of a 55-gallon drum with a door cut in the side, some holes for ventilation, and a metal pipe threaded through the center to make the bin easy to turn. In addition to keeping out rodents and processing compost quite quickly, Brian's bin has the added bonus that he is able to capture liquid seeping out the holes to use as compost tea. However, Brian wishes he'd drilled holes larger than 3/8" for better ventilation, and he would have liked the door to be bigger.

Photo credit: Brian Cooper

In addition to DIY compost systems, you'll find several types of bins and tumblers for sale online and at local garden centers. Many of these store-bought bins don't work any better than (or even as well as) home-made options, but they may make your neighbors feel better about the rotting plant waste in your backyard. On the other hand, a bed of tall flowers encircling a homemade compost bin can be even prettier than a store-bought bin—use your imagination, and chances are you can keep everyone happy.

## Urine as fertilizer

Don't have enough greens to make a good compost pile? You're flushing the solution away .

Urine is a potent fertilizer—it would be labeled with an N-P-K of 11-1-2.5 if you bought it in the store. Due to the high nitrogen level of your pee, you can pour it on compost piles to expedite the process, especially if you've added too many browns.

I know that some of you are quickly turning the page to escape this gross topic, so let me hasten to reassure you. Unless you have a urinary tract or kidney infection (or live in a tropical climate), urine is nearly always sterile. That means you can use *fresh* urine around food plants with very few concerns about food-borne illnesses. On the compost pile, urine is very safe.

Once you start collecting your urine (I recommend a five-gallon bucket for women and a milk jug for men), you'll start to find dozens of uses for it around your homestead. I like to water urine down with about eight parts water to one part pee and use the high-nitrogen fertilizer to feed my hungry houseplants. (Just don't let the urine sit around before applying, or it will stink up your house.) I also pour urine on our young *hugelkultur* mounds over the winter to hasten the decay of logs and branches. In general, use undiluted urine only on dormant ground or on high-carbon mulches or compost piles.

The one problem you might run into is salt buildup in your soil. This will only be a problem if you live in an arid climate and use large quantities of urine in a small area. If you get regular rains and are spreading a small family's urine out over several hundred square feet, you should be fine.

## Using compost in your garden

Whether you simply toss a hodgepodge of organic matter in a pile or carefully monitor conditions in a tumbler, you'll eventually have compost ready to go on your garden. Your compost is ready when the organic matter has broken down into moist, dark humus that looks a lot like fluffy chocolate cake crumbs, with no discernible apple cores or weed stems.

In a no-till garden, adding compost is as simple as raking back the mulch and spreading the humus across the soil surface. Be sure to add mulch on top of the new layer of compost to protect the high-quality organic matter from drying out in the sun. Worms will work the compost into lower layers of the soil, and soon your whole garden's earth will be darker and richer.

I like to add half an inch to an inch of compost before every crop (giving more compost to heavy feeders like squash and corn and less to plants like lettuce that only have to make leaves). If you keep your garden productive, you may put in two, three, or four crops each year in the same spot—lettuce gives way to bush beans, which are replaced by fall broccoli, for example. In that case, your garden may receive two or three inches of compost through the course of the year, ensuring that your vegetables have plenty of nitrogen and other nutrients to help them grow.

Adding compost to your garden does more than simply feed this year's crops, though. The organic matter promotes the growth of microorganisms, which hunt through the soil for minerals that might otherwise be deficient in your fruits and vegetables. And the humus itself acts as a sponge, sucking up water when it rains and then releasing the liquid slowly during subsequent dry spells. Over time, an organic garden fed with high-quality compost will require less care every year.

# Worm bin

**GOAL**: Build an under-the-sink worm bin
**COST**: $35 to $100
**TIME**: 1 hour to 2 hours
**DIFFICULTY**: Medium
**KID-FRIENDLY**: Yes

Animals are a large part of many folks' homesteading dreams, and we were no exception. During our first year on the farm, we fell for a team of mules despite having minimal pasture and no equine experience, and soon we were lugging bales of hay down our long, vehicle-impassible driveway to our "working team." When a drought struck and hay prices skyrocketed, we spent hours calling every feed store in the region, trying to track down scarce bales of hay. We sold our mules at the end of that nerve-racking summer and were so glad to see them go to a good home that we almost gave them away.

The moral of the story is: It's far too easy to turn your farm into a menagerie of animals that don't pull their weight but that do require an overwhelming amount of your time and financial resources. My advice? Start small! Worms are the easiest livestock you'll ever raise, they definitely do more work for the farm than you do for them, and you won't have to worry about leaving town for a week and ignoring your annelids. The worm bin in this exercise can be made easily and cheaply, fits under the sink, keeps waste out of the landfill even for apartment dwellers, and the nutrients produced are perfect for keeping a high-demand houseplant like a dwarf lemon tree thriving. Finally, worms are just plain cute—even the kids or spouses who think your homesteading tendencies are nuts can often be won over by a handful of wrigglers.

# Why worms?

Worm bins use a different species of worm than you would dig up out of your garden. *Eisenia fetida* is usually found in piles of horse manure in the wild.

Before I get too carried away, I feel obliged to tell you that your worm bin isn't going to produce gobs of compost. I mentioned that an under-the-sink worm bin will churn out enough nutrients for a potted lemon tree, and that's about as much as you should expect—to feed four or five small house plants or one heavier feeder. You can also apply the composted food scraps (castings) and liquid (worm tea) to favorite vegetables in your outdoors garden, but you might want to stick to babying one prize tomato.

That said, what your worm bin output lacks in quantity, it makes up for in quality. Worm castings are pure organic matter and seem to be higher in available micronutrients than any other compost, a fact that will make the resulting food you grow taste better. Castings are also a prime habitat for microorganisms, which work with your plants' roots to suck up far-flung nutrients and which also fight off diseases that might otherwise harm your crops. The castings are made up of a high percentage of humus, which is stable organic matter that resists breaking down and acts as a long-term amendment, keeping your soil more aerated during wet periods while at the same time allowing the ground to hold onto more water during droughts. With all these benefits over regular compost, you won't be surprised to learn that even adding miniscule amounts of castings to regular soil makes seedlings germinate more effectively and adult plants grow much better.

# Gathering your supplies

To build a small worm bin, you'll need the following tools and supplies:

- **Drill with 1/4 inch bit**
- **Scissors**
- **Ruler**
- **Marker**
- **2 plastic storage bins.** Eight- to ten-gallon storage bins can often be found on sale at the big-box stores for around $5 apiece. Make sure both of your bins are the same size so that they fit inside each other.
- **A sheet of cardboard** large enough to cover the top of one bin.
- **Bedding.** The best bedding for worms is machine-shredded newspaper. (Be sure to use a shredder that creates strips, not a cross-shredder that cuts the paper into smaller pieces.) Hand-shredded paper, torn-up cardboard boxes and egg cartons, autumn leaves, straw, coconut coir, and peat moss will also work, but each has failings. The first five alternatives tend to mat down in the bin, while coconut coir and peat moss have to be purchased and aren't sustainable products in most parts of the world.
- **Worms.** The worms you use in your compost bin aren't the same ones you see in your vegetable garden. Compost worms, also known as red wrigglers, redworms, or *Eisenia fetida*, are a communal species that enjoy living in close proximity to each other inside masses of decomposing food waste. If you're lucky, you might be able to gather compost worms from the wild by looking in piles of horse manure, but more likely you will need to buy your worms. Vermicomposters.com is an online community of compost worm enthusiasts who may help you get started, or you can just google "compost worms" to find one of the many businesses selling worms on the Internet. Either way, your bin will require two pounds of worms to reach full capacity (costing approximately $50), but you can also start with one pound and let the worms grow to fill the space. If you start with fewer worms, you'll need to feed fewer kitchen scraps for a few weeks until the bin is well colonized.
- **Soil.** Your worms need a small handful of soil added to their bin to help them grind up their food. No need to buy this—just go outside with a trowel and dig some up.

## Making the bin

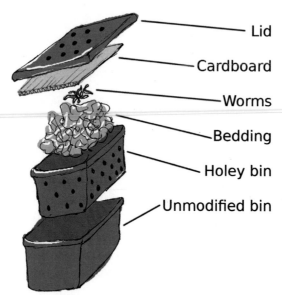

Lid

Cardboard

Worms

Bedding

Holey bin

Unmodified bin

You can make an under-the-sink worm bin out of a couple of plastic storage bins, shredded paper, and a sheet of cardboard.

Once you've gathered your supplies, it will probably only take an hour to throw your bin together. First, pour your worm bedding into the sink and let it soak in water for a few hours. You want the bedding to be well saturated since it will help your worms stay moist, but the bedding shouldn't be dripping water by the time it goes in the bin. When you're ready to start building the bin, pull the sink's plug and let the liquid seep away until the bedding is about the consistency of a wet sponge.

Meanwhile, get out your drill, scissors, marker, storage bins, and cardboard to make the worm bin. One of the storage bins will be used as a reservoir to capture worm tea and won't be modified in any way, but the other bin and one of the lids need regularly spaced holes drilled in the walls and bottom for drainage and aeration. You can measure and note the hole locations with your ruler and marker before drilling, or just have some fun and drill by eye. Either way, be sure to put about ten holes in the lid and eight to ten holes in each wall of the bin. The bottom of the bin should have about twenty holes in it. Your holes will be big enough for a worm to crawl through, but don't worry—if you make your worms happy, they won't want to leave.

Slip the holey bin into the unmodified bin. The unmodified bin will act like the saucer under a potted plant, protecting your floor. Now fill the holey bin with your moist bedding and mix in the handful of soil. Use your scissors to cut a piece of cardboard just large enough to fit inside the bin. The cardboard will sit flush with the top of your bedding to keep the worms moist and dark.

Take the cardboard back off and pour your worms (and any bedding they came with) into the bin. You don't need to mix them in—the worms will quickly migrate away from the light and into the bedding itself. Put the cardboard back on and add the plastic lid to the top of the bin. Your worm bin is complete!

## Caring for your worms

A healthy worm bin quickly converts food scraps into high-quality compost.

Give your worms a couple of days to settle in before you begin to feed them. After that, you can add food scraps daily, once a week, or on whatever schedule works for you, burying little caches of scraps in a different spot in the bin each time you feed the worms. Your worms will eat just about anything you can eat, but citrus peels are toxic in large quantities, and it's best to keep breads, meats, and oils out of your bin to prevent smells. You may need to add a fresh handful of moist bedding to the bin to cover up the scraps each time you put in food— the scraps should never be exposed on the bin surface.

The most common cause of worm bin failure is overfeeding—one pound of worms can handle half a pound of food scraps per day (which is equivalent to about a cup of liquid waste or two-thirds of an apple). If you bought two pounds of worms initially, you can add seven pounds of food scraps per week, but if you started with fewer worms, you should keep your feedings smaller until the worms have reproduced and colonized the whole bin. Rather than overfeeding the worms, why not start a compost pile outside to deal with any excess?

Your only other regular task is to keep the bedding moist in your bin. If you live in a hot, dry climate, you may need to water your bin at intervals; at the other extreme, if you add lots of wet food to the bin, you might end up with a bin that's sopping and needs dry bedding added. Either way, a clue to improper conditions is worms escaping into the lower bin. Finding a couple of worms per week down there is normal, but more than that is a sign that you need to tweak the conditions inside your worm condo.

Two other problems you may run into are stinky bins and fruit fly infestations. Fruit flies are nearly always a result of improperly feeding the worms—if you keep the food under bedding and don't provide too much, fruit flies won't find a spot to breed. Smelly bins can also result from not adding enough bedding, from adding too much food, or from keeping the bin too moist. In most cases, any worm bin problem can be solved by adding a fresh layer of bedding (moist or dry depending on the bin conditions) to the top of the bin and not feeding for a couple of weeks.

## *Harvesting tea and castings*

The dark compost tea that seeps out of the bottom of your worm bin is a top-notch fertilizer for plants.

In addition to caring for your worms, you will occasionally need to harvest castings and tea from your bin. Compost tea can be removed any time that liquid has built up in the lower bin. Just lift the holey bin out and pour the worm tea into a container; then apply it to your favorite plants. Worm tea acts like a quick boost of fertilizer while also providing a healthy dose of microorganisms than can perk up ailing plants.

When the contents of the holey bin start to look like compost, it's time to harvest the castings. For the highest-quality castings, make a second holey bin just like the one you built previously, fill the new bin with fresh bedding and a bit of food waste, and place it on top of the filled-up bin (with the cardboard and lid moved up to the top of the new bin). Worms will migrate into the new bin as they finish working the old bin, leaving you with nearly worm-free castings after a week or so.

There are a few simple rules to follow when applying castings to your garden.

**Worm castings should make up no more than 20 percent of your soil,** or your plants will suffer.

**Worm castings are best in the vegetable garden** rather than around trees, since they have a low fungi to bacteria ratio.

**Use your worm castings when they are fresh and damp.** If you allow your castings to dry out, be exposed to sunlight, or just wait around a few months before applying them to your garden, many of the positive benefits of worm castings disappear.

# Seasonings

**GOAL**: Expand your culinary horizons by trying out new spices and herbs
**COST**: $0 to $10
**TIME**: 1 hour to 2 hours
**DIFFICULTY**: Easy
**KID-FRIENDLY**: Yes

Turn your home-grown meals into gourmet feasts with easy to grow herbs.

Why do I think seasonings are important enough to serve as my second cooking lesson? Let me put it this way: Even the best of us get sick of cucumbers.

## Why seasonings are essential to homesteaders

In 2011, I finally figured out how to defeat the fungi that had kept our garden virtually cucumber-free for the previous four years. The trouble is, I overdid it. At first, my cucumber-loving spouse was thrilled by the spears of quartered baby cucumbers gracing his lunch and dinner plates, but after a month or two his interest began to wane. Neither of us likes pickles, and it just felt sinful to toss good food to the chickens, so I ended up eating the extra cucumbers for breakfast just to get them out of the house. Luckily, I realized I could perk up our jaded palates by dressing the cucumbers with balsamic vinegar and basil.

74

When you eat seasonally, your dinner plate represents one garden glut after another. We get sick of the same meal repeated endlessly, but I've discovered that I can take the same five vegetables, mix in slightly different seasonings, alter my cooking methods, and end up with half a dozen or more totally unique meals. My husband thinks I'm a genius, and I'm just glad he hasn't figured out yet that I've fed him broccoli for the last twenty meals in a row.

## Types of seasonings

Technically, there are several different kinds of seasonings.

**Herbs** are flavorings that come from the leaves of a plant. I'll discuss the herbs that you can easily grow in your garden in a later section.

**Spices** are seasonings made from a part of the plant other than the leaves. Many are tropical and are difficult or impossible to grow in the average U.S. garden, but you can produce chili peppers and fennel seeds at home.

**Black pepper** can't be grown in a nontropical climate, but this foreign spice is indispensable for most savory recipes, since a light sprinkle brings out hidden flavors; I recommend you give black pepper a try despite its exotic origins.

**Salt**—Since salt doesn't grow on a plant, it is neither an herb nor a spice. Like adding black pepper, lightly salting food enhances flavors.

**Onions and garlic** are technically vegetables, but both are generally used to season dishes rather than being served by themselves. Onions sweeten meals—especially when sautéed first until they become clear—as well as adding a distinctive onion flavor. Garlic provides a unique spiciness that is worth learning to love both for its ability to turn a single-vegetable-dish into a feast and for the bulb's healing properties.

**Vinegars**—Rather than pouring expensive (and often unhealthy) store-bought salad dressings on fresh vegetables, a bottle of balsamic or apple cider vinegar goes a long way toward enlivening salads. The former is sweeter and more subtle, the latter tarter and stronger.

# Starting with herbs you can grow

Celery requires a lot of TLC in the garden, but parsley is a plant-it-and-forget-it herb. As a result, I usually substitute parsley for celery in recipes like this delicious egg salad.

There are two ways of learning to cook with seasonings. You can try to figure out which herbs or spices flavor your favorite dishes, or you can experiment with herbs that can be grown easily in your garden. Although I think the best alternative is to combine both avenues of exploration, the self-sufficient homesteader could do worse than start this adventure by trying out the following easy-to-grow herbs:

**Basil**—Basil is frost-sensitive, but it is otherwise a very simple herb everywhere except in the Deep South where it may succumb to fusarium wilt. Start basil from seed soon after your frost-free date and keep picking the tops frequently so that the plants aren't able to bloom. Basil is indispensable in many tomato dishes, can be used to make pesto, and the leaves can be sliced up and layered atop fresh vegetables.

**Thyme**—This perennial is slow-growing, but some varieties are hardy down to zone 5, so once you plant thyme, you can keep harvesting indefinitely even through the winter. You can grow thyme from seed but will probably be better off buying a potted plant to get started. Thyme leaves go well with tomatoes and with most meats.

**Parsley**—Parsley is a biennial, usually seeded in early spring and enjoyed until extreme cold wipes out the roots or until the plant's second spring tempts the parsley to bolt. Parsley grows all summer but is tastiest during cold weather. I add parsley to tuna salad and egg salad in place of the harder-to-grow celery and also use the leaves and stalks to season soups.

**Oregano**—This perennial is hardy down to zone 5. Oregano grows quickly and can be started from seed, but flavors may not carry over from parent plants, so it's best to buy a cloned plant from a nursery. Oregano can take over your garden, so you might want to keep it in a pot or install a root barrier around your patch. Like basil and thyme, the flavor of oregano meshes well with tomatoes, and oregano is often used in Mexican meals as well.

**Coriander/cilantro**—These two seasonings come from the same plant—coriander usually refers to the seeds, while cilantro is the leaves. Coriander/cilantro is grown from seed in the spring and usually bolts in the middle of the summer. The leaves are used in salsas and other Mexican-style cooking.

**Egyptian onions** and **chives**—Egyptian onions and chives are primarily grown for their green leaves, which taste a bit like onions and/or garlic but lack the bite of either of those bulbs when eaten raw. Both Egyptian onions and chives are perennials, so they require very little care after establishment (from top bulbs for Egyptian onions or from seeds or sets for chives). Be careful to never cut more than half of the leaves on a single plant to keep your perennials thriving. Leaves from both chives and Egyptian onions can be used interchangeably, and both plants turn woody and inedible during the height of summer. Add greens of both sorts to sandwiches or mix them into lettuce, tuna, egg, or chicken salads.

**Rosemary**—This perennial will form a huge bush in the South but dies back during cold winters in zone 7 and colder. (Some varieties are hardier than others, and rosemary also does well as a potted plant.) However you grow rosemary, plan to start with a plant from a nursery and pick needles throughout the year. Rosemary can be added to tomato dishes and is often used by itself to flavor starches like bread or potatoes.

**Mint**—If you can think of uses for this herb, mint should definitely find a spot in your garden, since it is the easiest seasoning you can grow. Buy a start from a nursery and keep the mint in a pot or in a garden bed with serious root barriers, since mint spreads vigorously using runners. I just nibble on the leaves whenever I walk by our mint patch, but you can also make soothing cold teas from mint leaves. In my opinion, spearmint has the best flavor for fresh eating, although some people prefer peppermint.

**Chili peppers**—Chili peppers are grown just like sweet peppers; then you can use the fruits fresh or dry them for winter seasoning. These spicy peppers are used extensively in Mexican dishes and can also flavor Asian-inspired meals.

**Onions**—Onions are grown like vegetables, either from seeds or sets planted in early spring and harvested in midsummer. Nearly every meal I cook starts out with one or two onions. As I mentioned earlier, onions add a layer of sweetness to your dish that you won't notice as you eat but will notice the absence of if left out.

**Garlic**—Most American gardeners can grow garlic—see July's project "Fall planting" for cultivation tips. When I'm cooking with onions, I add three cloves of garlic per onion as a matter of course, and I also have several dishes in which garlic is the sole seasoning. Garlic can be used raw, but add less raw garlic than you would when cooking since heat mitigates the spiciness .

With the exception of onions and garlic, you can grow enough of each of these seasonings for a small household in just a pot or two on a sunny windowsill or balcony. Potted herbs are a great way for city-dwellers to at least dabble in producing their own food, or for gardeners up North to keep cooking with tender herbs far into the winter.

## *Testing new seasonings*

If you're very new to the world of seasoning food, I highly recommend trying out new seasonings one by one. Later, you can create more complex recipes, but you'll get a better feel for inventive seasoning if you understand each ingredient first. To that end, here are a few simple recipes (one serving apiece) to taste some of the easiest homegrown seasonings. You'll outgrow these recipes quickly, but hopefully each one will teach you whether that seasoning is worth adding to your repertoire.

**Scrambled eggs with green onions**—Break a couple of eggs into a bowl, add about a quarter of a cup of cut-up green onion leaves or chives, and whisk with a fork until the egg whites and yolks combine. Meanwhile, heat a bit of oil in a frying pan over medium heat until a drop of water flicked into the pan sizzles. Pour in the egg mixture and stir constantly with your fork until the eggs coagulate (about a minute or two). In general, adding herbs to scrambled eggs is a great way to get a feel for their flavor—the raw beginner might want to try this same technique with several other herbs from her garden.

**Parsley tuna salad**—Drain a can of tuna, add three stalks of parsley with leaves (cut up into small sections), and mix in mayonnaise until the salad hangs together. Eat alone or on a sandwich. If you don't like tuna, try this recipe with hard-boiled eggs to make egg salad instead.

**Garlic green beans**—Heat oil in a frying pan over medium-high heat and toss in about a cup of French filet-style green beans (the skinny, stringless ones). Stir constantly until the beans turn bright green and a few edges have blackened. Turn off the heat and put one or two cloves of garlic through a garlic press, adding the minced garlic along with salt and pepper to your beans. The residual heat will be enough to cook your garlic without burning it if you stir constantly for another minute or so. Even though this recipe is simple enough for beginners, it is so delicious that garlic green beans is one of our regular side dishes.

**Roasted rosemary potatoes**—Cut about a cup of potatoes (preferably new potatoes) into bite-size pieces (leaving on the skin) and toss with oil, salt, pepper, and a quarter- to a half-teaspoon of finely chopped rosemary leaves. Bake in a 425°F oven for about 25 minutes, until the potatoes are soft all the way through and are crispy on the outside.

# Easy and delicious cooked greens

A mixture of greens and chives sauteed in balsamic vinegar and peanut oil makes a tasty and easy side dish.

- about three quarts of loosely packed leafy greens
- about a pint of chicory or dandelion leaves
- about half a cup of Egyptian onion leaves or chives
- a healthy dash of balsamic vinegar
- a slightly less healthy dash of peanut oil

Cut the leafy greens, chicory or dandelion leaves, and Egyptian onion or chive leaves into bite-size sections. (I find it easiest to snip them up with scissors.) Put all of the above into a pot with balsamic vinegar and peanut oil and cook on medium-high, stirring frequently, until the leaves are barely cooked. This recipe cooks down so much that it barely serves two, and people always ask for more.

# Your real hourly wage

---

**GOAL**: Discover the true value of your time
**COST**: $0
**TIME**: 1 hour to 2 hours
**DIFFICULTY**: Easy
**KID-FRIENDLY**: No

---

If you have a job, you can probably tell me exactly how much you get paid per hour. Or can you? Pull out a pen and find out how much your time is really worth.

## Calculating your real hourly wage

Joe Dominguez and Vicki Robin's eye-opening book *Your Money or Your Life* is a must-read for anyone trying to simplify the financial side of life. This exercise is drawn almost verbatim from their book (and from their website www.financialintegrity.org) and is meant to help you figure out if your job is really worth the time you put into it.

The first step is to make some notes about how long you *really* spend working each week. Start with those 40 hours in your cubicle, of course, but then add in the hour you spend grooming, your daily commute, and the mandatory downtime you use up vegetating in front of the tube to wind down after work. Do you have to study or take classes to stay up-to-date in your field? Do you end up spending a week in bed because you're so run-down from work that you catch the flu? Add it all up!

Next, sum up your work-related expenses. These include the gas and upkeep on your car, those fancy duds you wear to the office, every meal or $5 cup of coffee you consume away from home because you're too busy to pack a lunch, the six-pack of beer you drink while winding down after work, the massages you pay for to wipe out the work stress, and the money you give other people to do your household chores (daycare, house cleaning, lawn upkeep, etc.), since you don't have time to do it yourself. Don't forget to include your taxes.

Finally, use the formula below to figure out your *real* hourly wage.

$$\frac{\text{Weekly income} - \text{Work-related expenses}}{\text{Total hours you really work in a week}} = \text{Real hourly wage}$$

The authors list extreme examples, like the white-collar worker who thought she was making $48 per hour but was really making $25.57 and the man being paid $11 per hour who was actually making $4. Without too much of a stretch of the imagination, I can see how working could send some job slaves into debt!

## Why do we work so hard?

Some scientists believe that early humans worked only about three hours per day. Why does the average American spend two or three times as many hours laboring as hunter-gatherers did?

**We want more stuff.** Most of us live in rich nations where the bare necessities—food, clothing, and shelter—can be met with very little cash. However, we're not content unless we're keeping up with the Joneses. Ways to minimize your monthly expenses organically (and thus reduce your work hours) include learning the difference between your wants and your needs, surrounding yourself with people who live simply, and cutting back your access to mainstream radio, television, and other media. See the chapter "Media consciousness" for more information.

**We don't have a life outside of work.** For many of us, our job title is our primary identity, so we strive to excel in the workplace, ignoring other facets of our personality. We spend more time around our coworkers than with our family and friends, so the latter wane in importance, and we go to work to socialize as much as to earn money. Eventually, we've gotten so used to working forty or fifty hours per week that we forget what we used to do for fun. If this sounds like you, don't worry—you can develop a life outside of work. Why not start by actually taking your vacation days this year rather than telling yourself you're too busy in the office to spare the time? It usually takes a week or two of being left to your own devices to rekindle smoldering passions.

## What to do with the numbers

Later projects will help you break free as much or as little as you want from the rat race, but for now, let's keep it simple. Maybe you're happy with your real hourly wage, but what can you do if that figure comes as a shock?

Some couples have discovered that it pays for one wage-earner to quit working entirely—the money the household saves on eating out and hiring someone to take care of housework is more than the salary they take in by working a job. If your household consists only of you, you can still decide to cut back your hours to spend more time on real life, making up for the lost income by growing your own food and mowing your own lawn. Or you might discover that your salary is simply not worth the commute, and you'd be better off accepting a lower-paying job closer to home. Even if you do nothing with your real hourly wage calculation, the exercise has merit for simply opening your eyes to the value of your time.

# JULY
*(January Down Under)*

# Fall planting

**GOAL**: Extend your harvest season into early to midwinter
**COST**: $0 to $20
**TIME**: 1 hour to 5 hours
**DIFFICULTY**: Medium
**KID-FRIENDLY**: Yes

Kale is one of the most frost-hardy greens, and it tastes even sweeter during cold weather.

This month heralds the beginning of the summer garden glut, and I know from experience that it's hard to think of carrots and lettuce when you're rolling in tomatoes and sweet corn. However, a little effort now will reward you with produce to pluck fresh from the garden in October, November, and December.

## No-till garden refresher

The instructions in this chapter assume you're managing a no-till garden, which is quite different from a conventional garden. Rather than rototill up the ground every time you want to plant, you just rake back the mulch, set down a layer of compost,

*(continued)*

## No-till garden refresher *(continued)*

then work the amendment in slightly if you're planting very small seeds, or leave the compost lying on the surface for transplants and larger seeds. The benefits of no-till gardens, methods of starting and managing no-till gardens, and the whys and hows of mulching were covered in previous chapters: "Kill mulch," "Plant your summer garden," and "Mulch." If you're just embarking on your journey, I highly recommend going back and skimming those sections before planting your fall garden. In the long run, I suspect that you'll find no-till gardening easier and better for the soil than conventional gardening.

## *What to plant*

Okra and squash thrive in summer heat, but a wide range of other crops need cooler, damper temperatures. Many of these fall crops convert starches to sugars after the first frost, resulting in sweeter kale and carrots than you'll ever find in the grocery store. If you're a relatively new gardener, I'll once again recommend you start with the easiest vegetables, but the truth is that few fall crops are all that hard. I've listed all the common fall vegetables below from simplest to most complex.

**Lettuce**—Leaf lettuce (where you cut individual leaves as soon as they're a couple of inches tall rather than wait to harvest the whole head) is by far the easiest vegetable I've grown in any season. As long as you get the planting time right, a lettuce bed is "plant it and forget it." I scatter the seeds very thickly on the soil surface so that I only have to weed once before the lettuce leaves fill in the gaps and shade out any further weeds. Then, after a mere month, you can start snipping lettuce leaves with your scissors as if you're giving the bed a haircut, continuing to harvest a few times a week for four weeks or more. My favorite variety of leaf lettuce is Black-seeded Simpson, but I recommend that you check with your local feed store to see which lettuce seeds they sell in bulk, as these are probably best-suited to your climate.

**Leafy greens**—Greens like kale, mustard, collards, Asian greens, and spinach rival lettuce for ease of growth but have a slightly tougher time germinating in hot summer soils. Greens are also more cold hardy and will last longer into the winter without any protection from the cold. For your first garden, I recommend trying several different types of leafy greens to discover which ones best fit your palate and climate. We find kale to be the sweetest and most cold hardy, but Eliot Coleman (author of *Winter Harvest Handbook*) notes that spinach will continue to put out new growth later in the season if you're willing to protect the plants from the worst of winter's cold. In addition, trials by the Seed Alliance in Washington State suggest that Fordhook Giant Swiss Chard may be as cold hardy as kale.

**Radishes**—Radishes are probably the easiest fall root crop to grow. Planted directly from seed, they come up quickly and turn into tender morsels within a month. That said, we don't like the spicy flavor, so I can't give you any firsthand information on radish cultivation.

Unless you live in the Deep South, garlic is one of the easiest vegetables to grow.

**Garlic**—As long as your winter has some bite to it, garlic is a nearly no-work winter crop that can be planted later in the fall than anything else. The trick with garlic is hunting down localized varieties, so don't buy your starter bulbs from the big-box stores (and definitely don't plant garlic sold at the grocery store); instead find a nearby nursery that raises its own. Southern Exposure Seed Exchange sent me the most amazing garlic varieties, but you might want to find something closer to you if you live out west. Once you have your seed garlic in hand, break apart the heads and plant the largest bulbs in well-drained soil, mulch around the plants once they come up, and ignore them until next year.

**Turnips**—Turnips are a root crop that you can plant for both roots and leaves. Be sure to read the seed packet for the variety you choose, to discover whether your turnips are primarily grown for large roots (and should be planted further apart and earlier in the season) or are grown for leaves (and can be scattered close together and planted at the same time as leafy greens).

**Carrots**—In general, root crops need loose, well-drained, organic-matter-filled soil, and carrots are even pickier about this than radishes and turnips—since the seeds are small and should be planted relatively close together, I tend to broadcast carrot seeds, then find that the seeds have a tough time germinating on the soil surface. The section "How to plant" will show a simple trick for getting carrot seeds to germinate even in summer heat. If you follow that planting guideline, carrots will be a delicious and easy addition to your fall garden. Just be sure to harvest after the first frost for maximum sweetness, but before the ground freezes. And keep the slow-growing seedlings well weeded for the first month, since they'll have a hard time competing with faster-growing weeds.

**Beets**—Beets can have many of the same troubles with poor soil and spotty germination that carrots can. To aid in germination, soak seeds before planting. In addition, beets (and Swiss chard and spinach, which share the same family) are the only plants that always require thinning. Each "seed" is actually a conglomeration of several seeds, so you'll see multiple seedlings pop up in the same spot. To thin clumps of beet seeds, carefully pull or (better) cut off the tops of all the seedlings except one in each spot to give your beets room to grow.

**Broccoli, cabbage, cauliflower, and brussels sprouts**—I lump all of these vegetables together because they are in the same species (along with kale) and are all grown pretty much alike. The main reason I've listed them relatively far down the complexity scale for fall vegetables is that broccoli and its ilk require three or four months from seed to harvest, and you can't just pick them young if the frost comes too soon, the way you can leafy greens. For next year's garden, I recommend marking your calendar in early summer (more on the exact date later) and starting your cabbage and similar crops in flats inside. For this year, you might choose to buy a few starts at the local feed store to transplant into your garden.

**Peas**—After several years of experimentation, I've decided that shelling peas just aren't worth the effort in our small garden—I recommend you try them only if you have plenty of willing hands to remove peas from their pods and lots of spare room to plant them. On the other hand, snow peas and the more sugar-laden snap peas make delicious additions to salads and stir fries. You'll need to build a simple trellis to hold the plants off the ground and might want to soak your seeds in a cup of water for twelve hours before planting if the ground is quite dry.

**Leeks**—Although leeks can be harvested far into the winter, they share the broccoli problem of needing to be started long before cold weather begins. They're also very slow growers that require lots of attention, so I recommend that people instead grow perennial Egyptian onions, which can be cooked in nearly the same way and require a fraction of the attention.

In the Deep South, you can also grow **potatoes** and **onions** as fall-planted crops that are harvested in the spring, but these vegetables will be killed by winter cold in most parts of the United States. If you live in Texas, you might even be planting tomatoes and other summer crops now to escape the punishing summer heat. This chapter assumes you live in a more moderate climate where you need to focus on planting cool-weather crops starting in July or August.

To sum it all up, I'd recommend that you start out with lettuce and leafy greens if you've never had a garden before, then expand into one or more of the root crops and perhaps broccoli and sugar snap peas if you embarked on your journey in May and are feeling confident about your gardening abilities.

## *When to plant*

Unless you live in an area with very short summers (zone 4 or colder), you've got quite a bit of wiggle room for setting out your summer crops. However, there is a hard deadline at the end of the fall garden—the first killing frost, when temperatures in the twenties (Fahrenheit) kill back all but the most hardy vegetables.

For most gardeners, I recommend the chart on page 92, which assumes that you'll be using no winter protection, will be starting everything from seed, and will be eating most of your vegetables before the killing frost. To use the chart, first determine your area's first frost date—for us it's October 10. (Your state extension agent is a good source for local information like average frost dates.) Write "10/10" (or your frost date) above the "00" at the top of the chart; then each column to the right of that date is 10 days after the first frost date and each column to the left of that date is 10 days before the first frost date.

Next, find the vegetable you're interested in; then look for the dates marked in green (planting times) and orange (harvest times). As you can see, fall carrots in my area should be planted between June 12 and July 12. If I waited to think about the fall garden until I felt the first hint of autumn chill in the air, it would be too late to plant anything except mustard, spinach, turnips (for greens), garlic, and radishes. However, you can plant broccoli, cabbage, brussels sprouts, cauliflower, and leeks up to a month later than the date on the chart as long as you buy sets rather than start the vegetables from seed.

But what do you do if your favorite vegetable isn't on the chart? Take out your seed packet and you'll notice that it usually contains a "days to maturity" number. Count back that many days from your average first frost date, add two weeks (since plants grow slower in the fall), and you have your last possible planting date.

| Example: | 5/13 | 5/23 | 6/2 | 6/12 | 6/22 | 7/2 | 7/12 | 7/22 | 8/1 | 8/11 | 8/21 | 8/31 | 9/10 | 9/20 | 9/30 | 10/10 | 10/20 | 10/30 | 11/9 | 11/19 | 11/29 |
|---|---|---|---|---|---|---|---|---|---|---|---|---|---|---|---|---|---|---|---|---|---|
| | 150 | 140 | 130 | 120 | 110 | 100 | 90 | 80 | 70 | 60 | 50 | 40 | 30 | 20 | 10 | 00 | 10 | 20 | 30 | 40 | 50 |
| beets | | | | | | | | | | | | | | | | | | | | | |
| broccoli | | | | | | | | | | | | | | | | | | | | | |
| brussels sprouts | | | | | | | | | | | | | | | | | | | | | |
| cabbage | | | | | | | | | | | | | | | | | | | | | |
| carrots | | | | | | | | | | | | | | | | | | | | | |
| cauliflower | | | | | | | | | | | | | | | | | | | | | |
| garlic | | | | | | | | | | | | | | | | | | | | | |
| kale | | | | | | | | | | | | | | | | | | | | | |
| lettuce (leaf) | | | | | | | | | | | | | | | | | | | | | |
| leeks | | | | | | | | | | | | | | | | | | | | | |
| mustard | | | | | | | | | | | | | | | | | | | | | |
| onions | | | | | | | | | | | | | | | | | | | | | |
| peas | | | | | | | | | | | | | | | | | | | | | |
| potatoes | | | | | | | | | | | | | | | | | | | | | |
| radishes | | | | | | | | | | | | | | | | | | | | | |
| spinach | | | | | | | | | | | | | | | | | | | | | |
| turnips | | | | | | | | | | | | | | | | | | | | | |

Fall planting times: Green denotes planting. Orange denotes harvest.

# Planning for quick hoops

A later chapter will walk you through building quick hoops to protect your fall crops from moderately cold weather. If you're willing to commit to building quick hoops now, you can put off fall planting a bit longer. But for how much longer?

After years of experimentation, Eliot Coleman (author of *Winter Harvest Handbook*) concluded that most plants stop growing when the day length drops below 10 hours. After this time, even if you protect your vegetables from the cold, they are merely existing in a semi-hibernatory state.

Coleman coined the term "Persephone Days" to refer to this deep winter period of short days, which occurs from November 5 to February 5 on his farm in Maine, from December 1 to January 10 in Charlotte, North Carolina, and from about November 22 to January 19 here in southwest Virginia. Those of you who are lucky enough to live south of the 32nd parallel have no Persephone Days and can keep your crops active all winter if you play your cards right.

The trick to a long winter harvest is to plant your crops at just the right stage of the late summer and fall so that they are just shy of maturity when the Persephone Days begin. Young plants are much hardier than older ones, so planting dates are even more important in the fall than in the spring—planting too early is just as bad as planting too late. You'll also need to pay close attention to succession planting so that you'll have a continuous harvest throughout the winter rather than a mass of lettuce one week and then no more for the rest of the year. In effect, you're not extending the growing season, just the harvest season.

To get a rough idea of when to plant under frost protection, use the same planting chart on page 92, but mark "00" as the onset of your Persephone Days (November 22 for us). You might want to plant two or three weeks earlier than the chart suggests, though, since vegetables will grow slower and slower as fall progresses.

# How to plant

In general, you will plant your fall garden the same way you planted your summer garden, but you have one new enemy—desiccation. The hot, dry days of summer quickly dry out the soil surface, which often leads to spotty germination of moisture-loving winter crops. I use two techniques to make sure my fall vegetables sprout.

Starting fall seedlings in flats indoors prevents problems with germination when the soil is hot and dry.

Some fall vegetables are best started inside in flats. Cabbage, broccoli, brussels sprouts, cauliflower, and leeks do well when started inside and then transplanted, and you might have better luck growing beets and turnips that way as well.

I find it far too labor-intensive to transplant other crops, so I instead rake the top inch of soil to the sides of my bed, scatter carrot, lettuce, or greens seeds on the surface, then gently pull the soil back on top of the seeds. Finally, I tamp the earth lightly with the head of a hoe to firm the ground up around my seeds. This method is a quick way of getting tiny seeds deeper in the soil without laboriously setting out lots of small rows, and the deeper planting will help maintain moisture around the seedlings' roots.

To prepare your no-till bed for fall planting, rake back the mulch and then pull the top inch of soil to the sides of the bed.

Other options exist to help fall seedlings germinate, but I find them a bit chancy. First, you can wait to plant right before rain is forecast, but one rain isn't always enough to get fall crops off to a good start if temperatures rise into the 90s for several days thereafter. If you've got the wherewithal, you can water the seedlings every day for a week or two—that will definitely work if you remember and have time. For best results, start your watering campaign a day or two before planting to premoisten the soil.

In general, planting seeds a bit deeper than you would in the spring is a good way of keeping moisture around their roots, and most fall seeds can be soaked in water for a few hours before planting to jumpstart the process. You can cover germinating seeds with an old board or thin layer of mulch to hold in moisture, but you will have to remember to remove either as soon as the seedlings sprout, so that they don't die for lack of sunlight. Finally, consider planting three to five seeds instead of one in each location. If they all come up, you can thin, or you can transplant the extra seedlings to fill in gaps.

# Freezing food

**GOAL**: Learn to freeze garden produce
**COST**: $0 to $20
**TIME**: 1 hour to 4 hours
**DIFFICULTY**: Medium
**KID-FRIENDLY**: Maybe

Broccoli maintains its flavor well in the freezer.

By the beginning of July, your garden should be overflowing with produce. Sure, you probably had a few failures, but at least one of your crops is bound to have taken off and dropped so much food in your lap that you're drowning in the output. The natural inclination is to give the excess away—and that's a good idea in moderation—but you should also look ahead to the long, cold winter. Wouldn't you rather eat your vitamin-rich, homegrown food rather than insipid grocery store vegetables? This project introduces you to the easiest method of storing fruits and vegetables—freezing.

## Types of food preservation

Cabbage can be stored by drying, freezing, or simply stashing away in a root cellar.

There are at least half a dozen good methods of storing food, including these:

**Storing food on the shelf**—Onions, garlic, sweet potatoes, and winter squash will last for several months on a dark shelf in your kitchen. It doesn't get much easier than that.

**Storing food in a root cellar**—Most root crops, including white potatoes, carrots, and parsnips, need a cool, damp environment. Given these conditions, they can be stored without any processing in a root cellar, basement, or hole in the ground.

**Canning food**—Once heated to a certain temperature and packed in a sterilized, sealed glass jar, food will last for years at a time without spoiling. Although canning is the standby storage method for many homesteaders, the extended cooking period makes the vegetables lose large quantities of nutrients, and the taste reflects that loss.

**Fermenting food**—Fermenting (think sauerkraut) uses microorganisms instead of heat to preserve food in a jar. The results tend to be highly nutritious, but the strong tastes can turn many people away.

**Drying food**—Dried food is more nutritious than canned food, and the process can require little or no store-bought energy if you use a solar dehydrator. I've found that fruits, especially, are tastiest dried. However, you'll need to plan on a lot of time cutting up the food and shifting it around on the trays, making drying one of the most labor-intensive storage methods.

**Freezing food**—Freezing requires much less cooking time than canning, so the results are more nutritious and tastier. The energy requirement is a bit of a tossup—you don't need to use so much electricity to process the food at the beginning, but you do need to run a freezer until you've eaten the bounty, and power outages can be a problem. That said, freezing is one of the simplest methods of preserving food, and you might as well fill up the freezer compartment on top of your fridge before moving on to more in-depth techniques.

This weekend's project walks you through learning what and how to freeze. Later projects will cover the basics of storing food on the shelf, canning, and drying, so feel free to flip ahead if you'd rather explore a different food-preservation project this month.

## What to freeze

After four years of using freezing as our main method of preserving produce, I've discovered that just about anything can go in the freezer. Of course, your food will never taste better than it does fresh, so gorge yourself on the bounty before turning to preservation, and don't put anything in the freezer that's not good enough to eat right now.

If you have limited freezer space, you might want to focus on freezing foods that don't taste as good dried or canned. In my opinion, fruits lose a lot when they're frozen, so they are often my last choice when meting out freezer space. Summer squash are also only moderately worthy of the freezer—I find that our summer squash gets watery and is fit only for soups and lasagna after freezing. Finally, tomatoes are just as good frozen but are one of the few types of homegrown produce that don't seem to mind being canned, so if I had a smaller freezer, I'd probably leave tomatoes out.

So what's tastiest frozen? My favorite frozen foods include green beans, sweet corn, vegetable soups, broccoli, and shelling peas, but we freeze a lot more than that. If you've got an excess of any kind of vegetable that is eaten cooked and that I haven't mentioned here, you might as well give freezing a shot.

# How to freeze food

For precooked foods like soup, freezing is as simple as putting the food in a suitable container and stacking it into the freezer. However, most vegetables will keep much better if you blanch them before freezing. Blanching is a process of steaming or boiling bite-size pieces of vegetables just long enough to deactivate the enzymes that cause food quality to degrade over time. You aren't cooking the food all the way, merely as long as it takes for the vegetables' colors to brighten. Blanching times for some common vegetables are shown below:

| Vegetable (cut into bite-size pieces) | Blanching Time (minutes) |
|---|---|
| asparagus | 3 |
| beets | cook until done |
| broccoli | 3 |
| brussels sprouts | 4 |
| carrots | 2 |
| cauliflower | 3 |
| celery | 3 |
| corn (kernels) | 1 |
| eggplant | 4 |
| reen beans | 3 |
| greens | 2 |
| mushrooms | 3 |
| okra | 3 |
| peas (edible pod) | 2 |
| peas (shelled) | 1.5 |
| peppers (sweet) | 2 |
| pumpkins | roast until done |
| summer squash | 3 |
| sweet potatoes | cook until done |
| turnips | 2 |
| winter squash | roast until done |

So, how do you blanch? The trick is to get the food hot quickly and then cold just as quickly. The traditional method is to drop chunks of produce into boiling water, lift them out with a slotted spoon, submerge the food in ice water, then let the blanched vegetables drain dry before packing them away in the freezer. However, this method of blanching results in the loss of many water-soluble vitamins, so I instead recommend steam blanching. Bring about an inch of water to a boil; then place a steamer full of vegetables into the pot and put on the lid. After the right amount of time has elapsed, quickly spoon the vegetables out onto a cookie sheet and place the sheet in the fridge's freezer while you blanch the next batch. By the time your second steamer-load of vegetables has been blanched and is ready to go in the freezer, the first set can be packed away in a sealed container to go out into the big freezer. Using this method, I can freeze a gallon of produce in short order.

## Labeling and rotation

Careful notes are the key to freezer success. Even though freezing slows food-quality degradation drastically, your vegetables will continue to age in the freezer. After twelve months, most food is much less tasty, and the nutritional value has declined markedly, so your freezer goals should be twofold:

- Freeze just enough food to last for a year.
- Eat a varied diet so that you don't run out of your favorites in the first month.

This freezer chart helps me keep track of my winter stores. I tack mine up on the refrigerator so it's handy when planning meals.

My solution to both of these problems is to make a freezer chart. Each type of food has a column, and I place an X in one square for each cup, pint, or quart packed away during the summer. In the winter, I shade out each square as I use up the frozen produce. A quick glance at my freezer chart lets me know that I've been eating too much pizza sauce if I want it to last until next summer, and that I need to hurry up and eat that okra so that our February meals aren't a monoculture.

My freezer chart is also handy when the time comes to plan next year's garden. If we didn't eat very much pesto, maybe I shouldn't grow so much basil this year. On the other hand, we ran out of broccoli by the middle of winter, so it looks like we need to expand that part of the garden.

Meanwhile, I keep each type of food segregated in the freezer and draw a map showing each food's location so that I can find things easily. Since I clean out the freezer entirely every spring and freeze food in clear plastic containers, I don't even need to label my produce. Instead, I plan to have the freezer completely empty by the time new food starts going in, which means that no food in the freezer is ever more than a year old.

## Eating out of the freezer

Stacking all of the green beans in one column, the pizza sauce in another, and the soup in yet another ensures that I can find what I'm looking for in a large chest freezer.

*(continued)*

## Eating out of the freezer *(continued)*

All summer as I frantically harvest garden goodies, I look forward to the ease of freezer cooking. Thaw out a package of broccoli, nuke it, and eat five minutes later. So restful . . .

What I forget is that winter cooking has its own challenges. Even though frozen produce is tastier than canned food, it loses that amazing flavor that allows me to steam vegetables and serve them plain during the growing season. Instead, frozen food can use a bit of dressing up, like sautéing green beans with garlic or roasting broccoli in a hot oven with olive oil, salt, and pepper.

The other trick to eating out of the freezer is what I call Berry Syndrome. Nearly everyone I know succumbs to this, and I suffer from it too. You freeze a pint or a quart or a gallon of those delicious summer berries (or sun-dried tomatoes, or whatever else is delectable and in short supply) and then you save the treat for a special occasion. By freezer cleaning time, it's still there! Don't fall into the Berry Syndrome trap—decide that today is a special day and thaw those berries out!

# Hanging your clothes out to dry

**GOAL**: Harness the power of the sun while simplifying your life
**COST**: $10 to $50
**TIME**: 10 minutes to 1 hour
**DIFFICULTY**: Easy to medium
**KID-FRIENDLY**: Yes

Hanging out clothes on a sunny spring day is more like playing than working.

No matter which source it comes from—coal, nuclear, even hydro, wind, and solar—the national power grid is synonymous with environmental degradation. On a more personal level, not only do the electric bills keep getting higher, we're also helpless if storms knock the power out for an hour, a day, or a week. Breaking free from this addiction is one of the goals of many homesteaders, but a full off-grid system is beyond reach for most of us. Nevertheless, we *can* take simple steps to make ourselves more self-sufficient in case of a power outage, at the same time lowering our monthly electric bills. This week's project can cost you as little as ten bucks while saving you $150 per year on your electric bill— a good first step.

## Solar clothes dryer

A sturdy laundry basket is a must when hanging out clothes. This plastic box was discarded by the U.S. Postal Service.

Photo credit: Adrianne Hess

Solar panels are pricey, but the sun's energy is quite easy to capture and turn to our advantage. Systems that harvest solar energy without converting that power to electricity are often called "passive solar" and include tricks like running water through black pipes on the roof to produce nearly free hot water, situating your house so that a bank of windows faces south for winter heating, and the easiest of all—hanging your clothes out to dry.

It's simple to separate the homesteading wheat from the chaff by tossing around the term *solar clothes dryer*. Folks more interested in gadgets than in simple living will perk up their ears and pull out their wallets, while the skinflints among us will snort and say, "You mean a clothesline, right?" The problem with clotheslines isn't that they don't work but that they're so inexpensive and easy to make yourself that "solar clothes dryers" are ignored by the advertising-driven homesteading magazines, websites, and TV shows.

I also run across naysayers with the following valid objections:

**Won't it take forever?** I estimate that hanging clothes on the line and then taking them back in requires perhaps five more minutes per load than tossing the wet clothes into a dryer. The average

American family dries 365 loads per year, meaning that their clothes dryer saved them 30 hours of labor annually. So far, modern equipment is sounding pretty good, right? Now, to put the number in perspective, you probably spent around $700 to $1,000 on a dryer that's going to last around eight to ten years—make that $100 per year—and you're burning $150 worth of electricity annually to run the dryer. That means you're spending a bit over $8 per hour for the time saved by using your clothes dryer. You have to decide for yourself whether an hour watching butterflies while pinning clothes on the line is better than the time spent on the job to purchase the labor-saving device.

**What do you do when it's wet and cold?** One of the most powerful things about hanging your clothes on the line is how the act tunes you into the weather and roots you in your own patch of earth. You'll learn to keep an eye out for hot, dry days and get your laundry washed first thing in the morning so that the clothes are dry before the dew falls that night. We live in one of the rainiest spots in the United States, but I almost never have a hard time finding enough sunny days to dry our clothes. If the weather really won't cooperate, you can always rig a line in the basement, garage, or barn (depending on your housing situation). In cold weather, drying your clothes inside will even help humidify that moisture-deficient winter air.

**Won't my clothes get dirty?** If you've never hung your clothes out to dry, it may seem counterintuitive to put clean clothes outside where they can accumulate car exhaust and bird droppings. However, in most cases, your clothes will not come in covered with bugs and pollen. As long as you don't locate your clothesline under a pine tree in the spring or directly downwind from a coal mine, the only bit of outdoors that will cling to your line-dried clothes is a refreshing scent. Plus, if you really care about your clothes, you'll find that using a clothesline rather than a dryer can extend the life of your wardrobe.

**I'm not hanging my underwear out in public.** I can definitely sympathize with this problem, since I was a bit chagrined as a teenager to be hanging up the family's undergarments in our suburban backyard. Luckily, there are easy tricks to save yourself from embarrassment. Just hang the outerwear on the side of the clothesline facing your neighbors and the underwear shielded on the other side. A sheet or towel works well to block prying eyes too. If you're extremely shy, underwear is small and easy to drape inside.

**My neighborhood won't allow clotheslines.** I have to admit that my knee-jerk response to this problem is: "You'd better get out of that neighborhood then, because they're not going to be too pleased with tomatoes in the front yard and chickens in the backyard either!" That said, it's tough to pull up roots, so there are a few tricks you can use to blend your clothesline into a ritzier neighborhood. You could try planting a living fence of bamboo to block off your backyard from snooping eyes or talk to your neighborhood association and see if they can be brought around to your point of view. If all else fails, you might not need a clothesline at all—why not get a few drying racks and drape your clothes in a spare room? Clothes on hangers can be lined up along your shower's curtain rod, or you can string up a clothesline above head height in a seldom-used garage, basement, or spare room.

## Clothesline options

A space-saving reel allows a family to fit its clothes into a small backyard, leaving room for a peach tree and a vegetable garden.

Photo credit: Adrianne Hess

You can buy a space-saving clothesline like the one shown above for $40, or you can make your own for nearly nothing. We cut cedar posts, attached scrap two-by-fours across the top, strung store-bought clothesline between them, and added clothespins, all for under $10. If your yard is set up so that you have a tall tree or building a good distance away, you can also buy two clothesline pulleys ($5 to $15 apiece) and make your clothes-hanging even easier.

No matter which route you choose, you should try to site your clothesline in one of the sunniest parts of the yard and use high-quality line. We started out with cotton clothesline from the dollar store, which fit our budget but rotted through within a couple of years. In the long run, plastic-coated line is more economical. Ditto with high-quality clothespins. Just don't use metal line or you'll end up with rust spots on your clothing.

## Advanced clothesline use

Gregory Smith made this simple clothesline prop by drilling a large hole near the end of a furring strip, then cutting the end of the wooden strip off to leave a notch.

Photo credit: Gregory Smith, www.fritzmonroe.com/fritz/

*(continued)*

## Advanced clothesline use  (continued)

My mother, Adrianne Hess, grew up outside Boston, "freeze drying" her family's clothes during frigid, snowy winters. Later, she moved down South and used a wringer washing machine on cloth diapers for all three of her kids, again drying them on a line. I asked her for some extra tips on clothes drying, and she responded as follows:

Before your father made my first T-structure clothesline, I had strung heavy wire going up the ditch behind the house, some of it tied to branches that hung over the electric fence on the other side. When I had heavy things, like jeans, or maybe big towels or even quilts or blankets, the line would sag.

I had already learned from my neighbors to **use tall props**, which is one reason I still keep my eye out for fairly straight branches over eight feet long. My props were sometimes ten feet long, and the best had a fork at the end, for the line to rest in. These were essential, for raising up the heavy load. (The worst part of hanging out is having your clothes drop in the mud!) Clothes dry so much faster when they're higher off the ground, which is why I now drape the socks and underwear on the high bars of my clothes reel.

When your father made the T-frame clothesline, I went down the creek to Onie, my nearest neighbor, and said, "He is trying to domesticate me!" I loved my rambling line!

In winter, especially, it is easier to dry sheets if you do not hang over the line (or they'll freeze). And if you fold the wet sheet in half, then in quarters as it comes out of the washer, it is easier to unfold and hang out in the cold. One of the ways I was taught to hang clothes out was to organize the clothes before going out, as one takes them out of the washing machine (or, in your case, as you rinse and wring)—so you have a pile of underwear that you already know where you will hang, and have the better clothes sort of shaken out and folded conveniently ready to hang.

You really need to be particular, on damp days, or if you have a lot to hang out and hope to be reusing your line the same day. Make sure the clothes are completely right-side out, even if you wash them wrong-side out. Shake them out so they don't clump but are flat. Above all, dry high, if possible, and don't drape over the line in the winter, unless you plan to turn and rehang the article for the underside to be dried. These are my life-tested rules!

## When and how to hang your clothes

If you grew up hanging your clothes on the line, you'll probably laugh at this section, but the truth is that many people don't know where to start with hanging clothes out to dry. The first thing to do, as I've mentioned earlier, is to look at the weather forecast. If you can find a day with temperatures above 80, low humidity, and no rain forecast, you can put your clothes out in the morning and bring them in that night—the lowest work option.

Most clothes are best hung with two pins, one on each side. If you're low on pins, you can double up your garments, using a single clothes-pin to attach the right side of one shirt and the left side of another. You can also hang several pairs of women's underwear, handkerchiefs, or cloth napkins from the same pin, but keep in mind that each of these pin-saving techniques will make the fabric under the pin slower to dry, which will mean more work on your part as you shift the garments end-to-end to encourage drying.

Tops are best hung upside down. T-shirts and sweaters are easy to attach with one pin on each side, but button-up shirts should be pinned at the seams. If you don't want the shirts to wrinkle, you can button each one closed so that it hangs evenly, or can even hang a very important shirt right-side-up on a clothes hanger. If you play your cards right, hanging clothes on the line can make ironing a thing of the past and can actually save you time if you're the sort who has to wear well-manicured clothes to work.

Pants can be hung in several different ways. You can hang them from the waistband, but most pants have extra fabric there and are heavy enough that they may tend to pull out of your pins. For nice pants, my mother taught me to fold each pants leg against the seam so that the two legs overlap each other, then hang the pants upside down. If you don't care about a crease partway down the clothing, you can also just drape the pants partway over the line then pin them in place.

Sheets can also be draped over the line—spread the long axis of the sheet along the length of the line so that the bottom won't dangle in the grass. When taking in dry sheets, fold them directly on the line and save yourself work later.

Underwear, napkins, washcloths, and handkerchiefs can either be pinned from one corner to save space and pins or can be hung like

T-shirts for fastest drying. Towels are usually hung from one side—they're slow to dry, so you won't want to drape your towels over the line the way you would a sheet.

After hanging your clothes in the morning, keep an eye on clouds and be prepared to run out and take in your laundry if it starts to rain. Your clothes will take twice as long to dry if they're drenched in a downpour, since they won't have gone through the spin cycle or the wringer to push out new moisture, and if you leave them on the line too long, the colors will bleach out. It's better to take the extra time to bring your clothes in and then either hang them around the house or put them back outside if the shower passes within a few hours.

Assuming the weather cooperates, check on your clothesline a couple of hours before dark. If you wait too long, dew will be falling and will dampen your clothes. Bring in anything that's dry and leave the rest of the clothes on the line to finish up in tomorrow morning's sun.

The one other factor you'll need to be aware of if you're line-drying your clothes for the first time is that your clean clothes will come in slightly crispy, as if they've been starched. In most cases, you won't even notice, since the crispness will wear out within minutes, but I sometimes find it necessary to rub a towel or cloth sanitary pad against itself a couple of times to soften it up.

## Beyond the clothesline

Hanging your clothes on the line can lead you in two different directions (assuming you don't hate the exercise and go back to your clothes dryer immediately). First, you might be intrigued by the idea of harnessing the sun's energy in such a simple, direct manner. If that's the case, projects to consider include solar water heaters, solar space heaters to warm your house in the winter, and solar food dehydrators.

Alternatively, you might be drawn to becoming more conscious of how care of your clothes impacts your life and the earth. Perhaps you'll want to reconsider the American obsession with cleanliness that requires a fresh outfit every day even for those who spend all their time in an air-conditioned office. If you earmark a set of clothes for going to town, another for farm chores, and yet a third set for lazing around the house, then change into the appropriate pair as necessary, you can cut your laundry time drastically. Although it's socially taboo in many places to wear the same outfit two days in a row, you can drape a lightly worn set of clothes over a chair, don a fresh outfit for the second day, and then return to the first outfit on the third day. Using these methods, we average about three loads of laundry for the two of us per month (10 percent of the national average), and I'm confident many of you can at least cut your laundry workload in half by making a few simple changes to your usage patterns.

# Budget

**GOAL**: Find out where your money goes
**COST**: $0
**TIME**: 2 hours to 5 hours (over the course of a month)
**DIFFICULTY**: Medium
**KID-FRIENDLY**: Maybe

One common homesteading goal is finding a way to escape the rat race. But quitting your job is an unattainable dream until you figure out on what you're currently spending your money. This weekend's project is a pen-and-paper break from the more hands-on exercises, and although it may seem less fun, making a budget is a mandatory step for any homesteader-to-be who isn't independently wealthy.

## *Why bother with a budget?*

The numbers say it all. Half of Americans have credit cards that they are unable to pay off in full each month. And if you factor in mortgages and other "intentional" debt, about 80 percent of us are in the red.

Although debt is the American norm, it is also the enemy of simple living. You're forced to stick to that full-time job to make your car payment each month, which means you also have to buy those fancy suits to look good in the office. You might as well eat your lunch at the restaurant down the road because you have so little time to cook real food, but then you wonder why your credit card bill is so startlingly huge at the end of every month.

A budget is the first step in the right direction. By figuring out what you're currently spending your money on, you can hang onto more of your cash and pay down your credit card balance. With your eye on the prize, you might be able to delete that mortgage in short order and can then cut back to half-time at work—now you have the flexibility to be more than a weekend homesteader!

## Figure out where your money goes

This project is going to take all month, but it's not that tough. Basically, all you have to do is keep track of where all your money comes from and goes to, which can be done in several different ways. Some folks carry around a little notebook with them and write down purchases on the spot—mark the date, price, and what you spent your money on. Others save receipts and tally them all up later. A third option is to use a credit card or bank card for all your purchases and just look at your statement a month later. Figuring out where your money comes from is probably easier unless you're running a very diversified business—just hold onto your paycheck stubs.

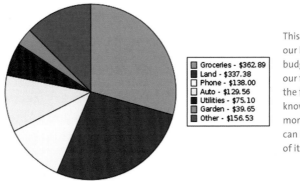

Groderies - $362.89
Land - $337.38
Phone - $138.00
Auto - $129.56
Utilities - $75.10
Garden - $39.65
Other - $156.53

This pie chart shows our household budget from one of our first months on the farm. Once you know where your money goes, you can hold onto more of it.

At the end of the month, you'll need to separate your expenditures into categories and sum up how much you spent in each one. The categories you choose should match your lifestyle; ours include basics like car expenses, groceries, restaurants, clothes, household supplies, tools, pet food, utilities, and so forth. This part of the project can be very laborious if you use pen and paper, so I highly recommend either figuring out how to use a spreadsheet or (even better) download some accounting software for your computer. I use GnuCash, which is a free program you can find at www.gnucash.org. Most accounting software will make it easy for you to create a pie chart to visualize where your money went.

If you want a really honest accounting of your month's expenditures, you will need to add a few expenses to the ones tallied from your monthly receipts. Chances are you pay for certain services once a year or once every six months, and if you didn't happen to get a bill this month, you might be tempted to leave out your real estate taxes, car insurance, and so forth when considering your monthly expenses. Make a list of these bills and figure out how much they cost you on a monthly basis, then add that total into your monthly expenses.

The last step in the number crunching phase is to figure out your monthly profit or loss. Was your income more or less than your expenditures? If you're running a deficit, that's the obvious first problem to correct on your way to financial security.

## What's next?

Making a budget is the beginning of a lengthy process, and where you go from here will depend on your own goals. Are you trying to pay off your debt as fast as possible? Do you just want to make ends meet? Are you trying to save up a nest egg to buy a bit of land? Each dream will send you off in a different direction, but I have a few suggestions before you tuck this project away:

> When you look at your expenses summary, **certain categories might jump out at you as ones on which you'd like to cut back.** If you're spending more on restaurant food than groceries, that's an obvious spot to scrimp, for example.

> **Calculate how much money it would cost per month to make your goals a reality.** If you didn't buy any new clothes for the next year, could you save enough to pay off your credit card debt?

> **Everyone should have a three-month emergency buffer**—enough cash socked away in an easily accessible savings or money market account so that you can pay the most important bills even if you have no money coming in. I highly recommend starting a separate bank account and filling it up until you reach your goal, then forgetting about the money until you really need it.

Some of you may be breathing a sigh of relief that this project is over, but if you can stand it, keeping track of your income and expenses is a good habit to get into. It only takes me about an hour per month to type receipts into my accounting program, and the exercise is a great way to maintain good financial habits. If you ever start a business, you'll need to have some basic accounting skills, so you might as well start now.

# AUGUST
## (February Down Under )

# Seed saving

**GOAL**: Save seeds from the easiest vegetables in your garden
**COST**: $0 to $10
**TIME**: 1 hour to 4 hours
**DIFFICULTY**: Easy to medium
**KID-FRIENDLY**: Yes

I like to save seeds while cooking dinner. I squeeze the guts out of tomatoes, then use the flesh to make spaghetti sauce.

What would you do if you fell in love with a certain variety of bean, but it dropped out of style and the big companies no longer sold its seed? Seed-savers don't have to worry, nor are they concerned about the sky-rocketing seed prices over the last few years. This week's project will walk you through saving the seeds from a few simple vegetables, but beware—you may get hooked and turn into a seed-saving hobbyist!

## Maintaining saved seeds

Even without setting foot in the garden, you can save money by taking better care of those half-full seed packets you bought in the spring. Nearly all vegetable seeds will last at least two years, and many are viable for much longer. The chart below shows the storage life of many types of vegetable seeds under optimal conditions.

| Seed type | Storage life (years) | Seed type | Storage life (years) |
|---|---|---|---|
| asparagus | 3–4 | lettuce | 4–5 |
| beans | 3–4 | onions | 1–2 |
| beets | 4–5 | parsley | 1–2 |
| broccoli | 3–4 | parsnips | 1–2 |
| brussels sprouts | 4–5 | peas | 3–4 |
| canteloupe | 4–5 | peppers | 1–2 |
| carrots | 3–4 | radishes | 4–5 |
| cauliflower | 4–5 | spinach | 3–4 |
| celery | 3–4 | squash | 4–5 |
| corn | 1–2 | Swiss chard | 4–5 |
| cucumbers | 4–5 | tomatoes | 4–5 |
| eggplant | 4–5 | turnips | 4–5 |
| leeks | 3–4 | watermelon | 4–5 |

The trick to giving your seeds as much longevity as possible is to keep water, heat, and light at bay. An airtight box with cardboard dividers will keep your seeds safe and organized, especially if you throw in a few packets of desiccant to soak up excess moisture. To maximize shelf life, keep your box in the freezer, garage, basement, or in another cool, dark place.

Cardboard dividers in an airtight box make it easy to find your stored seeds.

Once you optimize your seed storage tactics, you might be able to save yet more money by buying the larger, value packs of many seed varieties, since they can be used for two or three growing seasons. Whenever using seeds more than a couple of years old, I run a germination test to make sure my seeds are still viable. Just dampen a paper napkin or washcloth, fold it in half with five seeds inside, and put the cloth inside a sealed tupperware container or ziplock bag. Germination rates lower than 80 percent signal some loss of vigor, and I generally assume seeds will turn into spindly plants if less than 50 percent germinate. If you're trying to save an old variety, though, go ahead and plant seeds with low germination rates—just double or triple your seeding rate to ensure you get a good stand.

## Seed biology

Even though seeds can survive for years (or sometimes centuries) before sprouting and growing, they are using energy and are breathing that whole time. You can think of a dormant seed as a bit like a hibernating animal—both have slowed down their bodies and are living on the bare minimum amount of stored food.

*(continued)*

## Which seeds are difficult for beginners to save?

Now that you know how to store them, you can start saving seeds from your own garden. There are a few problems beginners might have with seed-saving, but you can easily work around them by skipping the following types of vegetables:

**Biennials.** Some of your garden plants take two years to produce seeds. Common biennials include carrots, beets, Swiss chard, cabbage, and parsley, all of which have to be protected over the winter and then given space in your garden next year if you want them to flower. I recommend that beginners start by saving seeds from annual crops only and keep buying biennials' seeds, at least for now.

**Outbreeders.** Strong outbreeders like corn, beets, broccoli, and spinach require pollen from a different plant in order to set viable seeds. This can be problematic for the backyard seed-saver since it means that your sweet corn plants are likely to cross with the neighboring field corn, which will give you a mish-mash of odd varieties when you grow out the seeds next year. Strong outbreeders also tend to become less vigorous if you save seeds from fewer than several dozen plants, which can present a space problem in the small garden. At the other extreme, some vegetables—like peas, beans, and most tomatoes—have flowers arranged so that they nearly always pollinate themselves. This latter group is known as strong inbreeders (or self-pollinators), and they are the easiest type of seeds to save.

**Multiple vegetables in the same species.** One way of making out-breeders into easy seed-savers is to only grow one variety of each species in your garden. However, some of our common vegetables share their species with a diverse array of other crops, all of which will cross-pollinate and produce strange mixtures in the next generation. For example, summer squash, acorn squash, and many gourds share the same species and will pollinate each other if grown close together.

**Hybrid seeds.** Finally, you'll want to steer clear of saving seeds from hybrids, since each seed will produce a different kind of plant than its parents. To be on the safe side, look for vegetable varieties listed as "heirloom" or "open-pollinated."

The good news is that there are certain vegetables that make seed-saving very easy. In the next few sections, I'll tell you how to save seeds from a handful of the easiest vegetables—sunflowers, okra, beans, peas, watermelon, squash, peppers, tomatoes, and cucumbers.

## Saving seeds from dry fruits

In this chapter, I'll be using the term *fruit* in the biological sense to refer to the part of the plant that contains the seeds, whether that's a pea pod or a tomato. Dry fruits are tough instead of fleshy when they're mature. Easy seeds you might want to save in this category include sunflowers, okra, beans, and peas. With the exception of the last two vegetables, you'll need to limit your garden to one variety of each species if you want your seeds to grow into plants that look just like their parents. Beans and peas are so highly self-pollinating that the flowers barely open, and you're unlikely to end up with hybrids even if you grow several different varieties side by side.

Allow beans to dry on the vine until the pods are brown.

With dry-fruited vegetables, the plant does nearly all the seed-saving work for you. Just leave fruits in the garden past their normal harvest date, and the seeds inside will mature while the pods turn brown and then dry up.

If you're growing vegetables that produce several rounds of fruit throughout the season (runner beans, indeterminate peas, and okra), you won't even have to designate certain plants for seed-saving. Unless you're a better gardener than I am, you'll miss fruits now and then while harvesting, and these fruits will become over-mature before you come by again. Leave the missed fruits on the vine, and you'll soon have pods to pluck for seed-saving.

On the other hand, sunflowers, bush beans, and determinate peas produce most of their fruits all at once, so a reasonably astute gardener won't miss many. I like to set aside a whole bed of bush beans for seed-saving to make sure I have enough mature pods to start next year's garden.

Sunflower seeds are ready to harvest when the heads nod down and the lower leaves turn brown.

You should be able to brush the flower parts away easily to reveal fat seeds.

If you live in a wet climate, you may need to bring your ripening pods in to hang under the porch roof or in an attic or garage so that they don't mold rather than dry. You can just cut off individual okra pods and sunflower heads, but it's easiest to pull up whole bush bean and pea plants and hang them upside down once the majority of the pods have lost all hint of green.

Be sure the wild birds don't eat your sunflower seeds if you hang the heads on your porch.

Once the pods are completely dry, crack them open with your fingers and pull the seeds out. If you're saving lots of seeds, you might want to learn to thresh (remove the seeds from their pods and stems) and winnow (separate the seeds from the chaff), but most backyard growers won't need to learn these tricks.

Each type of seed can be stored in a homemade envelope constructed out of a folded and taped piece of paper.

Be sure to label your packet with the variety, source, and date.

*Cock's comb from Rose Nell 2010*

Large seeds like beans, peas, and sunflowers should be placed in the freezer for a week after they're completely dry to kill off any insects that might gnaw on the seeds before spring. If your seeds are in a paper packet, place the packets in a ziplock bag, tupperware container, or glass jar before freezing so that the contents won't get wet. Don't open the container to remove your seed packets until the container has come back to room temperature.

## Saving seeds from wet fruits

Watermelons, summer squash, winter squash, and peppers have some of the easiest seeds to save, but they will cross-pollinate with plants in the same species. Check the list below to make sure you're not growing more than one variety of each species in your garden before deciding to save their seeds (and look over your neighbors' gardens, too, since bees will range quite a distance).

*Capsicum annuum*—sweet bell peppers, chili peppers

*Citrullus lanatus*—watermelon, citron

*Cucurbita maxima*—banana squash, Hubbard squash, winter marrow, turban squash, some pumpkins

*Cucurbita mixta*—some cushaws, some gourds

*Cucurbita moschata*—butternut squash, cheese squash, some cushaws

*Cucurbita pepo*—acorn squash, some pumpkins, crookneck squash, some gourds, scallop squash, vegetable marrow, zucchini

Pepper and watermelon seeds can be harvested at the same time you're preparing dinner, as long as you wait until the fruits are fully ripe. (Green peppers are not ripe, but orange, yellow, and red bell peppers are.) For peppers, I just cut out the core and brush the seeds off onto a plate to dry. I enlist the help of my spouse to set aside watermelon seeds as we eat, then rinse the seeds before drying.

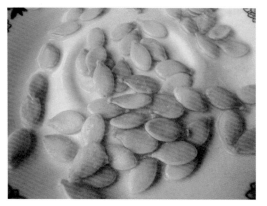

Wait until summer squashes have tough rinds, then cut the fruits in half, scoop out the seeds, and dry them on a saucer.

You'll need to let a few fruits go past their edible stage to save seeds from summer squash (such as zucchini and crookneck squash), but this happens quite naturally in most gardens if you forget to pick the zucchini for a day. Allow the monster squash to grow until they're full size, well colored, and the skin hardens so that you can't easily pierce it with your thumbnail. Then keep the squash on a shelf for another two weeks before cutting each one open and ripping out the seeds. Rinse the seeds and let them dry on a saucer.

The unpalatable flesh of an old squash saved for seeds is still enjoyed by the backyard flock.

Winter squash should be left on the vine until the plants die back all the way (or until frost threatens). Let the squash age on the shelf for a few more weeks just as you did with summer squash, then cut them open and take out the seeds to be saved. No need to waste the flesh—turn it into a pie!

## Fermenting

Gelatinous sacs surrounding the seeds of tomatoes and cucumbers need to be fermented off.

Two of the easy seed-saving vegetables—cucumbers and tomatoes—require their seeds to be fermented before they can be stored. Seeds from both of these vegetables grow inside a gelatinous sac that inhibits germination, and you need to let this sac rot away, or the seeds will have a low germination rate.

Cucumbers should be left on the vine until they turn yellow, then should be aged another week or two, but you can harvest tomato seeds as you cut up the ripe fruits to go into a sauce. Either way, cut the fruit open and squeeze or gouge out the seeds into a small container.

Squeeze the seeds out of a tomato, add a bit of water, and let the mixture ferment until a mold forms on top.

Add enough water to double or triple the contents of the container, then put it in a warm spot. (I use the top of my refrigerator.) Over the next few days, a mold will form on the water's surface, and then you'll notice that gently swishing or stirring the container causes seeds to fall to the bottom.

Pick off the moldy layer and carefully pour the turbid water off your seeds. Add more water, swish the seeds around, and pour the water off again until your seeds look clean. Alternatively, you might find it easier to clean the seeds by running water over them in a fine-meshed sieve. Either way, lay the clean seeds out on a plate to dry.

Cucumbers are vigorous outbreeders, so you won't want to save their seeds unless you're only growing one variety in your garden and there are no other cucumber plants nearby. On the other hand, most tomato varieties are obligate self-pollinators, with the exception of currant tomatoes (a small-fruited tomato that often has dozens of tomatoes in one cluster) and potato-leaf varieties. You can grow one potato-leaf tomato, one type of currant tomato, and any number of tomato-leaf tomatoes side by side in the garden without worrying about hybridization.

## Beyond the basics

Saving seeds from your backyard plants doesn't just maintain heirloom varieties; the process also allows you to select for traits that you want to see more of in your garden. The downside is that you need to be watchful and rogue out plants that aren't true to type so that they don't sully your saved seeds. For example, last year I grew bush beans and shelling beans side by side, and one bee must have managed to cross-pollinate what is usually an obligatory self-pollinating species. This year, nearly all my bush beans from saved seeds looked just how they ought, but one plant grew tendrils and resembled a mixture of a bush bean and a shelling bean. I pulled the plant out so that it wouldn't be able to pollinate nearby beans and dilute next year's seeds.

In a previous section, I alluded to another problem the backyard seed-saver can run across—inbreeding depression. If you save seeds from fewer than 100 outbreeding plants, recessive traits will build up in their offspring, and you'll start to see lower yields. To prevent this problem, swap half the seeds of the same variety with a seed-saving friend so that you can each double your gene pool. In extreme cases, you may need to buy new seeds of that variety and start over.

Since you never know what might happen, it's a good idea to hang onto a few seeds from previous years even though you've saved the same variety this year. If the blight wipes out my tomatoes before I'm able to save seeds, or if my squash cross-pollinates with a neighbor's plant and this year's fruits look odd, I'll have some good seeds to fall back on.

Finally, if you want to save seeds from vegetables not mentioned here, I highly recommend you pick up a copy of the comprehensive *Seed to Seed* by Suzanne Ashworth. The book will help you figure out if you need to use any special tricks to save seeds from your favorite crops.

# Drying food

**GOAL**: Preserve fruits and vegetables using no electricity
**COST**: $0–$20
**TIME**: 1 hour to 2 hours (over the course of 2 to 3 days)
**DIFFICULTY**: Medium
**KID-FRIENDLY**: Yes

The only supplies you need to dry fruits and tomatoes are a sunny car and some cookie sheets.

Last month, I started you off with one of the easiest methods of preserving food—freezing. But wouldn't it be nice to be able to save food for the winter with no input of electricity at any stage of the endeavor? Sun-drying is the answer.

## Why dry food?

Drying food has several advantages over other preservation methods, including these:

**Low start-up costs.** You may eventually decide to buy a dehydrator, as we did, but if you just want to dry the easiest fruits and vegetables, you can get away with buying absolutely no equipment as long as you have a few cookie sheets and a car on hand.

**High nutrition.** Every method of preserving removes some of the vitamins from your food, but drying rivals freezing for producing the most nutritious results. Dried foods tend to lose some vitamin A and vitamin C but hang onto everything else.

**Best flavor.** Although most vegetables taste better frozen, a few vegetables (tomatoes and summer squash especially) and most fruits maintain their flavor best when dried.

**Shelf stable.** Dried food won't last as long as canned food, but it will definitely sit on the shelf for at least a few months with no input of electricity. That makes drying far more helpful than freezing if your region is prone to power outages.

**Very safe.** Pretty much the only way you can hurt yourself while drying food is to cut your finger with a knife while slicing your fruits. Although dried food can go bad, you would see and smell the difference immediately. There's no threat of botulism the way there is with canned food, and your dehydrator definitely won't explode like a pressure canner might.

**Space saving.** Since food becomes much smaller when it's dried, you won't have much trouble finding spots to stash those sun-dried tomatoes and peach roll-ups. (The real trouble will be hiding them from your spouse so they don't disappear the first day.)

All of that said, drying does have one major disadvantage over other methods of food preservation—preparation time. If you end up using dehydration as your primary method of preserving the harvest, you'll probably want to invest in a good food processor and slicer as well as a designated dehydrator.

## *Preparing to sun-dry*

This weekend's project is to try out the easiest method of dehydrating food—sun-drying in your car. I recommend using either peaches or tomatoes for your first experiment for three reasons. First, sun-drying isn't as fast as using a dehydrator, so you can't dry nonacidic vegetables using this method—the veggies will go bad before they dehydrate. Second, tomatoes and peaches should be in bountiful supply in just about all parts of the United States at this time of year since they're at the peak of their season, so you can easily find locally grown produce if you haven't got enough in your garden. And, finally, sun-dried tomatoes and peach leather are some of the tastiest dried foods you'll ever put in your mouth, which will make you want to try more drying experiments on your own.

You won't need many supplies for this project, but it is helpful to have about half a dozen nonstick cookie sheets on hand along with a plastic spatula. The acidic foods you'll be drying can react with aluminum cookie sheets and change color, and they might stick to stainless steel. On the other hand, if you choose to dry halved tomatoes rather than making tomato puree, you can use any kind of flat surface you want. A food processor will make this project a lot easier and will speed up drying time. And, of course, you'll need some kind of vehicle with nontinted windows, preferably one that can be parked so that the majority of the windows point south (or north if you live in the southern hemisphere). You won't be able to drive the car until your fruit is dried, so plan to run your errands in advance.

After gathering your supplies, check the weather forecast. The best time for sun-drying is during a day with highs between 80 and the low 90s, with low humidity, and with no chance of clouds or rain. Cooler days will slow down drying so much that your food might mold, while hotter days will make temperatures inside your car exceed 135°F, at which point your food will burn. You want two of these perfect days in a row (three if the highs are on the low end of the range).

Once you find the right day, hunt down your peaches or tomatoes, keeping your number of cookie sheets and car surface area in mind. One cookie sheet will hold anywhere from 1 cup to 2 cups of fruit puree (depending on whether you want the leather to be thin and dry in a day or thick and take two or three days to dehydrate). Then wake up early and get started in time to put your peaches or tomatoes in the car by 10 a.m. at the latest.

## *How to make peach leather*

This section will assume you're making peach leather, but keep in mind that nearly the same technique can be used to prepare any other kind of fruit leather. I'll also tell you where you'd do things differently to make sun-dried tomatoes.

**Prepare your peaches.** Unless you bought your peaches from a commercial orchard, chances are the fruits need some bad spots cut out. Scoop out wormy centers, remove the pits, and slice off the skin. If your fruit is relatively pristine, the last step can be expedited by dropping the peaches in boiling water for just a few seconds until the skins can be slipped right off.

If you're drying tomatoes instead of peaches, just cut out the cores and slice the tomatoes in half. Seeds and skins are fine.

Pureeing fruits speeds their drying time.

**Puree the raw peaches in a food processor.** Even though most people dry their tomatoes merely cut in half, I've found that you'll get faster and more even dehydration by pureeing tomatoes the same way you would peaches. Since we usually use sun-dried tomatoes as a condiment rather than eating them whole, pureeing the tomatoes at this step also saves preparation time later.

**Add a bit of honey and lemon juice.** This step should be skipped when drying tomatoes, and it can also be skipped with fruit if you wish. However, lemon juice is helpful to maintain color and prevent mold formation during drying, while honey counteracts the lemon's sourness and adds pliancy to the fruit leather so that it rolls rather than tears. A tablespoon of honey and half a tablespoon of lemon juice per cup of fruit puree seems to be just about right.

Pour the puree and honey mixture onto cookie sheets. The official method of making fruit leather involves spreading your puree on skins of saran wrap, but we don't keep that kind of disposable in the house. Cookie sheets work fine, although you probably won't get perfect-looking fruit leather.

Jiggle the pan, and your fruit puree will form an even layer.

**Spread the puree evenly across the cookie sheet.** Just jiggle the pan, and your pureed fruit will quickly settle across the entire surface.

If you are drying halved tomatoes instead of puree, simply set the tomatoes cut-side up on the cookie sheet. Optionally, you may sprinkle the cut sides very lightly with salt and pepper.

**Lay your cookie sheets in a sunny car to dry.** The trickiest part will be adding wedges underneath different parts of your sheets so that the puree doesn't puddle on one end of the tray. You'll also want to check on your fruit puree at least two or three times a day, moving pans that are drying fastest to cooler parts of the car and replacing them with slower-drying sheets. Maximum drying time should not exceed two and a half days.

**Scrape the fruit leather off the trays with a spatula.** Depending on how much moisture is left in your leather, it may peel off or crumple up. I prefer the slightly wetter leather even though it's less pretty, but you should taste your first batch at various stages to decide what you like best.

**Store your fruit leather.** Fruit leather will last at room temperature for about a month, or you can stash it in the fridge or freezer where it will last for a few months or a year, respectively. Dried tomatoes will sit on the shelf even longer since you'll probably dry them to a lower moisture content. Either way, seal your dried produce in an airtight container and store it in a dark, dry place.

## Hollywood Sun-Dried Tomatoes

Makes one cup.

Actor Frank Hoyt Taylor introduced me to this delicious garnish made of sun-dried tomatoes marinated in garlic, basil, and olive oil.

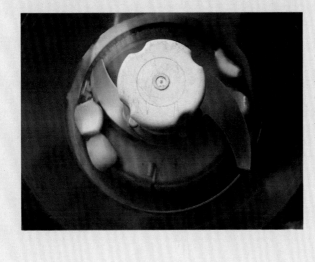

Put three large cloves of garlic in the food processor and cover them up with olive oil. Blend. (Yes, I can count. I figure those two small cloves on the right equal one large clove.)

*(continued)*

# Hollywood Sun-Dried Tomatoes *(continued)*

Add about a cup of loosely packed basil leaves to the food processor. Blend again. Add a bit of salt and pepper if you didn't salt your tomatoes in the drying stage.

Line the bottom of your container with one layer of sun-dried tomatoes or sun-dried tomato puree. Spoon on enough of your garlic, basil, and oil mixture to liberally cover the tomatoes. Lay down another layer of tomatoes, another layer of goop, another layer of tomatoes, and so forth until you reach the top of your container.

Pour olive oil over your tomatoes until the oil completely fills the container. Put on the lid and let your concoction marinate in the fridge for a few days. The tomatoes will plump back out and become infused with herb flavors.

*(continued)*

## Hollywood Sun-Dried Tomatoes *(continued)*

We consider Hollywood sun-dried tomatoes to be a winter treat, so we toss them in the freezer immediately. After they've frozen, then thawed back out in the fridge months later, the flavors have blended perfectly. We use the result in egg salad, as a spread on sandwiches, a topping on pizza or fried eggs, or eaten alone as a snack.

Once you pull the tomatoes out of the juices, you're left with flavored oil that will spice up just about any dish. If you can't think of any other way to use it, try brushing the oil mixture over a piece of stale bread and toasting it for instant, delicious garlic bread.

The only thing to be careful of is the threat of botulism if you let your Hollywood sun-dried tomatoes sit out on the counter, or if you leave them in the fridge for a few weeks. We never seem to have a problem eating up a cup of these tomatoes in a day or two, so I don't think you'll have a problem enjoying them in time!

## *Beyond the basics*

Very few people ask what to do with dried fruits and tomatoes—they're so good plain that you mostly just eat them. If you do decide to cook with dried produce, you'll get best results if you soak the food in a liquid for a few hours until the pieces plump back up, then toss them in soups, pies, etc. Water works fine as the reconstituting agent, but you can use broth if you're hydrating vegetables, or fruit juice if you're plumping up fruit; both liquids will add a little additional flavor.

Reusable fruit leather inserts make it easy to peel whole sheets of leather off your tray.

If you fall in love with drying food, you'll want more control over the process and the ability to dry more types of food. That means buying or making a designated food dehydrator that heats food more evenly and at a higher temperature. Solar dehydrators work well in arid climates, while electric dehydrators are more appropriate for cloudy, humid areas.

# Building a chicken coop or tractor

---

**GOAL**: Prepare a spot for a small laying flock to call home
**COST**: $20 to $200
**TIME**: 5 hours to 15 hours
**DIFFICULTY**: Hard
**KID-FRIENDLY**: Maybe

---

Chickens have a multitude of uses on the permaculture homestead.

Once you figure out their living arrangements, chickens become fun and easy garden companions that nearly any homesteader can handle. This week's project walks you through making (or buying) the perfect coop or tractor for your farm.

## *Are you ready for chickens?*

Does your vision of a farm include a milk cow, a couple of draft horses, goats clearing brush, and sheep grazing your pastures into lawns? While it's possible to work up to such a diverse menagerie, I recommend that beginning homesteaders keep a firm handle on their animal urges and stick to the following low-work livestock—compost worms, honeybees, rabbits, and chickens.

139

I'll sing the praises of chickens in a moment, but before you get too excited, you should make sure that you're ready for these feathered companions. Although chickens are small, they require a relatively extensive pasture if you don't want them to end up living in a smelly and barren run. You'll need to allow at least 100 square feet per bird (preferably two or three times that amount). Using the diverse pasturing systems outlined below, that space could include the woods behind your house, your lawn, parts of your garden, your orchard, and more. But if you live on a postage-stamp lot and your entire outdoor area amounts to 250 square feet, you'll have to get very creative to keep chickens happy.

Chickens also require a certain amount of caretaking time. If you streamline their housing with an automatic waterer and deep bedding, chicken-related chores may amount to about 15 minutes per day. You'll probably spend a lot more time with your flock than that, though, because they're just a pleasure to watch and to be around.

Growing your own meat is spiritually satisfying and also provides quality nutrition you can't buy in the store.

Finally, and most importantly, you need to find peace with where your meat comes from if you raise chickens. Yes, you can buy a pair of laying hens and ignore the fact that their brothers were slaughtered, but a chicken only lays well for a couple of years before her egg production dwindles. Unless you want your farm to turn into a petting zoo for dozens of old, nonproductive hens, you'll need to learn to butcher your birds eventually. The experience can be somewhat traumatic for newbies, but in the long run, I feel empowered knowing how to raise my own meat, and I suspect you will too. And you'll be better prepared to deal with those useless male kids your milk goat churns out if you're able to butcher meat animals. (If the idea of raising meat animals appeals to you but feels a bit daunting, why not use this as the impetus for your "Teamwork" or "Apprenticeships" project?)

I hope I haven't scared you away from raising poultry (or livestock of any kind), because chickens are some of the most productive and rewarding partners you can have on a homestead. They'll eat up your kitchen scraps, turning them into much higher quality eggs than you can buy in the grocery store. Your flock's manure can be made into luscious compost to feed your plants. And you can even allow your chickens to eat weeds in the garden before planting time. If you've got the space, time, and willingness to be part of the food chain, chickens will find a place on your homestead and in your heart.

## Are chickens legal?

Photo credit: Shoshana Glick

Many cities allow urban homesteaders to keep a backyard flock.

*(continued)*

## Are chickens legal? *(continued)*

Those of you living in a town or city may be wondering whether you're allowed to keep livestock in your backyard. If you don't know anyone in your town who is already raising chickens, it's worth taking a field trip to town hall to find out the rules. Urban areas that allow chickens often have certain restrictions in place—for example, you might be allowed up to four chickens but no rooster, and you might have to keep your flock at least ten feet away from the property boundaries.

If your zoning laws prohibit chickens, are you out of luck? Across the nation, urban homesteaders are showing their neighbors that chickens—and honeybees and rabbits and even goats—cause no more noise, smell, or health problems than a large dog. Dozens of cities have already relaxed their zoning laws to allow chickens within city limits, and your planning offices may follow suit if you approach them politely with the facts in hand.

## Deciding on a chicken housing system

Do you want to raise your birds in a tractor or stationary coop? Will their manure drop through a screened bottom or be captured in carbon-rich bedding? How large does the flock's interior and exterior living area need to be? There's no one set answer to these thorny chicken questions, which is why I labeled this exercise "hard." You have to consider your neighborhood association, your gardening prowess, and several other factors while developing the housing system that's best for your flock. Hopefully, the information below will help you clarify your needs and get those creative juices flowing.

*Coop vs. tractor vs. pasture vs. free range*   I can't recommend the traditional coop and stationary run system to anyone, since it tends to turn into a smelly and muddy mess, but each of the other options has its own appeal.

Chicken tractors are best in suburban areas where the chickens' pasture doubles as your lawn and garden. These small coop-and-run combos are moved to a new patch of earth every day, allowing the chickens access to some greenery and bugs without scratching any single spot bare.

Chickens raised on pasture lay eggs with bright orange yolks and lots of omega-3s.

If you've got more space, rotational pastures surrounding a stationary coop let your birds find more free food, which lowers feed bills and increases the quality of their eggs. Coops are also more water- and windproof than tractors, which generally results in healthier birds. The downside of coops is that you'll have to clean out manure and mow the pastures a few times each year to keep the chicken yard from growing up in brush.

A third option is to entirely free range your birds, which gives them access to even more wild food and reduces or eliminates your need to manicure pastures. Free ranging has a variety of downfalls, though, including predators, garden damage, half-feral chickens that roost in trees instead of in the coop, chicken poop on your front porch, eggs hidden under bushes, and unhappy neighbors. I suspect free ranging will only work for a small percentage of my readers, and even those may choose to restrict free ranging to winter when the garden is less sensitive to scratching feet.

*Manure management*   Another choice you'll need to make is how to deal with chicken manure. Your birds' excrement is a high-quality input to your garden, but it can also be a vector for disease within the flock, as well as a smelly and unsightly mess. No matter which system you choose, you'll know you're doing it wrong if your chicken coop stinks, you're breeding flies, and you aren't willing to kneel down inside.

Chicken tractors make manure management easy. You simply pull the tractor to a fresh spot in the lawn or garden daily, and the bit of manure left behind melts into the soil within a few days. The only problem you may run into is if your tractor is too heavy to move easily and you leave it in one spot too long.

Some chicken coops are raised off the ground and have a screened bottom so that the chicken manure falls through onto the earth below.

I really can't recommend this system, which looks a lot better on paper than it does in reality. First of all, poop inevitably builds up on the screen in certain spots, so your chickens are walking through their excrement. And the manure on the ground is still out in the open where it quickly loses high-quality nitrogen into the air and attracts flies.

Deep bedding is a manure management system that creates a virtually odorless compost pile on the coop floor.

My favorite manure management option is deep bedding. Plan your coop to have no floor and then layer several inches of high-carbon bedding (like wood shavings, autumn leaves, or straw) on the ground. You'll need to add a bit more bedding every few days or weeks (depending on your stocking density) so that the bedding soaks up your chickens' manure and doesn't get wet or covered with poop. The result is a compost pile right on the floor of your coop, which heats your birds in the winter and provides certain essential vitamins. Studies have shown that chickens on deep bedding are healthier than those in any other type of stationary coop manure-management system, since beneficial microorganisms build up in the deep bedding and outcompete disease-causing organisms. In addition, once the bedding gets to be a foot thick, you can clean out the bottom few inches of well-composted manure and bedding to feed the garden (but be sure to leave several inches in the coop as composting inoculant). What's not to like?

*Square footage and number of chickens*   The size of your coop or tractor will depend on how many birds you're housing and on how much access they have to the outdoors. At the minimum, plan on four square feet per bird, but be aware that these are very cramped quarters unless your chickens spend all day outside roaming around and just come in to jump on the roost at night. Chickens are short, so they don't really need their coop to be more than three feet tall, but you might choose to make the ceiling high enough so you can walk in (which will also make your chickens feel a bit more secure when they roost).

So how many chickens should be in your first flock? Chickens are social animals, so it's cruel to keep one chicken by itself, and at the other extreme I think that you should split groups of more than twenty-five birds into multiple living areas so that each hen doesn't have to keep track of her pecking order in such a large flock. Figure out how many eggs your family eats per day and multiply the number by two to find out how many hens you need to provide all your eggs even in the winter.

A rooster is not necessary for eggs but will be required if you want to raise your own chicks. He will overmate your hens if you keep him in a small tractor or with fewer than three or four hens, and he'll also crow in the morning, which might be a problem if you live in the city. On the other hand, if you want to free range your birds, or if predators are common on your homestead, I've found that a rooster pays for himself by keeping the flock in line and out of foxes' bellies.

*Nest boxes and perches*   Chickens require very little infrastructure in their coop, but you'll want to build one nest box for every three to five hens and provide a linear foot of roost for each bird.

Nest boxes can be as simple as a plastic milk crate or five gallon bucket turned on its side, with a short section of wood along the bottom of the front to form a lip, holding in the bedding. Alternatively, you can build a nest box out of plywood, preferably with a removable bottom to make it easier to clean. A door on the back of the box allows you to reach inside and gather the day's eggs without entering the coop.

Roosts can be made from wooden dowels, two-by-fours, two-by-twos, or even sticks you gather in the woods. Laying hens often like to roost up high, and if you provide perches at various levels, most will end up huddled together on the tallest one. Heavier birds sometimes have trouble flapping up to such high perches, though.

*Ventilation*   Don't seal your coop or tractor the way you would a house built for humans. Chickens don't like drafts (which you can think of as a breeze rustling their feathers) but do like lots of airflow that vents moisture and smells to the outdoors. We live in zone 6 and have successfully wintered our birds in open tractors with one section enclosed on three sides by a tarp or old carpet. The chickens were fine overnight, although they did complain about having to jump down onto the snowy ground during the day. If you're building a coop with store-bought materials, be sure to provide windows or vents to allow for airflow.

*Doors*   You'll need one human-sized door in your chicken coop so you can maintain the bedding, but any other doors can be "popholes"—just as tall and as wide as your chicken. We have four popholes in each of our coops so that we can rotate chickens through different pastures each week, ensuring that our busy flock doesn't scratch any one area bare.

A pophole is a chicken-sized door.

If you're building a chicken tractor, you'll probably want multiple doors as well. You won't be walking into the tractor, but it's useful to have a large door that will let you reach in and catch a troublesome bird. At some point, you may want to install temporary fencing around the tractor and open a smaller door to give your chickens a quick and dirty pasture, especially if you're leaving town for a week and won't be able to move their tractor.

In addition to wild predators, you need to protect your chickens from cats and dogs.

*Predators*　We aren't the only animals that think chickens are tasty. So do owls, hawks, raccoons, weasels, cats, dogs, and many more wild and tame predators. When planning your tractor or coop and pasture, you'll need to think about your predator pressure and how much protection you should provide to keep your flock safe.

A well-trained outdoor dog like ours makes predator-proofing the coop nearly unnecessary. At the other extreme, if you have heavy predator pressure, you may need to take steps such as using hardware cloth instead of chicken wire around pastures and in tractors, burying a solid barrier several inches into the ground around the base of pastures and coops, making sure there are no holes in the coop larger than about two inches in diameter and shutting your chickens in every night. You're more likely to have predators around if you live in a rural area and regularly see wildlife, but even in town, neighborhood dogs can take their toll on your flock.

When raising chicks, you have to be even more careful, since rats and snakes can slip through very small holes. The best way to keep out rats is prevention—never leave more food out in the open than your chickens will eat in one sitting, and store unused feed in a metal container. To keep out snakes, simply cover any holes in the walls.

*Cheap vs. pretty*   The final factor to consider when building your coop or tractor is how much money you want to spend and how well the building needs to blend into its surroundings. My husband is quite adept at making do, and he was able to scrounge up old boards, cut down small cedar trees, and build a tractor for under $20. You can house your chickens equally cheaply if you're willing to use found supplies.

On the other hand, our tractors might not fly in suburbia. Buying all new lumber and roofing tin and adding a coat of paint might make your tractor cost a couple of hundred dollars or more. But that price tag will be worth it if it keeps your neighbors from calling Animal Control.

## Gallery of chicken tractors

Building a home for your chickens is the most intense project in this book, and you shouldn't feel bad if you decide to buy a premade coop or tractor. (You should, however, expect to spend up to a thousand dollars to get a quality product.) On the other hand, if you've got the time, I recommend trying your hand at building your own.

The most important factor to consider when designing a chicken tractor is weight. An extremely common mistake is for the husband to build a fancy chicken tractor that's too heavy for his wife to tug onto a new patch of ground every day, so the beautiful structure turns into a tiny stationary coop that crowds birds and makes them sick.

Otherwise, the design of your chicken tractor will be determined by the factors listed in the last section. The photos below should get your creative juices flowing.

Photo credit: RDG

RDG from WeekendHomestead.net constructed a simple chicken tractor to house his extra roosters while they were growing up to broiler size. He wrote: "The chicken tractor I built is made from 2" x 6" pressure-treated lumber for the frame. The frame is 12 feet by 4 feet. Half inch EMT metal electrical conduit is used for the hoops. Chicken wire is used to enclose the structure. The ends are made from half inch pressure treated plywood. I have hung a feeder and automatic watering bucket from the conduit. I used the only 4-foot tarp I could find to keep rain off the broilers." RDG's design could be made with lighter framing components (a 2" x 4" bottom and PVC pipe hoops) for an easier to pull tractor that's just as simple to build.

Photo credit: Neil Brooks

Neil Brooks built the 4 feet x 4 feet chicken tractor above based on Joel Salatin's design. The 2" x 2" construction, low profile, and open sides give a lot of living area for very little weight. Judicious cross-bracing will allow you to build even larger tractors while still using thin, light lumber.

Photo credit: Duncan Sickler

Duncan Sickler's chicken tractor would fit into any neighborhood, no matter how nice. He built his tractor using the Catawba coop plans available online. The tractor is an A-frame structure with an open-bottomed "downstairs" and a wood-floored upstairs. Chickens hang out on the ground but head up a ramp to lay eggs or roost for the night.

Photo credit: Duncan Sickler

Winter can be a tough time for chickens in tractors, so Duncan designed a deep bedding box to go beneath his tractor and keep his flock clean and dry during the cold season. The box is a simple rectangular structure filled with wood shavings and straw.

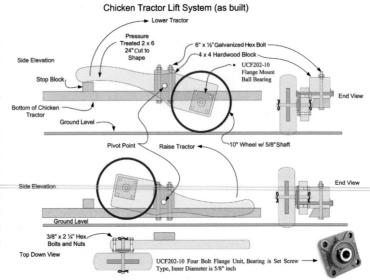

**Chicken Tractor Lift System (as built)**

Lower Tractor

Pressure Treated 2 x 6 24" Cut to Shape

6" x ½" Galvanized Hex Bolt

4 x 4 Hardwood Block

Side Elevation

Stop Block

UCF202-10 Flange Mount Ball Bearing

End View

Bottom of Chicken Tractor

Ground Level

Pivot Point

Raise Tractor

10" Wheel w/ 5/8" Shaft

Side Elevation

End View

Ground Level

3/8" x 2 ¼" Hex Bolts and Nuts

Top Down View

UCF202-10 Four Bolt Flange Unit, Bearing is Set Screw Type, Inner Diameter is 5/8" inch

Duncan also developed the wheel lift system shown above for his chicken tractor. Although a bit complex, the system solves a problematic feature of chicken tractors—you either make them wheel-less so the chickens can't slip underneath the walls, or you add wheels to make the tractor easier to move but risk escaped hens. With the wheel lift in place, you can pull a wheeled tractor, then flip a switch and set the tractor back down to ground level.

## Gallery of chicken coops

An existing outbuilding can be converted into a roomy chicken coop.

Chicken coops are easier to design than chicken tractors because you don't have to worry about mobility. If you live on an established farm, chances are there's already a shed, outbuilding, or corner of your barn that could be turned into a coop without much effort. I've even heard of suburbanites who built a coop in the corner of their garage.

If you're starting from scratch with store-bought materials, I recommend using basic "stick house" construction practices. Walls are framed one at a time using two-by-fours for structural integrity and sheets of plywood to close up the space. The roof begins with two-by-four or two-by-six rafters, topped with plywood and then some sort of roofing material. You can make a lot of mistakes on your chicken coop and then be a pro when the time comes to put an addition on your house!

You can build a new chicken coop out of 2" x 4" lumber and plywood.

My husband built one of our chicken coops out of used roofing tin, old doors, and free pallets. While our coop might not pass muster in suburbia, the only store-bought components were a handful of screws and a couple of hinges.

We're skinflints, so our chicken coops are cobbled together out of old lumber, pallets, doors, tin, and even cardboard. The supplies cost next to nothing, and we have no neighbors to complain.

## Designing a chicken pasture system

If you're making a tractor, once you create the structure, you're done for the week. However, if you've built a coop, you need to spend some time designing and building pastures to give your birds access to bugs and weeds. Your pasture can be a separate area set aside specifically for your chickens, or it can be an integral part of your homestead, encompassing your orchard, garden, and lawn. Either way, you should follow these guidelines:

**Fencing.** If you have no predator pressure, your fencing can be as simple as a roll of four- or five-foot-tall chicken wire stretched between metal fence posts about fifteen feet apart. We've also had good luck using plastic garden trellis material for temporary fencing. In either case, be sure to tack down the bottom of the wire so that chickens don't slip underneath—logs and old boards work great. If you don't have a guard dog, though, you will probably want to use some sort of electric fencing or heavy-duty materials like chain link. Dogs and foxes can chew right through chicken wire. Hog, horse, or cattle panels are expensive but make fencing extremely easy while allowing you to branch out into miniature goats, sheep, or other livestock using the same infrastructure.

The simplest design for a rotational chicken pasture system consists of a coop in the center with paddocks radiating out like the spokes on a wheel.

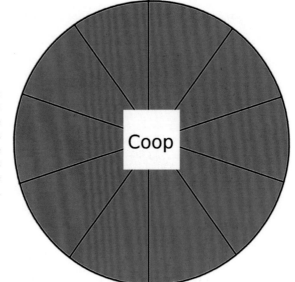

**Paddocks.** Rather than building one pasture that will eventually get scratched bare, split your area into several smaller paddocks. At the very least, build four paddocks, but six or more will keep your pasture healthier.

**Space.** Allow as much room as you can. As an absolute, bare minimum, your pasture should have forty square feet of space per bird, but I find that my chickens are happiest with about ten times that much grazing area.

**Sun and shade.** Your chickens will prefer sun in the winter and shade in the summer, so either give them separate pasture areas for the hot and cold seasons or provide a bit of both. Also, be aware that trees and bushes will protect your chickens from hawks (and will make the flock more inclined to hunt for food since they'll feel safer).

**Mowing.** You'll need to mow your pasture at intervals, especially in the spring, to keep the grasses at peak palatability. Think about pasture maintenance when you design the layout.

I highly recommend that you do a bit more reading on rotational pasturing so you don't spend your first year reinventing the wheel the way I did. Although the book is really about ruminants, *Greener Pasture on Your Side of the Fence* by Bill Murphy is the best text I've found to help you get the most out of rotational pastures. You might also enjoy reading about my own trials with chicken pasturing at www.avianaquamiser.com/news. Finally, Harvey Ussery's *The Small-Scale Poultry Flock* is the best possible introduction to making chickens a part of your permaculture homestead.

# Rain barrel

**GOAL**: Collect free water from the sky to hydrate your garden
**COST**: $15–$40
**TIME**: 2 hours to 3 hours
**DIFFICULTY**: Medium
**KID-FRIENDLY**: Yes

As long as you have gutters, making a rain barrel is an easy exercise that will save money on your water bill.

Photo credit: Rain barrels. Water Resources Program at Rutgers NJAES, 31 Oct. 2011. Web. 23 Nov. 2011.

Collecting rainwater is one of the few homesteading techniques in this book that I consider important enough to share but don't use in my own life. My husband and I live in the central Appalachian mountains, in an area that's sometimes called a temperate rainforest because of the sheer quantity of rain that falls every year—averaging around an inch a week. Sometimes the rain doesn't fall quite on schedule, but we also have a huge creek that doesn't seem impacted by the bit of water we draw off at intervals for irrigation. We drink from a well that never runs dry (and that is fed by a completely wooded watershed that we manage), so we don't worry much about water. (We also don't have gutters, so rain barrels aren't low-hanging fruit for us.)

That said, I suspect that at least 90 percent of our readers either pay a water bill every month or live in a hotter, drier climate where their well can't meet the demands of a big garden. If that's true for you, then collecting free water from the sky will help your pocketbook and will give your plants a chance to thrive without sucking already stressed rivers dry. City dwellers will find that collecting rainwater also keeps the precious liquid from being treated like sewage in their municipal wastewater plant, a process that increases taxes and uses up valuable energy. Finally, many people prefer using the soft water they collect from their roofs to wash their hair or clothes rather than end up with soap scum from hard well water.

## Supplies and tools

Here are the materials you'll need to make a simple 55-gallon rain barrel:

- 55-gallon barrel with closed top (You can often find used 55-gallon barrels at feed stores for about $10. Be sure to choose a barrel that has carried food rather than chemicals, and wash the barrel out if it's dirty inside.)
- 2 cinder blocks
- 1 spigot
- plumber's tape (optional)
- plastic colander or basket
- 2 square feet of wire mesh (like a window screen) or of air filtration material
- 1 flexible connector arm that fits on the end of your gutter's downspout (optional)
- 1 tube of silicone
- 1 small piece of PVC pipe (or a second spigot or various connector pieces)

Have these tools on hand:

- drill
- jigsaw
- caulk gun
- staple gun
- hacksaw or reciprocating saw

# Rain is a perfect season

Rain is a perfect season to plant seeds.
When the skies flooded the earth,
We stood strong, out of doors,
Where we could watch the birds swoop
For worms.

Our parents seemed to hibernate in a
Different world completely.
If they lived through us, warm, rain-drenched
Soggy-haired creatures,
It did not show.

We were immune to thunder,
We repelled lightning.
Mom and Daddy would stand
Out on the porch, barely braving
The roof, shouting,

"Come in if the lightning gets too close!"
The neighbors thought they were cop-out parents.
We were glad for it.
We took five-gallon buckets,
Filled them with gutter water,

And dumped them on our heads.
We smelled our small southern city
Clean as the water washed off
The cars, the industrial grime,
And our own boredom,

All of which accumulated on roofs,
Ran into the drain pipes,
And journeyed to the gutter,
Where we would race sticks
To the bottom of the hill.

After the sticks circled around over the drain,
And the gushing water pulled them down
Into the underworld, after that, neither me,
Nor my siblings, could guess where our
Rain day stream must go.

Maggie Hess, livingwithmaggie.branchable.com

# Construction

Downspout

Leaf strainer

Overflow pipe

Spigot

You can build this rain barrel for $40, or much less if you use found supplies.

In essence, all you're doing is channeling water from your gutter into a modified barrel. Let's start at the bottom and work our way up.

Your rain barrel should be located as close as possible to the downspout of your gutter system. Lay down two cinder blocks and set the 55-gallon barrel atop the blocks. The purpose of the cinder blocks is to raise your barrel off the ground (so you'll have a bit of elbow room when hooking up hoses to your spigot) and to increase your water pressure slightly. If you're a more accomplished DIYer, you can build a tower to raise your rain barrel off the ground and increase your water pressure even more, but be sure your tower is stable—55 gallons of water weighs almost 500 pounds!

Near the bottom of the barrel, a spigot will allow you to drain water from your barrel to use in the garden. To install the spigot, either drill a large hole or start with a pilot hole and then cut the rest of the opening with your jigsaw. Either way, try to make the hole as round and properly sized as possible so it won't leak. Wrap one thickness of plumber's tape around the threaded part of the spigot and screw it into the hole. (If you don't have plumber's tape, you can instead coat the threads with silicone before screwing the spigot in. Be aware that if you use silicone anywhere on the barrel, you'll need to allow the silicone to cure for a couple of days before letting rain flow into the barrel.)

Next, install an overflow pipe near the top of the barrel. There are a variety of ways to create an overflow pipe, the easiest of which is to use silicone to attach a small length of PVC pipe to the barrel, as shown in the diagram on page 157. If you don't want excess water to puddle on the ground near the barrel, you can instead attach a spigot and hose to channel the water into the garden. Or you can go to a bit more trouble and use various connector pieces to channel the overflow water back into the original drainage system for your gutters.

Working as a team makes rain barrel production easier and more fun.

Photo credit: Rain barrels. Water Resources Program at Rutgers NJAES, 31 Oct. 2011. Web. 23 Nov. 2011.

Now you're ready to move up to the top of the barrel where water flows in. You'll be adding two layers of screening to this area—a plastic colander or basket underneath to give the inlet structural integrity, and then window screening or air filtration material to catch leaves and mosquitoes. After each storm, you can scoop the leaves out and add them to your compost pile.

Mark the outside of your hole by tracing around the colander or basket, but plan to cut about half an inch inside the line so that the colander will sit in the hole rather than fall through into the barrel. Use a drill to make a pilot hole, then cut out the opening with your jigsaw. Apply a bead of silicone around the rim of your hole and set the basket or colander inside, gluing it down. Drape your window screen or air filtration material on top and staple that in place.

Next, connect the downspout to the barrel. This step may be as simple as cutting the downspout with your hacksaw or reciprocating saw and letting the water flow into your colander, or you might install a flexible connector arm onto your downspout to make sure the water doesn't splash around and that it ends up just where you want it.

Finally, use the last of your silicone to seal up any holes through which a mosquito could make its way into the rain barrel. It may also be necessary to add a screen to your overflow spout.

If all this sounds too tough, many nonprofits and municipal systems sell premade rain barrels for $60 to $190, and some offer workshops where experts help you build a rain barrel for a far lower price. On the other hand, if price is what's holding you back, you might be able to find all the parts for your rain barrel for free by browsing the throwaway items on the curb during the next trash day. No matter how you find or make your barrel, you'll no longer have to feel guilty about using expensive potable water to feed your garden!

## Daisy-chained rain barrels

Photo credit: Brian Cooper

Brian Cooper daisy-chained four barrels together and added a feature to drain the first flush of water out the back.

*(continued)*

## Daisy-chained rain barrels  *(continued)*

Photo credit: Brian Cooper

Brian Cooper found several local sources of free or cheap 55-gallon barrels, so he decided to put them to use. He warns those of you following his lead to find out what the barrels contained before bringing them home. Barrels that were used to haul soap and food products are generally safe to wash out and reuse, but steer clear of barrels that contained oils or toxic chemicals.

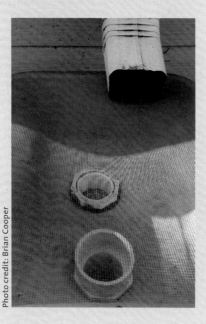

Photo credit: Brian Cooper

Brian hooked the rain barrels together so that they all fed one spigot and were filled by a single downspout. Under the downspout, he installed a screened tub with two outlets—one flush with the bottom of the tub that catches the first rain, and a slightly taller outlet that feeds the rain barrels as the storm continues. This system allows Brian to discard the initial gallon of water, which is generally full of dirt and debris that accumulated on the roof since the last storm. The screen in the tub also catches leaves, which Brian brushes off after each rainfall.

*(continued)*

**Daisy-chained rain barrels** *(continued)*

Although Brian's system may seem like overkill, removing the first flush of water keeps the contents of his rain barrels very clean. If you installed this type of system on a building with a metal roof, you could use the contents of the rain barrels as backup drinking water, potable after just a bit of treatment.

## *Watering your garden*

One of the best uses for rain-barrel water is to irrigate your garden. Even if you live in a damp climate, giving your garden a hand during small droughts can increase your yields and also ensure that young fruit trees survive before they are able to establish deep roots.

Your first step is to decide on an irrigation system. If your garden is quite small, you can simply fill a bucket and scoop out water to spot irrigate, or hook up a hose to do the same. Alternatively, you can use pitcher irrigation in key areas—bury an unglazed, hole-free ceramic pot in the soil, fill it with water, and the liquid will seep out into a three- to six-foot-diameter area, keeping the soil at a constant 80 percent saturation. For larger gardens, I recommend spending more money to set up either drip irrigation (great for water conservation but expensive and nitpicky) or pulsating sprinklers (cheap, can handle dirty water, and last for years with little maintenance). Be aware that you'll need to install a pump in your rain barrel to build up enough water pressure to make a pulsating sprinkler run.

How much water does your garden need? Most plants benefit from around an inch of water per week during the summer, which equals a little less than two-thirds of a gallon (0.62 gallons) per square foot. So, if you want to make sure your twenty-square-foot strawberry bed gets enough water, you need to apply at least 12 gallons of water ($20 \times 0.62 = 12.4$) once a week. Don't wait to water until your plants begin to wilt, or you'll see lowered production, but do keep an eye on rainfall and hold back on watering if precipitation has already achieved your weekly goal.

For more accurate watering, consider your unique garden characteristics. Water drains out of sandy soil quickly but can stick around in clay soil for extended periods of time. Climate also matters—a hot summer day in the dry southwestern United States can see nearly half an inch of water evaporating from the soil surface between dawn and dusk, while summer in the Pacific Northwest is generally cloudy, so a garden in Washington state may lose only a fifth of an inch of water per day in August. If you have sandy soil and live in a hot, sunny climate, you'll definitely want to mitigate water loss by adding lots of organic matter to your soil, keeping a constant mulch cover, and watering deeply and more often.

Finally, it's essential to understand the negative effects of improper watering.

**Frequent shallow watering tempts plants to keep all their roots close to the soil surface.** Then when you forget to water for a few days, your plants shrivel up and die. Instead, you should water deeply (about an inch of water at a time) once or twice a week to promote the growth of far-reaching roots.

**Sprinkler irrigation in the evening can promote the growth of fungi,** especially among sensitive vegetables like tomatoes and cucumbers. For these plants, water first thing in the morning on a sunny day so that their leaves can dry off quickly, or use drip irrigation.

**Rapid watering with a hose can cause soil crust formation in clayey soils,** especially if you tilled your soil too finely or are watering very dry earth. A soil crust forms when tiny soil particles are washed into the air pores between larger soil particles, forming a solid mass which prevents further water from soaking into the ground. To prevent crusting, water clay soil slowly and use no-till techniques.

**Excess water can flush micronutrients out of the topsoil.** Many micronutrients are soluble in water, so if you forget and leave the sprinkler on overnight, you'll wash these essential minerals deep into the subsoil where plant roots can't reach them. Your vegetables won't be too thrilled about sitting in soggy ground for days there-after either.

Despite these potential pitfalls, once you see the results of a well-watered garden, you may realize that one rain barrel isn't enough. Soon you'll be putting gutters on your barn and filling up thousand-gallon tanks, creating an oasis in your backyard.

# SEPTEMBER
*(March Down Under)*

# Eating seasonally

**GOAL**: Stock up on local produce when it's in season
**COST**: As much or as little as you like
**TIME**: 1 hour to 4 hours
**DIFFICULTY**: Easy
**KID-FRIENDLY**: Yes

Homesteading provides food tastier than you could buy in any store at a cost less than you'd spend at the cheapest grocery. While growing your own food is the long-term goal, you can realize some of the same benefits just by learning to eat seasonally.

## Why eat in season?

If you grew up eating food from a fully stocked grocery store, you are probably used to cooking with just a few favorite vegetables. I know that before I started gardening, a trip to the store always resulted in a couple of heads of broccoli, some carrots and onions, cabbage, lettuce, and tomatoes. I was able to make salad, soup, a stir-fry, and steamed broccoli—that was pretty much my entire repertoire, and I cycled through each meal a few times a month.

In stark contrast, I eat just about every vegetable under the sun now, but I wouldn't dream of putting lettuce on my plate in August and tomatoes in January. Instead, frost-sweetened kale sautéed with green onion tops and balsamic vinegar is one of my family's favorite winter dishes; we nibble on snap peas in the spring, and we gorge on cucumbers in the summer. Some vegetables—mostly bulbs, roots, and tubers—can be stored raw for months, so garlic and onions transcend the seasons and make an appearance on our plates every week of the year. Otherwise, we've discovered that we don't miss having broccoli year-round, and instead think that eating what's ripe now tastes better (and is better for us).

If you purchase—rather than grow—your food, cost is another major benefit of eating in season. Using the techniques I'll outline in the next section, you can find seasonal produce for half the price those same vegetables would go for in the grocery store . . . or much less. The joke goes that in rural America, the only time you have to lock your car is July; otherwise you'll return to find it full of zucchinis.

If you need one more reason to eat in season, here it is—the environment. Keeping warm-weather crops like tomatoes alive in the winter requires a heated greenhouse, which drastically increases your food's carbon footprint. In stark contrast, seasonal produce at the fruit stand or farmer's market hasn't been transported very far, probably wasn't raised in a greenhouse, and is just plain easier on the earth.

However, the real reason that I think something as simple as a trip to the farmer's market merits a place in *Weekend Homesteader* is that the open-minded seasonal eater is already well on his way to growing his own food. You'll learn the varieties you like and dislike and will also work your mind around cooking with unfamiliar (but delicious) vegetables. Friends of mine who get baskets from CSAs (more on those later) are constantly complaining in the fall about the masses of winter squash and leafy greens. Although I look forward to these foods, I'll admit that butternut squash is not a common item on most modern Americans' plates, so you'll need to learn to be more flexible with your culinary habits. Being willing to substitute and try new things will help you discover that butternuts are like pumpkins (only tastier) and make great pies and soups, while mustard greens can be slipped into nearly any stew or casserole. Epicurious.com and other recipe websites allow you to input a few ingredients into the search box then peruse dozens of possible meal ideas. Soon, your friends and family will think of you as a gourmet chef.

## *Where to buy in-season produce*

I've listed in-season produce options from cheapest to most expensive below:

**Straight from the farm.** This is a very hit-or-miss approach, but if you keep your eyes peeled while driving down country roads, you'll probably see little hand-lettered signs alerting you to "Cucumbers 4 Sale" or "Sweet Corn." In some cases, there won't be anyone there, just produce sitting beside a jar of cash; drop in your dollar and take home the bounty. In other cases, you might be able to chat with the farmer and even tour his farm to learn whether he fertilizes with horse manure or 10-10-10 and what he sprays on his fields. The downside is that this type of farmer usually just hangs up his sign when he's got a bit more produce than he can handle, so you might not find anything for sale tomorrow or next week.

Fruit stands usually sell fruits and vegetables produced locally, with some selections from far away.

**Farmer's markets.** Next cheapest is visiting your local farmer's market, where you still get a chance to chat with the farmer, although not to tour the farm. Here you can choose between two strategies. Either arrive early to snap up the produce that's in short supply (but is probably more expensive, possibly even pricier than in the grocery store) or wait until the end of the market's hours and make out like a bandit. In many cases, the vegetables being sold won't be any good next week and are bound for the compost pile or the feed manger if no one buys them, so you can bring home a week's worth of vegetables for a song just as the farmers are packing up to go home. The downside of this method is that you'll probably have to learn to like some unusual vegetables and might need to preserve the bounty before it goes bad, but both of those abilities are important for homesteaders to learn anyway. Finally, I should note that farmer's markets in some cities cater to an upscale audience, making them more expensive than similar establishments in rural areas. On the other hand, many of these farmer's markets now accept food stamps as part of the SNAP program, which makes fresh produce more affordable if you live on a very limited income .

**CSA.** CSA is short for "community supported agriculture" and is a system where you pay a set amount at the beginning of the year in exchange for a basket of seasonal produce every week. You really learn a lot about the local farming scene this way, since you'll share the farmer's losses if the green beans get eaten up by beetles, and you'll also take part in the bounty when tomatoes have a bumper year. Many CSAs allow (or require) you to volunteer on the farm for a few hours, too, giving you yet more gardening experience. The main downside of the CSA model is that you need to commit hundreds of dollars up front, which is tough to do if you're living on a shoestring budget. That said, over the course of the year, CSA produce tends to be very cost competitive with other direct-from-the-farmer methods of buying food.

**Produce/fruit stands.** Most towns of any size will have a fruit stand or two where a middleman hunts down local (or not so local) farmers and sells their produce during normal nine to five hours (at least during the summer). This is the easiest, and most expensive, way of buying locally, since you're paying the middleman's wages as well as the farmer's. You should also be aware that produce stands may source their vegetables from hundreds of miles away, so the food could be no healthier or better tasting than it would be in the grocery store (although it does tend to be a bit cheaper, especially in rural areas). On the positive side, the proprietor is often willing to tell you where his food came from, so you can pick and choose seasonal and local produce if you like.

Many websites allow you to search for farmer's markets, CSAs, and other local food options. The most inclusive sites for farmer's markets (at least in my area) seem to be localharvest.org (which also allows you to search for other types of local food) and the USDA's Agricultural Marketing Service (search.ams.usda.gov/farmersmarkets/). Eatwellguide.org has a more comprehensive listing of CSAs in my area (along with many other sources of local food). Since these websites are by no means exhaustive, flipping through the phone book or asking friends might turn up more local options.

# Roast summer vegetables

Roasting is a great way to bring out flavors and sweeten vegetables. Cooking okra in this manner has the added benefit of avoiding the vegetable's usually slimy texture.

Summer vegetables are often so delicious that you will enjoy eating them raw or lightly steamed, but I've included a recipe below that can be tweaked to fit just about any summer harvest basket. Start with any of the following:

- aummer squash (zucchini, crookneck, etc. )
- okra
- tomatoes
- eggplant
- bell peppers (yellow, orange, or red are tastier than green)
- sweet corn (cut off the cob)

Choosing at least three different vegetables from the list above will make your meal more interesting. Chop the vegetables into bite-size pieces and estimate how much volume you've got. For each gallon of vegetables, add the following:

- 2 onions (chopped into half-inch pieces)
- 6 cloves of garlic (minced or pressed)

Mix all the vegetables together and drizzle on olive oil until the chunks are lightly coated. Sprinkle on salt and pepper—less than you might think, since the vegetables will cook down and the flavors will intensify. (You can always add salt and pepper after cooking if you're unsure of yourself.) Then spread the mixture on cookie sheets and bake in a 450°F oven, stirring occasionally until the onions are completely clear and some vegetables show signs of browning (30 minutes to 1 hour, depending on how thickly layered your vegetables are on the tray).

Dress with balsamic vinegar and fresh basil leaves, cut into small slivers. You can turn this dish into a meal by adding precooked beans or meat, or just serve as a delicious side.

# Canning

**GOAL**: Preserve crushed tomatoes in a hot-water-bath canner
**COST**: Up to $50
**TIME**: 4 hours to 6 hours
**DIFFICULTY**: Medium
**KID-FRIENDLY**: No

Canning is the first option many homesteaders consider when they want to preserve their homegrown food for the winter. Although canning won't be the best choice for everyone, most would-be homesteaders should at least know the basics of the easiest canning method—the hot water bath. This week's project will walk you through canning seven quarts of crushed tomatoes.

## Why you should can (or maybe not)

Canning is a method of heating food to a high-enough temperature that will kill microorganisms, then sealing the container so that no new critters can get in. Don't be confused by the name—although canned food from the store often comes in cans, most homesteading-scale canning takes place in jars. In either case, properly canned food will last between one and five years on the shelf, and some canned food might still be edible as much as three decades later.

Compared to other methods of food preservation, canning has some major selling points for the homesteader.

**No energy input after the initial canning.** Since you don't need to expend any energy to keep your food safe after it has been sealed in a jar, canned food makes a great emergency backup for power outages. Although you do need a lot of heat to get the jars sealed in the first place, you could can your vegetables over a wood fire if necessary, which makes canning one of the most sustainable preservation options.

**Aesthetics.** It's hard to argue with the beauty of shelf after shelf of multicolored future meals, and the canning process itself is one long art project.

**Moderate cost.** Depending on whether you're only going to can fruit or want to be able to branch out into meats and vegetables, canning has a low to moderate price tag. Home food preservation techniques with the lowest start-up costs include storing food on the shelf, sun-drying, and fermenting, followed by canning, drying with a dehydrator, freezing, and root cellaring (if you don't already have a root cellar). Of course, you also have to consider the ongoing costs, which for canning involve replacing broken jars (rare if you're careful) and buying new lids every year, as well as the electricity or gas involved in canning itself. Ongoing costs for most types of preservation are generally on par, although storing food on the shelf or in a root cellar costs nothing once you have your space set up.

On the other hand, canning has the following disadvantages:

**Tricky for beginners.** All that hot water and the low but real threat of botulism and exploding pressure canners scare many beginners away from food preservation if they think canning is their only choice.

**Taste and nutrition.** The longer you cook food, the more vitamins are lost, so you shouldn't be surprised to hear that canned food tends to be less tasty and less nutritious than dried or frozen food. On the other hand, a few foods are just as flavorful canned—pickles, jams, applesauce, and tomatoes are among the top contenders for delicious canned foods.

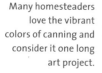

Many homesteaders love the vibrant colors of canning and consider it one long art project.

**Large batches.** The last problem with canning is the necessity of preserving your produce in large batches. Most of the other preservation techniques allow you to put away a bit of food here and there, tucking an extra pint of spaghetti sauce in the freezer when you have some left over from dinner or throwing one tray of peaches in the car to dry. To fill a hot-water-bath canner, however, you'll need around half a bushel of vegetables, which turns canning into a lengthy undertaking.

I have to admit that the cons outweigh the pros for me, and I rarely can food in my day-to-day life. However, I'm glad to know how to can, and I think you'll feel more empowered if you have this trick up your sleeve as well.

## Botulism and canned food safety

Botulism is the best-known danger of home canning. The bacterium *Clostridium botulinum* flourishes in anaerobic (air-free) environments like the food in canning jars and, when ingested, can cause serious illness or even death. The real trouble is that you often can't see, smell, or taste any change in the food to signal that *Clostridium botulinum* is present, so there's no way to know whether your home-canned green beans are safe.

As scary as that sounds, the botulism bacterium can't survive either extremely high temperatures or extremely low pH conditions, so as long as you follow approved recipes to the letter, you'll be fine. (Approved recipes are those that have been laboratory tested and are disseminated by sources like the USDA, state extension services, or the *Ball Blue Book*.) Botulism prevention is the reason hot-water-bath canning is only appropriate for fruits and tomatoes, and why you need to add lemon juice if you're not sure of the acidity of the produce.

Nevertheless, you shouldn't be too scared of botulism when you try out home canning. There are about 24 cases of botulism-induced death resulting from canned foods in the United States every year ... which is less than half the number of Americans who die from bee stings and a quarter of the Americans who are killed by lightning strikes. Canning your own food is far safer than your commute to work.

*(continued)*

## *Hot-water-bath canning*

There are two main types of canning—hot-water-bath canning and pressure canning. While both are appropriate for home preservers, the former requires much less equipment and knowledge, so it's the one we'll focus on in this week's exercise.

Hot-water-bath canning involves filling sterilized jars with food, then putting the jars in a big pot of boiling water for anywhere from a few minutes to an hour or more. This process kills many, but not all, microorganisms. Luckily for us, the low pH (high acidity) of certain foods suffices to kill any remaining microorganisms, so we can get away with this relatively simple canning method when preserving fruits, tomatoes, and pickles. All other vegetables and meats must be canned using a pressure canner.

When hot-water-bath canning, it's important to pay attention to everything that goes in the jar. Sweeteners like honey and sugar can be added with impunity, but including basil and onions in a tomato sauce will raise the pH so much that you'll have to pressure can. To stay on the safe side, look for proven recipes or can only unadulterated fruits or tomatoes.

While I'm on the topic of acidity, I should mention that the acidity levels of tomatoes may sometimes be too low for hot-water-bath canning unless you add a bit of bottled (not fresh) lemon juice or citric acid. The magic cutoff point is 4.6—tomatoes with a pH at or above this pH are not safe to hot-water-bath can on their own. Low acid tomatoes that definitely have been proven to need lemon juice include these:

Ace, Ace 55VF, Beefmaster Hybrid, Big Early Hybrid, Big Girl, Big Set, Burpee VF Hybrid, Cal Ace, Delicious, Fireball, Garden State, Royal Chico

Depending on whom you talk to, San Marzano tomatoes may or may not be safe.

Varieties that definitely have a pH low enough to allow you to hot-water-bath can them without adding any lemon juice or citric acid include the following:

Abraham Lincoln, Amana Orange, Anna Banana, Antique Roman, Aunt Ruby's German Green, Beefsteak Extra Large, Big Rainbow, Bisignano #2, Black, Black from Tula, Black Krim, Burpees Delicious, Caspian Pink, Cherokee Purple, Climbing Trip L Crop, Costoluto Fiorentino, Costoluto Genovese, Currant Tuscan Bombolino, Ernie's Plump, Evergreen, Giant Syrian, Goliath, Grappoli D'Inverno, Hillbilly, Howard German, Ingegnoli Gigante Liscio, Italian Giant Beefsteak, Italian Heirloom, Italian Plum Canning, Joe's Plum, Jubilee, Kellog's Breakfast, Kootenai, Large Polish Paste, Laurano, Le Case Di Apulia, Lilian's Yellow Heirloom, Long Keeper, Lycopersicon Cheesemanii, Marglobe, Mortgage Lifter, Moskvitch, Mr. Stripey, Napoli, Nebraska Wedding, New Hampshire, New Jersey, Opalka, Oregon Spring, Oscar, Pantano Romanesco, Persimmon, Pink Brandywine, Platillo, Polish Giant, Pomadoro Grosso, Prairie Fire, Principe Borghese, Red Brandywine, Riesentraube, Rio de Fuego, Rio Grande, Roman Candle, Rutgers, San Marzano (listed by some as being above), Santiam, Saucy, Silvery Fir Tree, Siletz, Soldacki, Striped Stuffer, Stupice, Super Italian Plum, Super Sioux, Tondino Di Manduria, Tyboroski, Yellow Brandywine, Yellow Pear, Yellow Perfection, Watermelon Beefsteak, Zebra, Zogola.

However, to make the decision even more complex, a high-acid tomato variety may produce low-acid tomatoes if the fruits are over-ripe, bruised, cracked, affected by blossom-end rot, or nibbled by insects. In addition, tomatoes ripened off the vine, in the fall when days are shorter, in the shade, or on dead vines can all have a pH too high to allow hot-water-bath canning without added lemon juice. To play it safe, you might as well add the lemon juice recommended in the recipe below.

## Hot-water-bath canning supplies

The equipment you'll need to hot-water-bath can includes the following:

Always use designated canning jars. Although these jars are expensive if bought new, you can often pick them up at yard sales or in thrift stores.

**Canner.** Big blue or black pots with lids can often be picked up for just a few dollars at yard sales or thrift stores, or bought new for around $25. These designated hot-water-bath canners are large enough to hold seven quart jars, and they come with a wire basket inside to make it easy to lift the jars in and out. In a pinch, you can use any pot that's capacious enough to contain at least four quart jars with two inches of water over the tops, but canning without a real canner is more difficult, since you have to struggle to get the jars in and out safely.

**Jars.** It's important to use only designated canning jars. These jars will have raised letters or symbols on them, often "Mason" or "Ball" or "Kerr." Don't use old peanut butter jars, mayonnaise jars, or any jars not meant for home canning (although local honey often comes in canning jars in our area, and these can be reused). Canning jars can be pricey ($1.75 apiece, with rings and lids included, brand new), but you can almost always find jars much cheaper at yard sales, flea markets, or thrift stores. Carefully inspect used jars to make sure the rims are smooth, since chips or cracks will prevent a perfect seal. For this exercise, try to find seven quart jars, either wide-mouth or regular-mouth. (Lids will be easier to find for the latter.)

**Lids.** Canning lids can't be reused safely, so you have no option except to buy new ones. A package of twelve is usually under $5 and can be found in mainstream grocery stores. If you buy new canning jars, they often come with lids and rings.

**Rings.** Rings can be reused, but it's best to discard rusty or warped equipment. Look for rings when you hunt down used jars. Or you can buy a package of new rings in your grocery store for under $10.

**Funnel.** A small metal funnel is very helpful for filling regular-mouth canning jars. You can pick up a canning funnel very cheaply at yard sales or buy a new one for under $10.

**Tongs.** You probably already have a pair of metal tongs in your kitchen that will work for canning.

Your stove needs to accommodate a large canner and a pot of boiling water, and you'll also need room to cook your tomatoes down.

**Stove.** It's best to use a large burner to get the water in your canner heated all the way to a rolling boil, and you'll need at least two other burners to cook the tomatoes and sterilize the lids. An electric stove will work, but some people prefer to can outside over a propane flame or wood fire to keep the kitchen cool.

**Knives, cutting board, bowls, ladle, spoons, hot pads, dish towels, etc.** Your well-stocked kitchen should supply everything else that you need.

I recommend that those of you who haven't canned before don't invest a lot of money in equipment until you decide whether canning will be one of your favorite preservation methods. Chances are you have a friend who will loan you her canner for the weekend, and she might even come over and show you how to use it in exchange for a quart or two of tomatoes.

## *How to can crushed tomatoes*

Preserve only your best garden produce. No matter whether you're canning, drying, or freezing, vegetables never taste better than the day they were picked out of the garden.

Now it's time for the hands-on part of the project—canning seven quarts of crushed tomatoes. Most of the steps below can be followed even if you choose to can applesauce or another fruit instead, but canning times differ widely, so consult a recipe if you want to branch out.

After assembling the kitchenware outlined in the last section, the first step is to find your tomatoes. You'll need about half a bushel of tomatoes to fill your jars, so if you can't save that many from your garden, you should check out one of the local food sources listed in the "Eating seasonally" chapter. Either way, select only the best tomatoes—preserved food will never get better than it is at the moment you pick it, so set aside rotten or unripe fruit.

Remove cores and bad spots. I like to leave skins on and seeds in for increased nutrition.

Next, prepare the tomatoes as if you're going to cook with them. Wash each fruit and decide if you're going to remove the skins—I usually leave the skins on for nutrition, but some people don't like the taste or texture. To remove tomato skins, submerge the tomatoes in a pot of boiling water for a bit more than a minute, let cool, and the skins can be peeled off. Whether you skin or not, you will want to cut out the core of slicing tomatoes or just trim off the top of romas, then chop the tomatoes into two-inch sections. Cherry tomatoes can simply be cut in half.

While you're cutting up your tomatoes, you should also be bringing your canner to a boil and preparing the canning jars. Take a minute to look over the rims of your jars a second time and discard any that have nicks or cracks; then wash the jars thoroughly. If you don't have a dishwasher with a sterilizer feature, the easiest way to sterilize your washed jars is to put a few inches of water in each one and place the jars into the canner as water comes to a boil. Your goal is to have enough water in the canner so that the liquid will eventually cover the full jars and extend two inches above their lids.

Once your canner is on the stove, you can turn back to your tomatoes. For this recipe, you will be hot packing, which means the tomatoes need to be cooked on the stove until they boil, then simmered for five minutes longer. You can add a bit of water to the bottom of your pot of tomatoes to keep them from sticking, but I like to simply squeeze the tomato sections in my hands several times until tomato juice comes up to cover the chunks. (If you prefer, you can use a potato masher to crush your tomatoes instead.) Then I put the pot of squashed tomatoes on medium-high heat and stir often (turning down the heat if necessary) until the tomatoes are ready.

While your tomatoes are cooking, add a third pot to your stove. This pot will be full of boiling water to sterilize your lids and also to top off the canner in case you didn't put in enough water to begin with. Before moving on to the next step, wait until your canner has been at a full boil for ten minutes, your tomatoes have simmered for five minutes, and your small pot of water is boiling.

Place a clean cloth on a counter to create your sterile work space and then sterilize anything you want to work with—a ladle, tongs, your canning funnel, and perhaps a spoon. You can sterilize these items by dipping them in the boiling water of the canner. Meanwhile, drop one canning lid into the small pot of boiling water to sterilize.

You can sterilize your jars as you heat up your canning water.

Very carefully, use your tongs to take a jar out of the canner, pouring all the boiling water back into the pot. Set the jar rim-side-up on the clean cloth, put the funnel on top, and measure out two tablespoons of bottled lemon juice to pour into the jar.

Now you can ladle in your tomatoes. Don't fill the jar all the way to the top; instead, leave half an inch of head space (air) between the tomatoes and the rim of the jar.

A canning funnel makes it easy to fill jars without spilling. You should be able to find used canning funnels at thrift stores or yard sales for pennies.

Sterilize the corner of a clean dishcloth by dipping it in boiling water and use the cloth to wipe the rim of the jar clean. This is an essential step—if you leave any particles of food on the top, the jar will not seal.

If the rim isn't clean, your jar won't seal.

With your tongs, fish your sterilized jar lid out of the boiling water . . .

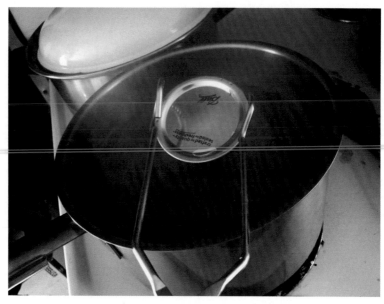

Sterilize lids in a pot of boiling water.

. . . and place it on top of the jar without touching either the rim of the jar or the underside of the lid with your fingers.

When putting on the lid, don't touch the underside with your fingers.

Gently screw a clean ring on top. The ring shouldn't be screwed on too tight—it's merely holding the lid in place, not forming the seal.

Gently screw on the ring while holding the lid in place.

Repeat with the other six jars, then remove the wire cage from the canner and place it on a flat surface. Carefully put your filled jars in the rack . . .

Place the filled jars in your rack.

. . . and lower the rack and jars into the boiling water. If the water doesn't cover the jars by at least two inches, pour in additional hot water from your small pot to achieve that water level. Replace the canner lid to keep heat inside.

Very carefully lower your jars into the boiling water.

Even though the contents of the jars are hot, they'll still lower the temperature in the canner a bit, so it will take a few minutes for the water to come back to a rolling boil. When it does, leave the heat on high and start counting your processing time. From sea level up to 1,000 feet in elevation, you'll need to boil your jars for 45 minutes; from 1,001 feet to 3,000 feet, boil for 50 minutes; from 3,001 feet to 6,000 feet, boil for 55 minutes; and above 6,000 feet, boil for a full hour. Rolling up dishtowels to encircle the base of your canner will prevent water that boils over from running all over your stove, but don't let the cloth catch fire!

Once the required processing time has elapsed, turn off the heat and raise the canner lid away from you so you don't get burned by the steam. Using potholders, carefully lift the wire basket and jars out and place them in a draft-free location. My mother likes to drape the jars with a towel to slow cooling and keep cold air at bay.

As the jars cool, the contents will shrink, and a vacuum will form inside. You should be able to hear a metallic ping as each jar lid pops down to create a depression in its center. Leave the jars alone for at least twelve hours until they are completely cool; then carefully screw off the rings (if you want to reuse them immediately) or tighten them down. Feel for the depression in the center of each lid that indicates a seal—the lid shouldn't pop up and down when you press on it, and it should instead remain firm. If any jars didn't seal, you can put the tomatoes in the fridge or cook up a pot of soup immediately to use them up.

Finally, find a spot to store your preserved harvest. From a scientific point of view, the best location for your filled canning jars is in a dry, cool (but above freezing) larder out of direct sunlight, but many of us are so proud of our colorful creations that we store them in the open to add vibrancy to the room. Homesteader decorating!

## Cannery alternative

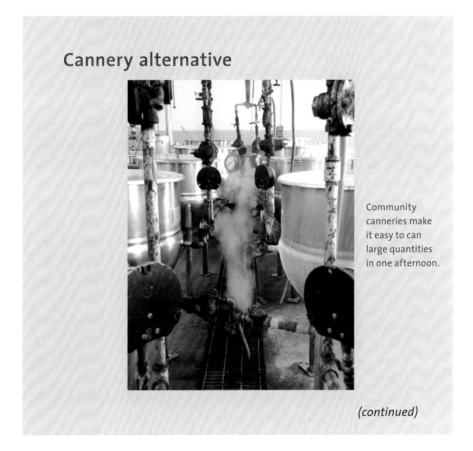

Community canneries make it easy to can large quantities in one afternoon.

*(continued)*

## Cannery alternative *(continued)*

There's one more option you might want to consider if you'd like to try out canning but don't want to do everything at home. Community canneries used to be quite widespread across the United States and can still be found in certain regions. These facilities have industrial-scale canning equipment including vats where you can cook up huge masses of apple butter, preparation counters and sinks, pressure canners, and more. There is usually a staff person present who can answer your questions, and you may meet other canning enthusiasts glad to help out as well.

Using a community cannery isn't free, but the experience tends to be cost-competitive with buying your own equipment. Our local cannery charges a few pennies per jar for use of their facilities and is also stocked with metal cans that expedite canning (sold for less than a quarter apiece). Overall, the cannery is a great choice if you've got huge amounts of produce ready to be processed on the same day and want to preserve your year's harvest in a clean, utilitarian environment. See www.frugalliving.about.com/od/canningfoods/a/Community-Cannery-Locations.htm to find a community cannery in your area.

# Bringing your chickens home

**GOAL**: Purchase a small laying flock and learn about its daily needs
**COST**: $30–$100
**TIME**: 2 hours to 4 hours
**DIFFICULTY**: Easy
**KID-FRIENDLY**: Yes

A rooster guards a free-range flock.

An August exercise helped you decide whether chickens were right for your homestead and then walked you through designing and building their pasture and housing. Now you're ready to bring home your flock and start eating homegrown eggs!

# Planning your flock

An oat cover crop can feed the garden soil, and your chickens too.

You'll need to answer three questions before going out to find your new birds:

**How many?**   The housing exercise explained the space requirements per bird and some of the pros and cons of including a rooster. If you've never kept livestock before, I'd recommend starting small—with two to four hens. Your flock won't be self-sufficient without a rooster, and you'll probably want more eggs than this starter flock can provide (especially if you have a large family), but it's much better to begin with just a few birds and then add more than to get overwhelmed by a huge flock and decide chickens aren't for you.

**How old?**   Chickens start laying eggs when they're around six months old. They lay very well for one year and moderately well for a second year, then provide fewer and fewer eggs each year after that. I recommend against taking in someone's old hens—the previous owners might give their chickens away free, but old hens are actually quite expensive, since you'll be stuck feeding the flock large amounts of expensive grain while getting very little in return. At the other extreme, I think that raising chicks is a project beyond the weekend homesteader level (although those of you with a bit more time and experience will enjoy learning to raise your own chicks). Instead, look for "point of lay" pullets, which are chickens just beginning to lay eggs at the age of six to twelve months. Since you're beginning your flock in September, the hens might not actually be laying at the moment, but you should make sure they're old enough to start laying by next month at the latest.

**What kind?** There are dozens of heirloom and modern hybrid varieties to choose from, and there's no one-size-fits-all bird. I recommend that the serious homesteader steer clear of exhibition birds (the ones that have been bred for aesthetics, often with feathered feet, funky combs, or beautiful plumage). Another category to avoid is dual purpose birds, which are supposed to be good at producing both eggs and meat, but which usually do neither very well. Instead, look for good egg-layers. I've found that Black Australorps are experts at rustling up a lot of free food on pasture, although they're a bit skittish and don't lay quite as many eggs as some other breeds. Golden Comets are a modern hybrid that lay a huge number of extraordinarily large eggs; the birds are very friendly but are only moderately adept at foraging. Other very prolific egg-layers include White Leghorns (very flighty and lay white eggs), Red or Black Sex-links, and select types of Rhode Island Reds. If you want to explore less well-known breeds of chickens, I recommend starting your research at www.ithaca.edu/staff/jhenderson/chooks/chooks.html.

## Feeding your chickens

Chickens enjoy nearly every food humans eat.

A previous exercise walked you through providing housing, roosts, and nest boxes for your new flock, so the only extra items you need to add to the coop this week are food and water.

Adult hens are usually given either laying pellets or laying mash for food, both of which are mixtures of milled grains, soybeans, and minerals available in fifty-pound bags at your local feed store. Be sure to plan a dry, rodent-proof spot to store the excess feed—we use a metal trashcan that can sit out in the pasture rather than use up space inside. You can buy a feed trough for your birds, but I prefer to simply scatter the proper amount of food on the ground each day to give my chickens an incentive to get up and exercise. Assuming they're being fed nothing else, each hen needs about a quarter of a pound of feed per day (approximately a cup of laying pellets) in the summer and perhaps a bit more in the winter if your weather is cold.

There are many ways to supplement your chickens' diets with fresh, healthy edibles that will reduce your expenditures on store-bought feed. The most obvious option is to provide them with pasture, especially during the growing season, when grass and insects can make up between 10 and 20 percent of your birds' diet.

Kitchen scraps are the other low-hanging fruit—your flock can eat just about anything you can, so give them your apple cores, that container of leftover lasagna that went bad before you remembered it, and all other food waste that comes out of your kitchen. Feeding your eggshells back to the hens is a good way to provide additional calcium; just step on the shells as you drop them on the ground so they look less egglike and won't tempt your hens to peck at the eggs in the nest boxes.

Chickens are omnivores, so there's no problem with giving them meat scraps, bits of cheese, bread, and other food products that would cause problems in a compost pile. On the other hand, your chickens will almost certainly ignore citrus and onion peels; I throw those skins in the chicken bucket anyway and simply let the excess scraps compost in the corner of the pasture, but you should separate out those items if you're pasturing your chickens on a lawn and want it to look pristine.

Extra garden produce is a special treat for your flock.

If you're feeling ambitious, you might consider raising earthworms or black soldier fly larvae for your flock or growing your own grains. A century ago, most farmers knew that an everbearing mulberry tree could feed a flock of chickens their entire rations for three months in the summer, and other trees and berries in the pasture can provide additional treats for the flock. For more outside-the-box chicken-feed ideas, visit my website at www.avianaquamiser.com/tag/chicken_feed/ and check out Harvey Ussery's *The Small-Scale Poultry Flock.*

## Watering your chickens

Photo credit: Barbara von Oppenfeld

My husband invented the Avian Aqua Miser to make sure our chickens always have access to clean water.

Chicken coops have a bad reputation for being filthy, unsightly environments, and if you follow conventional practices, that notoriety is well deserved. However, if you understand that manure on the ground or in the chickens' water is a sign of mismanagement, you can keep your chickens happy and healthy and ensure that they make good neighbors.

When we started keeping chickens, I was not thrilled by the daily task of emptying out traditional waterers full of manure. Meanwhile, my husband knew that our chickens weren't as healthy as they could be since they were consuming their own waste. So Mark developed a nipple-based chicken waterer that keeps the water clean in an enclosed reservoir and doles out the precious fluid a drop at a time when the chickens peck at the nipple. See www.AvianAquaMiser.com for more information about our POOP-free chicken waterers.

Of course, you can also pick up a traditional waterer at your local feed store and commit to cleaning it out a few times a day. But whatever you do, make sure your flock has constant access to clean, unfrozen water.

## Finding your chickens

Now for the fun part—bringing your flock home! Although newly hatched chicks can be shipped through the mail, if you're following my advice and starting with adult hens, you'll need to find them locally. Craigslist is a good place to start your search, or you can keep an eye on bulletin boards around town. If you're drawing a blank, you might even ask a clerk at the feed store, since he will probably know who comes in regularly to purchase chicken feed and might be willing to give those local chicken-keepers a call to see if they've got a few hens to sell. No matter how you find them, expect to spend about $10 apiece for point-of-lay hens.

Chickens don't like being transported, so try to minimize their trauma as much as possible when picking them up. Bring some cardboard boxes with holes in the side, a dog or cat crate, or one of the wire cages made specifically for transporting chickens. Don't let your flock get too cold or too hot—lay down some newspaper and put your box of chickens in the backseat rather than hauling them in the bed of a pickup truck. And, if you've got a choice between several potential suppliers, buy your chickens as close to home as possible.

Once you've brought your flock home, lock them in the coop or tractor for a few days before letting them out to roam around. This is an important period when your birds will bond with their new home, and you don't want them to get used to roosting in trees or under bushes at night.

Now is also a good time to introduce your cats and dogs to your chickens. Dogs, especially, can turn into chicken-killers very easily, so you'll need to spend significant time with the family pet and make sure he understands that chickens aren't dinner.

Finally, be aware that your chickens may stop laying as soon as you bring them home. The trip is traumatic for them, and they could take a few weeks to get their act back together. Don't worry—they'll start laying once they feel settled.

When introducing dogs to chickens for the first time, make sure your pets are restrained.

## Daily care

With a well-designed system, chickens nearly take care of themselves.

Daily care of a laying flock is extremely simple. I feed the birds and check their water in the morning; then my husband brings in the eggs in the evening. If you're tractoring your chickens, you'll want to pull their tractor to a new patch of ground every morning (and perhaps in the afternoon as well if you've crammed a lot of birds inside). Chickens living in coops and pastures can be pretty self-sufficient, but your predator pressure might mandate closing them into the coop at night and then opening the door each morning.

Chickens are very low maintenance, but they're also a joy to observe. Don't forget to factor time into your busy schedule to watch them hunt for bugs or play "chicken soccer" as each hen tries to steal that juicy tomato you threw in the coop. Finally, get ready to cook the most delicious eggs you've ever tasted.

# Voluntary simplicity

**GOAL**: Spend a week buying only the bare essentials
**COST**: $0
**TIME**: 1 hour
**DIFFICULTY**: Medium
**KID-FRIENDLY**: Maybe

This week's exercise will help you overcome the largest stumbling block on your path to financial self-sufficiency: fear.

## *Afraid of independence*

My husband and I make a living by selling chicken waterers over the Internet, and we highlight the steps to replicate our journey in the ebook *Microbusiness Independence*. Hundreds of would-be entrepreneurs have bought our ebook, and many of them send us emails telling how much they would love to become financially independent. But they always end by explaining why they can't afford the risk right now.

Unlike most get-rich-quick books, we're up-front with our readers, telling them that they'll probably need to tighten their belts for six months to a year before their microbusiness starts paying the bills. We admit that in year one, our microbusiness barely pushed us above the poverty line. Even though our profits increased dramatically from there, the mainstream, middle-class American is terrified of the idea that he might not be able to pay to fix a flat tire immediately or that he might have to shoulder his own health insurance costs. That fear holds him back from taking the plunge into financial independence.

I feel very lucky that my parents were believers in voluntary simplicity and raised three kids on less than $20,000 per year in the 1980s. I've never been afraid of poverty because I've learned that—once you pay for the basics—extra money really doesn't make you any happier.

The first few years that my husband and I lived on the farm, we were poor as church mice, but we felt richer than our peers because we got to spend every day working together and falling more and more in love. We had time to explore whatever permaculture notions or inventions took our fancy, and we always managed to pay all our bills as well as protect our health with a catastrophic health insurance plan. That was in 2006 when we reported a whopping $11,746.41 on our joint tax return and didn't go a penny into debt.

Even with such a low income, though, I was afraid to quit my job and try to become financially independent. Similarly, I suspect that the biggest stumbling block most homesteaders face is their full-time job. This week, you'll see if you can live without it.

## Income and social class

Most proponents of simple living are members of the middle or upper classes dreaming of the "simplicity" of a back-to-basics lifestyle. However, people who raised themselves up out of poverty often believe they are ethically obliged to maintain a middle-class lifestyle to give their children a good start on life. Can you achieve both dreams at once?

In the United States, income is often used as an indicator of a family's social status, but money doesn't have to determine your place in life. Education and the arts are key to becoming culturally middle class, and neither depends on a high family income. I like to tell people that I was raised economically lower class and socially upper class, an upbringing that gave me the best of both worlds.

At least one of my parents was at home full time for most of my childhood, so I spent hours reveling in the most important gift any child can receive—the full attention of an adult. My mother read me Dickens when I was an infant, and we made weekly trips to the library throughout my formative years. When I expressed an interest in going to the theater, my father figured out that all we had to do was sign up to be ushers, don black pants and white shirts, and we'd get in free.

It's becoming even easier to be culturally upper class while living simply. For example, many top-notch colleges have need-based financial aid programs, and there is an increasing trend of giving full scholarships to students whose parents make less than around $60,000 per year.

Although there were times during my childhood when I wished I had as much spending money as my peers, I now feel that my parents did me a favor by raising me in voluntary simplicity. Knowing that I can live on very little has opened doors that many people are afraid to access, and I believe a caring father or mother could do worse than to follow my parents' lead.

## What is the poverty line?

The poverty line is a figure that tells how much money you need per year to keep body and soul together. The world average in 2008 was $456, but the poverty line specific to the United States is much higher. The chart below lists the poverty line figures used by the U.S. Department of Health and Human Services in 2011.

| People in your family | 48 contiguous states and DC | Alaska | Hawaii |
|---|---|---|---|
| 1 | $10,890 | $13,600 | $12,540 |
| 2 | $14,710 | $18,380 | $16,930 |
| 3 | $18,530 | $23,160 | $21,320 |
| 4 | $22,350 | $27,940 | $25,710 |
| 5 | $26,170 | $32,720 | $30,100 |
| 6 | $29,990 | $37,500 | $34,490 |
| 7 | $33,810 | $42,280 | $38,880 |
| 8 | $37,630 | $47,060 | $43,270 |
| Each additional person adds | $3,820 | $4,780 | $4,390 |

The chart shows that my husband and I, living in Virginia, would need to make at least $14,710 annually to be above the poverty line. An Alaskan family consisting of mom, dad, and three kids would need $32,720 per year.

## Living with just the bare essentials

The first step in this week's exercise is to figure out what your weekly income would be if you lived at the poverty line. For us, that would be $282.88 per week, and our hypothetical Alaskan family would have a weekly income of $629.23. Now head to the bank and take out the exact amount of cash you figured above, then hide your credit and debit cards and checkbook until next week. Your mission is to make ends meet on the cash in your wallet.

If you're playing by the rules, you won't fill up your gas tank and stock your kitchen shelves before starting, and neither will you plan to go on a spending spree as soon as the week is over. On the other hand, you don't need to pay your credit card bill from last month, your mortgage, or any other debt with the cash in your wallet. The goal is to pretend you're living debt-free on your poverty line allotment.

The more advanced reader may want to figure out what the weekly portion of his monthly utility payment would be, but that isn't mandatory. Still, if you know that you're spending $150 on electricity every month largely because you rely on electric heat and keep the thermostat up to 75 degrees, maybe you should figure out how much of your weekly allotment you're willing to commit to electricity. Check the meter at the beginning of the week and tell yourself you're only allowed a certain number of kilowatt-hours, then turn down the heat and pile on sweaters.

You might be surprised to discover that once you start packing a lunch, decide to carpool to the office, and skip buying nonessentials, you have money left over at the end of the week. After all, those of you who started reading in April should have quite a bit of produce stored up from the summer garden or local produce stand. And surely your closet is full enough that you didn't go naked by not buying any clothes. Maybe it's not so terrifying to tighten your belt after all.

## *Beyond the basics*

To be fair, life at the poverty line can be tough if you come down with the flu, can't work for two weeks, and need to scrape together enough money to pay the rent. That's why I recommend that everyone have three to six months worth of living expenses socked away in a bank account they never touch. An emergency buffer keeps you from going into debt when you knock a hole in your gas tank and need a few hundred dollars to get it repaired.

Which returns us to the topic of debt. Eighty percent of Americans are in debt, and those mandatory monthly payments often keep them in jobs they hate. You are the only one who can decide whether that fancy house and car are worth the result—coming home so exhausted that you have no energy to enjoy your home and family. Is fear the only thing keeping you in suburbia?

# OCTOBER
## *(April Down Under)*

# Quick hoops

**GOAL**: Extend your growing season by one month or more
**COST**: $50
**TIME**: 3 hours to 4 hours
**DIFFICULTY**: Hard
**KID-FRIENDLY**: Maybe

Wouldn't you like to be eating lettuce fresh from your garden when snow is on the ground? Quick hoops are a fast, inexpensive, and easy way to extend your growing season by a month or more.

## *Season extension*

Quick hoops can extend your growing season into the dead of winter. In my zone 6 garden, I ate homegrown kale every week of the 2011-2012 cold season.

Assuming you don't want to sink the time and money into building a full-size greenhouse or hoophouse, there are three main methods of protecting your winter vegetables so you can harvest more food later in the season. Row covers are made of water- and light-permeable fabric that can be thrown over your garden plants. These work well for growers in zones 7 and 8, but not so well further north. Cold frames are wooden boxes topped with windows or row cover fabric. And then there's my favorite method—quick hoops.

Quick hoops were invented by the masterful gardener Eliot Coleman, who uses them in combination with larger structures to harvest leafy greens nearly year-round in his Maine garden. I'll explain how to make a quick hoop in a later section, but the idea is simple—you cover bent PVC pipes with fabric to create a slightly warmer microhabitat for your cool-season crops.

Compared to cold frames, quick hoops have the following advantages:

**Light penetration**—Cold frames have wooden walls that shade a relatively large area on the south side of the bed, and in early spring I've noticed that seeds just won't germinate in that cold spot. Quick hoops don't create any shady areas, and so far I've seen no cold spots that restrict germination. In a winter garden, light penetration during the day is the most important factor for keeping plants and soil warm, so this advantage trumps all other comparisons of the two season-extension methods.

**Snow load**—The rounded profile of a quick hoop makes snow more likely to slide off the sides (especially if you add a sheet of plastic on top of the fabric). In contrast, when heavy snow falls on fabric-covered cold frames, the cloth tends to bow down and squash your plants, sometimes tearing the fabric beyond repair.

**Cost**—If you have old lumber lying around like we do, cold frames are a big winner since they only cost as much as the fabric and screws. On the other hand, if you're buying the materials new, I estimate that the quick hoop I'll describe below costs 29 cents per square foot versus 64 cents per square foot for a cold frame made with untreated two-by-tens.

**Longevity of fabric**—After the initial construction, the only regular cost for either system is replacing tattered row cover fabric. I've discovered that cold frames covered with row cover fabric look like beds or toys to small children, cats, and dogs. One leap onto the cold frame and the fabric is often ruined (not to mention that your plants are demolished). Quick hoops don't seem to be as enticing.

**Modularity**—Our raised beds aren't all the same width or length, so I've found it difficult to move cold frames from bed to bed. With my rotten, salvaged lumber, cold frames also tend to fall apart when I move them. Quick hoops are much more modular and allow you to cover irregularly shaped beds, using the same raw materials in different years to protect beds with somewhat different dimensions.

**Speed of construction**—Your first quick hoop might take longer to build, but once you get the hang of it, you can make a twenty-five-foot-long quick hoop in just two and a half man-hours. In later years, you'll be able to erect that quick hoop from precut parts in half an hour or less. Most of the process requires only one person, in stark contrast to my experience building cold frames—lots of swearing seems to ensue if there aren't four hands involved in that process.

**Ease of storage**—Quick hoops win big here. During the summer, when I don't need our cold frames, they're leaning up against a fence or wall, which creates a weedy spot that's hard to mow around. Quick hoops disassemble into a few long poles and a bit of fabric, all of which can be packed away into the barn or garage in short order.

**Aesthetics**—Our cold frames are pretty enough, but there's just something striking about the domed quick hoops that tempts me out into the winter garden.

On the other hand, if you're changing over from cold frames to quick hoops, you should be aware that quick hoops have the following disadvantages:

**Water penetration**—The flat top of cold frames lets water pool on the row cover fabric just long enough to drip through and water your bed, but water mostly runs off the quick hoop. I was surprised to see dry spots inside our quick hoops one spring despite about eight inches of rain in as many days. You may need to water your plants if the soil inside gets too dry.

**Wind**—The higher profile of quick hoops catches wind much more than our cold frames did. If you live in a treeless area, you might be better off with cold frames.

Comparisons between the two methods aside, some sort of simple season extension is a must in the homesteader's garden. Not only do you need to preserve less food (which means less energy used and less time spent in the hot summer kitchen), you also get to treat yourself to fresh produce during the winter months. When you're depending on your larder instead of the grocery store for December meals, crisp kale is a luxury.

## Using quick hoops in the garden

Leaf lettuce is a good choice for growing under quick hoops. You can give your lettuce bed a haircut at least once a week, enjoying homegrown salads for months from the same planting.

Depending on where you currently are in your annual growing cycle, you can use a quick hoop in several different ways. Those of you reading this chapter in late fall will probably opt to cover up your broccoli, lettuce, greens, or other cool season crops to extend their harvest further into the winter. If the first frost hasn't yet nipped the garden, you could place a quick hoop over tender annuals like peppers or basil and perhaps gain another week or two of summer bounty. Since quick hoops are so easy to move, you can actually use them for both purposes, transferring the quick hoops to your winter crops once killing frosts penetrate the thin fabric and wipe out your tomatoes.

Come spring, quick hoops are even more useful. I've discovered that the primary factor preventing cool-season crops from sprouting in late winter is actually soil temperature, not air temperature. If you erect your quick hoop over a bed in January or February, you might be able to warm the soil enough to plant spring vegetables a couple of weeks earlier than usual and have the neighborhood's first peas and greens. Of course, those cool-weather crops don't need the quick hoop's protection for more than about a month, so once spring arrives, you can move the quick hoops to new beds and start your tomato sets outdoors or give yourself a jump-start on watermelon season.

## Gather your supplies

Once you've settled on a spot for your first quick hoop, you'll need to know the length and width of the area you want to cover. Our garden beds are about 4.5 feet wide, so I spent a bit more cash than I needed to when building each quick hoop, but it made more sense to cover what I had than to create new beds. If you're starting a garden area from scratch, though, you'll get the most bang for your buck by protecting an area 6 feet wide. Length is relevant only because this dimension will determine how much row cover fabric and how many pieces of PVC pipe you need to buy.

Here's your shopping list:

**1/2-inch PVC pipe.** These pipes will be the supports that arc from one side of the bed to the other, so they need to be long enough to create a gentle curve with space underneath for your plants, but not so long that the quick hoop catches a lot of wind. You probably won't have much choice in the store and will have to cut the pipes later, but if you do have an option, a 10-foot pipe is perfect for arching over a 6-foot-wide bed and you'll need about 7.5 feet of pipe to cover a 4.5-foot-wide bed. To find out how many pipes you need, take the length of your bed, divide it by 3, and add 1. For example, our 25-foot-long quick hoop needed nine pieces of PVC pipe.

**3/8-inch rebar stakes.** Take the number of PVC pipes you need, multiply it by two, and you have the number of rebar stakes you'll need. Each stake should be about one foot long, but you might need longer stakes if you have very sandy soil or lots of wind. Rebar comes in four- to ten-foot lengths, with the longer sections more economical but the shorter ones requiring less cutting on your part.

**Row cover fabric.** The best row cover fabric to use for quick hoops is Agribon AG-19 (or a similar weight fabric by another manufacturer).

You'll be tempted to buy heavier row cover fabric rated down to colder temperatures, but Eliot Coleman has discovered that lighter weight fabric actually keeps your plants warmer because it allows more sun penetration. Your fabric needs to be at least 2 feet wider than the length of your PVC pipe (so, 12 feet wide if you are covering a 6-foot bed or 9.5 feet wide if you're covering a 4.5-foot bed) and at least 6 feet longer than your bed. Some feed stores or garden centers sell row cover fabric by the foot, or you can buy packages or rolls of the fabric online.

**Rebar sides.** The easiest method we've found for keeping wind from whipping up the sides of the quick hoop is to wrap the fabric around long pieces of rebar. You can use any diameter rebar you want (the cheapest is probably a good idea), and the rebar will need to be able to run the length of both sides of your beds. It's fine to use two or three pieces of rebar per side, but it's easier to get into your quick hoop without tearing the fabric if you only use one.

**Bricks, rocks, sandbags, or other heavy objects** to weigh down the sides of the quick hoop. I like to use one brick every four feet or so on both sides.

**Tent stakes.** No matter how long your quick hoop is, you just need two stakes for the ends. I like to use tent stakes—either the plastic or metal ones that can be found for less than a quarter apiece—but you can make wooden stakes by cutting a two-by-four on an angle if you'd rather. The wooden stakes will stand up better under heavy winds in sandy soil but will be harder to drive into the ground.

**Twine or rope.** If you mulched your garden with straw, the plastic twine that held the bales together is perfect for this project. Natural-fiber twine won't last.

**Thin, translucent plastic**. This optional addition is helpful if you're erecting a quick hoop in a very snowy climate and want to give the snow some help sliding off the top. On the other hand, adding plastic means you'll have to manually vent hot air on warm days. The sheet of plastic needs to be the same size as your piece of row cover fabric.

You'll also need the following tools:

**Hacksaw.** For cutting the PVC pipe.

**Reciprocating saw or rebar cutter.** Cutting the rebar stakes to the right length is the trickiest part of this project. We used a reciprocating saw with a metal blade and ran through two blades to make one quick hoop. The rebar also shook like crazy, so one of us had to hold the rebar flat while the other cut. The proper way to cut rebar is using a big bolt cutter known as a rebar cutter, but the tool isn't worth the expense for this one project. You could also use your hacksaw, but cutting all the stakes would take hours. In my opinion, your best option is to sweet-talk an employee at the hardware store into cutting your rebar before you check out.

**Hammer.** Optional, unless your ground is too hard to push the rebar stakes in by hand.

**Scissors.** For cutting the row cover fabric and twine.

**Tape measure.** For lining up your stakes.

This sounds like a lot of supplies, but if you have the right tools, you should be able to buy everything you need to build a 25-foot quick hoop for around $50.

## Quick hoops in the snow

Metal hoops make quick hoops sturdy enough to withstand northern winters.

Photo courtesy Barbara Damrosch, Four Season Farm

*(continued)*

## Quick hoops in the snow *(continued)*

Photo courtesy Johnny's Selected Seeds

The Quick Hoops™ Bender streamlines the production of metal hoops.

PVC quick hoops are easy to build, but they can be crushed by heavy snow in areas with severe winters. If you live in the far north, you may choose to make metal hoops from galvanized electrical conduit (also known as EMT), which costs only a bit more than PVC pipe at your local hardware store. Johnny's Selected Seeds (www.johnnyseeds.com) sells a Quick Hoops™ Bender for $59 that makes it easy to mold metal pipes into a curve.

Johnny's recommends using their metal-supported Quick Hoops™ with different types of coverings depending on the season. AG-19 row cover fabric protects crops in spring, AG-15 is an insect barrier in the summer, and a combination of AG-19 and clear greenhouse plastic is used for winter frost protection. This more heavy-duty option has helped gardeners as far north as zone 0a (Northern Canada or Alaska) grow winter crops with ease.

## *Building your quick hoop*

Before erecting your quick hoop, make sure there's nothing obstructing its path. That might mean pulling out large weeds, clearing rocks, or cutting out stumps.

Next, cut your 3/8" rebar into one foot stakes. See the "Gather your supplies" section to determine how many stakes you need and for cutting suggestions.

I space my stakes three feet apart, but you might choose to set them closer if you live in an area with heavy snow loads.

Drive your stakes about nine inches into the ground every three feet along both sides of your bed. Don't worry if you need to change that spacing to 2.5 feet or 3.5 feet to cover the entire bed—quick hoops are very flexible when it comes to construction. I was able to push my stakes into our soft garden soil with a gloved hand, but you might need to use a hammer.

Now cut your PVC pipes into appropriate lengths with a hacksaw. You can use 7.5 feet to cover 4.5-foot-wide beds, while 10-foot lengths cover 6-foot-wide beds.

When bending the PVC pipes, try not to stand on your raised bed like I did.

Stick one end of the PVC pipe onto a rebar stake on one side of the bed, gently bent the pipe over, and slide the other end onto the rebar stake on the other side of the bed. The pipe should slide easily over the rebar stakes without much wiggle room, and the resulting arc should feel firmly affixed to the ground.

Cut your fabric to the right length, but don't worry about taking off extra width. You'll need enough fabric to completely cover the hoops and then bunch together at each end—I figure on at least six feet more fabric than the bed is long, and a little extra wiggle room is helpful. It's simplest to unroll the fabric, drape it over the hoops, then eyeball where to cut the piece free. This process is much easier if you choose a day with no wind.

Quick hoop construction goes much more smoothly if you wait for a day with no wind.

Bunch the end of the row cover fabric together and tie it with a piece of twine. Repeat at the other end.

Your quick hoop gets its structural integrity from the tension you apply when you attach the twine at each end to a stake. Pound a stake into the ground a few feet beyond each end of the quick hoop, then use the knot shown on page 212 to tighten your row cover fabric over your PVC pipe frame.

I use a come-along knot to attach each end of my quick hoops to a stake in the ground. First, make a solid loop partway down the twine:

a) make a loop,

b) turn the loop into a knot by passing it through itself,

c) pull the knot tight.

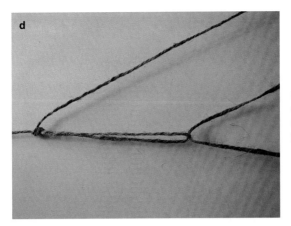

d) Next, hook the free end of the twine around the tent stake and double it back to pass through your solid loop.

e) Pull the twine taut by tugging on the free end of the twine, then pinch the twine in place with one hand to preserve the tension.

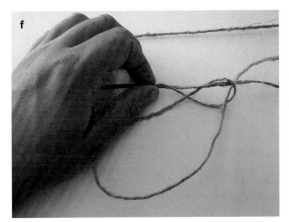

f) Use your other hand to make another loop with the free end of your twine and pass that loop around the portion of the twine leading to the stake.

g) Pull the loop up to where you have the twine pinched to tighten the knot.

h) To untie the knot, simply pull on the free end of the twine. Then skip to step d) to retie the knot.

Now that you have your fabric tied down on each end, it's time to secure the sides. Simply lay your long pieces of rebar on top of the fabric and roll the fabric up around the rebar until the bundle lies flush with your PVC walls. A few bricks or heavy objects placed on top will make sure the rebar doesn't move. Be sure to put weights on the fabric close to the tent stakes too since this part of the quick hoop has no rebar to weigh it down and is the most likely point for wind to invade.

Once built, the easiest way to get into a quick hoop is to remove the bricks from one side and carefully lift the rebar to sit on top of the hoops (or raise the rebar all the way across the top to lay it on the other side if you need more room). In some cases, you may have to untie the twine connecting the fabric to the tent stake, but other times you can just slip under the edge and cut a bowl of salad greens without going to all that trouble.

Roll the extra row cover fabric around lengths of rebar, then use rocks, bricks, or sandbags to weigh down the edges.

# Storing vegetables on the shelf

**GOAL**: Stock up on winter vegetables that require no special preservation

**COST**: $0 to $20

**TIME**: 1 hour to 4 hours

**DIFFICULTY**: Easy

**KID-FRIENDLY**: Yes

Winter squash, like pumpkins and butternuts, can be stored on a kitchen shelf all winter.

Once the leafy greens in your quick hoops finally give out, you will still be eating fresh produce if you plan ahead now. Vegetables like pumpkins, sweet potatoes, and onions can all be stored with little or no special equipment on a kitchen shelf and eaten right through until spring.

## Types of storage vegetables

Most of you are probably aware that potatoes and carrots can be kept all winter long in a root cellar, but building a good cellar is out of the reach of most weekend homesteaders. (After five years on the farm, we

216

still haven't managed to find time to make one of our own.) But once you start looking at the nooks and crannies in your house, you might discover that between your closet, attic, garage, guest room, basement, and kitchen, you have the right environment to store half a dozen types of vegetables right now. That means homegrown, fresh food in the dead of winter—delicious!

The trick to keeping your storage vegetables fresh all winter is understanding the type of conditions each one prefers. Storage conditions can be measured by temperature, humidity, ventilation, and darkness. Nearly all crops like it dark and airy, but each vegetable has a favorite range of temperature and humidity.

These carrots are just as fresh in February as they were in November. To keep potatoes and carrots in your fridge, simply cover the the roots with a damp towel to prevent them from drying out.

In practice, I divide our storers up into two categories—cool, wet storers and warm, dry storers. Cool, wet storers thrive in root cellars and can also be kept well in simpler storage areas like mulched garden rows, storage mounds ("clamps"), trenches, a basement, under the sink in a damp and chilly bathroom, or in the crisper drawer in your fridge (not in a plastic bag, but covered with a damp towel). Warm, dry storers will do much better in your attic, in an unheated guest room, or under your kitchen sink (if you keep the winter thermostat low).

I'm vastly oversimplifying by dividing crops into these two categories, but it's easy to get carried away trying to provide a dozen different storage conditions to make all your crops happy. The table below lists some storage data for common vegetables.

| Vegetable | Optimal storage conditions | My storage conditions | My storage location |
|---|---|---|---|
| beets | 32–40°F, 90–95% humidity | cool, moist | |
| cabbage | 32–40°F, 80–90% humidity | cool, moist | |
| carrots | 32–40°F, 90–95% humidity | cool, moist | crisper drawer of the fridge |
| garlic | 32–50°F, 60–70% humidity | warm, dry | kitchen shelf |
| onions | 32–50°F, 60–70% humidity | warm, dry | kitchen shelf |
| parsnips | 32–40°F, 90–95% humidity | cool, moist | |
| potatoes | 32–40°F, 80–90% humidity | cool, moist | storage mound, crisper drawer of the fridge, under my bed |
| sweet potatoes | 50–60°F, 60–70% humidity | warm, dry | kitchen shelf |
| turnips | 32–40°F, 90–95% humidity | cool, moist | |
| winter squash (including pumpkins) | 50–60°F, 60–70% humidity | warm, dry | kitchen shelf |

Despite ignoring some of the optimal conditions, I've had great luck keeping all the storage vegetables I've tried fresh until they're eaten up. Some years, sweet potatoes and butternut squash have lasted more than twelve months (at which point they turned into chicken feed since we had new crops coming in to take their place), and we always manage to have garlic year-round. Suboptimal conditions just mean that your storage vegetables might not last quite as long, but if you don't let them freeze, most will still taste great several weeks or months later.

## Growing or finding storage vegetables

Whether or not you've grown a bushel of winter squash, you should be thinking about storage vegetables in October. Right now, farmer's markets are chock-full of these crops, and storage vegetables tend to sell for a very low price since most Americans don't know what to do with them. The "Eating seasonally" chapter gave you some tips for finding sources of locally grown food, and if you don't have vegetables from your own garden to store, foraging for food from nearby farmers is your project for this week.

If you are harvesting storage vegetables from your own garden, you should take a bit of extra care to make sure they'll last as long as possible. Next year, you'll want to think about your storage vegetables as early as April when you consider the following:

**Check the soil conditions.** Soils deficient in nutrients (especially potassium) produce vegetables that don't store long, but excess nitrogen can have the same effect.

**Plant later.** The summer garden is so bountiful that you barely need a potato to round out your meal, so it's best to plan your storage vegetables to ripen in early to late fall. Winter squash may need to go in the ground as much as a month after your frost-free date so that they ripen just a few weeks before the first frost, and spring carrots will be woody and bitter by fall, so you'll want to put in a second planting for winter storage. Basically, you should plant your storage vegetables as late as possible to still get a mature crop.

When you harvest (or buy) your crops, handling also affects longevity. Many storage vegetables look so tough that you'll be tempted to toss them from the garden row into a bucket or drop your store-bought sack of potatoes on the ground, but the tiniest nick or bruise will make those crops more likely to spoil. Use a little extra care now, and you'll be enjoying your reward in February.

Wait to harvest winter squash until the vines have died back.

Harvesting at the right time is also key. Many storage vegetables don't mind being harvested late, but onions, garlic, winter squash, and sweet potatoes should be taken in before frost nips the ground. On the other hand, carrots and parsnips sweeten after cold weather hits, so wait until just before the first killing frost to harvest these roots.

For winter squash, white potatoes, and onions, you want to harvest after the stems and leaves have died back, but sweet potatoes won't lose their leaves until after a frost (at which point the tubers are slightly injured). You can unearth one sweet potato plant and test the size of the tubers before digging your whole plot, which is also the approved method for determining garlic ripeness. (Keep in mind that although I'm discussing garlic and onions now, you should have harvested both of these crops in the middle of the summer).

When harvesting vegetables for storage, try to dig them in dry weather when less soil is clinging to the roots and the vegetables themselves are less filled with water. Choose a sunny day and leave underground vegetables sitting on top of the soil for a few hours after harvesting to dry their skins. Gently brush off the dirt, but don't scrub or wash the vegetables.

Root crops should be left on the soil surface to dry for a few hours before collecting.

## Curing storage vegetables

If you bought vegetables, they probably all look pretty good, but you should expect a certain percentage of imperfect crops when you grow your own. Right after harvest, I like to pick through vegetables (especially potatoes) to pull out any that are bruised or cut—these will be eaten as soon as possible since they won't last long otherwise.

The next step is to figure out if your crops need to be cured. If you cure vegetables that don't need to be cured, they'll rot. And if you don't cure vegetables that do need to be cured, they'll rot too. So take a minute to check your vegetables against the chart below before putting them in their final storage spot.

| Vegetable | Curing method |
|-----------|---------------|
| beets | none |
| cabbage | none |
| carrots | none |
| garlic | 1–2 weeks in a warm, dry place |
| onions | 2–3 weeks in a warm, dry place |
| parsnips | none |

*(Continued)*

| Vegetable | Curing method |
|---|---|
| potatoes | 2 weeks at 50–60°F and 95% humidity (slightly warmer than a root cellar) |
| sweet potatoes | 2 weeks at 80–85°F (dry) |
| turnips | none |
| winter squash (including pumpkins) | 2 weeks in a warm, dry place; don't cure acorn squash |

Curing serves a couple of purposes. In all crops except white potatoes, a primary purpose is to lower the water content so that the vegetable won't rot in storage. White and sweet potatoes and winter squash develop a hard skin during curing that will protect the crop during storage. And I've noticed that flavors also tend to intensify during curing—garlic eaten fresh out of the ground is watery and doesn't lend as much zing to soups, while sweet potatoes are starchy instead of sweet if eaten right away.

There are dozens of different ways to cure vegetables at home, but the main idea is to allow for maximum airflow around the plants without exposing them to direct sunlight and rain. I've shown some of my favorite curing methods below.

Old window screens make great drying stations if set up on cinder blocks and separated from each other by bricks. If you live in a suburban location, keep your eyes open on trash day, and chances are you'll find quite an assortment of screens being thrown away.

We cure our garlic by hanging the plants under the porch eaves. Just tie the garlic into bunches small enough that air can get into the center and let them cure until the leaves turn brown.

Onions can be braided and hung just like garlic, but their more slender leaves tend to break apart, bruising the onions as they drop to the ground. For best results, include a sturdy piece of twine or wire in the full length of the braid for structural integrity.

For small harvests, you might be able to get away with curing the vegetables in a garden cart like the one shown here, or in baskets propped up above the ground. Just make sure that the vegetables aren't sitting on top of one another—they shouldn't touch each other at all.

If you have more space inside than we do, you might get away with curing your vegetables in the house. But if you're curing under a porch or tarp outside, you'll need to take temperature into account. We harvest our sweet potatoes a couple of weeks before the first frost so that they'll have time to harden their skins before we need to move them inside to their final storage spots.

## Sorting and storing vegetables

After their curing period is complete, it's time for one more round of sorting before you store your vegetables. Once again, pull out any obviously bruised vegetables—a light squeeze will turn up onions that are starting to rot inside or garlic that is already drying out. These problem vegetables, along with any unusually small ones, are set aside for eating soon.

While you sort, cut off leaves and excess roots, but don't cut close enough to expose the living parts of the vegetables. Then put them away in baskets or bags for storage.

Airflow is nearly as important during storage as during curing, and you also don't want to stack too many vegetables on top of each other or they'll bruise. The mesh bags in which onions, oranges, and potatoes are packaged in the grocery store are perfect—you can either save your own throughout the year or ask in the produce section, where the staff often have empty bags headed for the dumpster.

Baskets also make good storage containers, especially the rectangular half-bushel baskets in which peaches are sold. Larger vegetables, like winter squash, might not need any storage containers at all and can just sit on a shelf.

Refer back to the first section of this chapter to decide where to stash your vegetables for the winter, but before you put them away, take a few minutes to note down how much of each type you have. You can weigh the veggies or measure them by the bag or basket. If you also make a note when you run out of each type (or of how much extra you have in the spring), you'll know how much to buy or grow next year.

## Maintaining your storage vegetables

Later chapters will give you some good recipes for using up those butternut squash and potatoes, so you'll want to make sure they last. I take a look at my bags and baskets whenever I pull out some of the contents to see if anything is rotten. "One bad apple will spoil the barrel," and so will one bad potato, so remove any problem crops as soon as they appear.

If you're keeping vegetables out in your garage or barn, you'll also want to ensure critters don't make off with your stores. You may need to use hardware cloth or some other mouseproof lid to cover up your baskets and bags. It's also important to ensure that your storage vegetables don't freeze.

When storing vegetables (like carrots and potatoes) that prefer high humidity in a lower humidity location, I like to drape a damp dish towel over them. Once a week (or whenever I go into the crisper drawer after a carrot), I dampen the towel again to keep the crops moist.

Otherwise, just sit back and enjoy homegrown vegetables preserved with no outlay of cash or energy.

# Scavenging biomass

**GOAL**: Find free mulch and compost for your garden
**COST**: $0
**TIME**: 1 hour to 4 hours
**DIFFICULTY**: Medium
**KID-FRIENDLY**: Yes

Mulch and compost are expensive, but you can often pick up the ingredients for free. This week's project walks you through finding the best sources of free biomass in your area.

## Deciding how to use free biomass

On a homestead, there's a nearly unlimited need for compost, mulch, and bedding for animals. But which type of biomass should be used where? The characteristics below will help determine each material's best use in your garden.

In the "Mulch" chapter, I explained how a material's carbon to nitrogen ratio (C:N ratio) determines its usefulness as mulch or compost. Here is the short version:

Materials (like manure and spring grass clippings) that are **high in nitrogen** compost quickly and feed your plants within the first year. A C:N ratio of 10:1 is found in high-quality, finished compost. It's possible to have too much nitrogen in some biomass to apply it directly to your garden without composting, so materials like chicken manure (C:N of 8:1) are better used to heat up a compost pile.

Materials (like wood chips and paper) that are **high in carbon** compost slowly and work better as mulch. A C:N ratio above 60:1 is too low in nitrogen to apply directly to your garden even as a mulch until allowed to compost for a year or more.

Another factor to consider when deciding what to do with scavenged biomass is the presence of seeds. Seed-free biomass—like coffee grounds—can be applied straight to the garden, but if you use seedy grass clippings as mulch, you'll be sorry. I made that mistake a few years ago and ended up with a massive weeding job when the mulch sprouted a lawn around the roots of my sweet corn.

But don't turn up your nose at uncomposted manure or other potentially seedy biomass—there are several ways to make use of the materials without creating a weeding problem. If you've got the time, you can simply compost them. A well-built compost pile will get so hot inside that it will kill any weed seeds, allowing you to use the result on your garden with impunity. An alternative is to lay the seedy materials on the ground as the base of a kill mulch, in which case the seeds will never sprout. Finally, if you have chickens, your flock will love picking through weedy biomass on the floor of their coop, mixing in their high-nitrogen droppings to create stellar compost.

The final problem you might run into when using free biomass is poisons. Try to collect your grass clippings from uglier lawns rather than from beautiful green swards treated with herbicides. You might also want to steer clear of tree leaves grown downwind of industrial facilities. Colored inks, especially those found on paper heavier than newsprint, may occasionally contain heavy metals. As long as you compost questionable biomass well, fungi will deal with most chemical problems for you—heavy metals are the only issue that seems to be too tough for fungi to handle. (See the "Growing edible mushrooms" chapter for more information.)

## Finding free biomass

A century ago, many products that we think of as "waste" were cherished as sources of garden fertility. The invention of chemical fertilizers, though, made most farmers turn to easier-to-handle (and less smelly) sources of nutrients. Although this sea change has damaged our environment and degraded the nutritional quality of our food supply, there is a silver lining—the backyard homesteader has dozens of kinds of free biomass to choose from.

The type of biomass you hunt down for this week's project will depend on where you spend your time. Many of you live out in the country but commute into a city every day to work—you can scavenge in both places without going out of your way. If you spend most of your time in one setting or the other, though, it's probably not worthwhile to drive too far outside your usual stomping grounds for free biomass. I've separated sources of biomass into those found in your household, in rural areas, and in urban areas to help you simplify your scrounging.

## Household biomass

Before heading out into the neighborhood, it's best to make sure you're fully utilizing all the sources of biomass your own household churns out as waste. If you decide you like any of these products, you can collect them on a larger scale in the typical city, or even talk your rural neighbors into setting aside their waste for you.

**Kitchen scraps** tend to be high in nitrogen and (generally) seed-free, making them good for adding to worm bins or for heating up compost piles. (Of course, if you have chickens, you should give the flock first dibs.) The downside of kitchen scraps is that they tend to smell and can attract vermin, so be sure to cover them with high-carbon materials.

**Grass clippings** can be collected from your lawn using a bagging mower. You'll only want to remove between a third and a half of the clippings from your lawn to keep the grasses happy (letting the rest of the clippings melt back into the ground) unless you fertilize the soil using a chicken tractor or other sustainable method. The highest-quality clippings are harvested in the spring, when grass leaves are full of nitrogen and make a great mulch if applied immediately to garden beds. Spring clippings will also heat up compost piles quickly, as long as you mix them in well so that they don't turn slimy. Later in the year, grass clippings are higher in carbon and tend to be full of seeds, so you'll need to compost summer and fall clippings or put them on the floor of your chicken coop.

**Paper** is very high in carbon, so it is best mixed into a compost pile with high-nitrogen materials. A quality shredder will make paper much easier to compost or to use as bedding in the worm bin. In both cases, newsprint works best, and you should steer clear of colored inks. Heavier papers are best utilized to start fires in your woodstove.

**Wood ashes** from your stove are high in the nutrients potassium and calcium. They will raise the pH of your soil or compost pile, though, so use ashes only if you know that your soil is too acidic.

Biochar is a very long-lasting form of organic matter that may remain in your soil for hundreds or thousands of years. The charcoal favors beneficial micro-organisms, retains nutrients that might otherwise wash out of your soil, helps soil aggregation, and holds onto water without leading to waterlogged conditions. You may not see improved yields right away after adding biochar, but chances are the benefits will become apparent by year two.

**Charcoal** can be sifted out of your wood ashes and turned into biochar. Wait until the coals have cooled and then use hardware cloth attached to a wooden frame to remove the charcoal. Soak charcoal in urine for a day or so; then apply the activated biochar to your garden the same way you would top-dress or work in compost. Biochar acts like humus, providing safe havens for soil microorganisms to grow and thrive.

**Hair** and **feathers** are very high in nitrogen, but both resist absorbing moisture, so they break down slowly. If you cut your own hair, it's worth saving the results and mixing them with wetter, high-carbon materials (like soaked hay) in a compost pile. Ditto if you kill and pluck your own chickens.

## Urban biomass

The typical city or town is so full of biomass going to waste that you could spend all day harvesting. In addition to the materials listed in the last section, you'll find the following:

**Coffee grounds** are produced in large quantities at coffee shops. Grounds are seed-free and high in nitrogen (C:N of 12:1), so they can be used straight in the garden or in the worm bin.

**Cardboard** looks like it should be lower in quality than paper, but the corrugated version is bound together with biodegradable glues that soil microorganisms love. I can never get enough corrugated cardboard for making kill mulches, but if I had excess, I would tear it up and use it as worm-bin bedding or in the compost pile. Corrugated cardboard can also be used to propagate edible mushrooms, as I'll explain in a later chapter. Most stores have cardboard boxes to give away, but furniture stores will have the largest boxes that are best for kill mulches.

**Tree leaves** are one of my favorite curbside attractions in the fall. Their C:N ratio of around 50:1 (and lack of seeds) makes deciduous tree leaves a good source of mulch, especially if you can find a way to shred the leaves so that they don't blow away. Since trees suck up micronutrients from deep in the earth, their leaves are rich in elements like calcium that your soil may lack. To compost leaves, shred them if possible and then mix with a higher-nitrogen material like manure.

**Spent hops and mash** are a waste product of microbreweries. These wet, high-nitrogen materials are best added to a compost pile with dry, high-carbon materials.

**Fish waste** can be found at seafood processors and canneries. Fish waste stinks to high heaven, so you'll want to mix it into the ground or bury it deep in a compost pile immediately, but the fish are high in nitrogen and trace minerals.

## Rural biomass

If your neighbors are farmers, you may be in luck. Animal manure (especially manure from dairy cows and well-fed horses) is some of the highest quality biomass you can add to your garden. Here's a rundown on the pros and cons of some of the main types of manures, along with other rural products:

Don't let the mess factor turn you away from using free sources of manure. You can bring home small quantities easily using a shovel and a few five-gallon buckets. Of course, you can haul much more in a pickup truck, loaded by hand with a pitchfork or by a helpful neighbor with a scoop.

**Horse manure mixed with straw bedding** is my favorite kind of manure, especially if you can find a pile out behind someone's barn that has been ignored for a year, so that hot-composting has killed the ubiquitous weed seeds. Compost worms adore mixtures of horse manure and straw, so you can easily increase the size of your worm bin to take advantage of any amount of the stuff. Or just make a big compost pile for next year's garden. The C:N ratio of plain horse manure is about 12:1 without bedding, but manure will inevitably be mixed with straw (for a high-quality result) or sawdust (for a lower-quality result that needs longer composting).

**Cow manure** is similar to horse manure but wetter, so it might gross you out if not mixed with plenty of bedding. The highest-quality cow manure comes from dairy cows because they are fed well.

**Rabbit manure** has a C:N of around 12:1 and is dry, so you can get away with using fresh droppings straight on your garden. Rabbit manure tends to be seed-free and doesn't smell. You'll get more nitrogen if you include the urine-soaked bedding.

**Chicken manure** (or manure from other types of poultry) has a C:N of 8:1 and is high in phosphorus (which is often in short supply in the typical compost mix). Too rich to be applied directly to your plants, chicken manure doesn't add much long-term organic matter to the soil, so using the manure is a bit like pouring on chemical fertilizers. A monotonous diet of only chicken-manure compost will tend to build up salts in your soil and result in an oversupply of phosphorus. Finally, chicken manure stinks if it's not enclosed in bedding. On the positive side, the high nitrogen content of chicken manure makes it a great addition to a slow-to-heat compost pile made of materials like autumn leaves or wood chips, and chicken manure is usually seed-free. I consider chicken manure a good source of nitrogen and phosphorus in a well-rounded compost pile, and I use halfway-composted, deep bedding to mulch and fertilize my woody perennials.

**Spoiled hay** is another type of biomass that can sometimes be found for free in rural areas. Hay is cut and dried pasture grass, often full of seeds, which is meant to be fed to livestock like cows and horses. (Even though hay looks like straw, the two are very different materials and have different uses on the farm.) If hay gets damp, it can mildew and is no longer safe to feed to your animals, so farmers will often give away the spoiled hay. From a gardening point of view, the quality of hay varies widely depending on whether you've found spring hay (high in nitrogen, low in seeds) or summer hay (high in carbon and seeds). Either way, though, you can't go wrong by laying down spoiled hay under a kill mulch to make a rich raised bed or using the organic matter as bedding in your chicken coop.

**Sawdust** might be free for the hauling at carpentry shops or saw mills. Meanwhile, if you flag down one of the crews that trim trees off the power line or along the sides of roads, they may dump a whole truckload of wood chips in your yard. Both types of wood products have an extremely high C:N, so you'll need to mix them with lots of high-nitrogen materials and compost for quite a while before using the result on your garden. I let piles of plain wood chips rot for a couple of years and then use the mulch around my fruit trees—beneficial fungi love well-rotted wood chips, and the soil around my trees' roots gets fluffier every year.

**Rotten fruits and pomace** can sometimes be scavenged from orchards and cider mills. Pomace is the pulp, skins, and seeds left behind after you make apple cider. Both of these materials are wet and attract painfully stinging yellow jackets, so they're best mixed deep into a compost pile amid absorbent materials like dry hay or sawdust. The fruit waste is high in nitrogen, and the seeds will add phosphorus to your compost pile. Alternatively, you could feed both rotten fruits and pomace to your chickens, goats, or other livestock.

**Seaweed** can often be picked right off the beach if you live by the ocean. Seaweed is high in nitrogen (19:1), so it can be used as a quickly rotting mulch or can be added to a compost pile. The major bonuses of seaweed are the trace minerals and potassium provided.

## Wild biomass

If your farm has a woodland attached, you can collect organic matter amid the trees without impacting the forest's ability to host wildflowers, raccoons, and warblers. My favorite sources of woodland biomass include these:

*(continued)*

# Wild biomass  *(continued)*

**Stump dirt** is the moist, dark, earthy-smelling organic matter found inside decaying trees or logs. Nearly pure humus, stump dirt can be used in place of store-bought potting soil when starting seeds. If you're potting up a longer-lived house plant, mix some compost with your stump dirt since the latter is low in macronutrients (although high in micronutrients).

**Wood** is generally gathered for firewood or building, but it is also handy in the garden when building *hugelkultur* mounds. See the "Kill mulch" chapter for more information.

**Tree leaves** can be raked off the forest floor and stuffed into a duffel bag to carry home. In addition to working as a quality garden amendment in the ways I described in a previous section, wild-gathered tree leaves will inoculate your perennial garden with mycorrhizal fungi to help your fruit trees thrive.

The key to managing woodlands sustainably is to keep your impact as light as possible. For example, I try to gather leaves from different areas each time, only scooping up the duff at the same spot once every decade or so. Similarly, you can cut a single tree out of an acre of woodland every year without changing the structure of the forest at all.

Invasive species are another factor to consider when using wild biomass. Many states prohibit moving firewood more than fifty miles, in hopes of preventing invasive insects and diseases from spreading into formerly untouched areas. From a biological standpoint, you don't need to be concerned about moving sterile organic matter (such as coffee grounds straight from a restaurant), and you're unlikely to cause many problems if you move cultivated organic matter (such as spoiled hay and grass clippings), but you might choose to limit transporting wild biomass more than ten miles, to be on the safe side.

Finally, invasive plants are an issue when you gather leaves off the forest floor. I like to scoop up leaves in the most mature forest areas on my property since I've walked through these spots in the summer and know there are no invasive plants to spread around. On the other hand, my young forests are infested with Japanese stiltgrass, which can turn into a weed hazard in the garden if I gather seeds along with my leaf mulch. If you don't know which invasive species are a problem in your area, the easiest way to find out is to visit a local park and ask a naturalist.

## The rewards of free biomass

Gathering free sources of biomass can be time consuming and physically strenuous, but the rewards are many. Since you'll usually want to ask for permission before grabbing biomass out of someone's dumpster, scavenging will help you meet new people and form connections in your community. In many cases, you'll be keeping "waste" from ending up in the landfill while building the long-term fertility of your soil. Last of all, it's just plain fun to get something so useful for free.

# Apprenticeships

**GOAL**: Learn a skill hands-on
**COST**: $0
**TIME**: 3 hours to 8 hours
**DIFFICULTY**: Medium
**KID-FRIENDLY**: Maybe

Working with animals on someone else's farm can help you decide if you want to commit to the time and equipment needed to bring mules, bees, or other livestock home.

Some homesteading skills are much easier to learn hands-on. This week, you'll hunt down an expert and spend an afternoon picking his brains about a technique or project you've been itching to try out.

## Choosing an apprentice project

A century ago, most of us would have learned basic homesteading skills from our parents, but nowadays, even grandparents often know nothing about milking a cow or shearing a sheep. Books fill in a lot of the gaps but may spend a whole chapter struggling to explain basic physical skills that are easy to teach in person. If you've gotten your hands dirty with homesteading even a little bit, you've probably already stumbled across skills you want to master. Here are some options:

**Tools**—There's a knack to using any tool effectively, so if you weren't raised with a shovel in your hand, it might be worth helping a neighbor dig a ditch to become a pro. Personally, I'm itching to figure out how to choose and use a scythe that fits my short stature. You might want to learn about loosening soil with a broadfork, digging potatoes with a potato fork, or killing weeds with a propane torch.

**Animals**—A great way to see if those animals you dream of really suit you is to visit a farm and spend an afternoon participating in their care. You might learn to shear a sheep, clip a goat's hooves, milk a cow, slaughter chickens, or guide a team of mules. Having an expert show you his or her beehive or guide you in extracting honey can make beekeeping seem much less complex.

**Construction**—If building your own chicken coop seemed too daunting, perhaps it would be worth helping someone build a shed. You could pick up the vocabulary of lumber and learn to use power tools safely. Or maybe you're interested in electrical wiring, plumbing, or another related skill.

**Household**—Do you want to learn to make your own soap, use a pressure canner, knead bread dough, ferment grapes into wine, or spin wool into yarn?

Don't feel obliged to pick a skill from the suggestions above—your apprenticeship should be specific to your own needs. But do put at least three or four items on your list so that it'll be easier to find a mentor.

## Searching for teachers

Another way to start your apprenticeship search is to make a list of people who seem chock-full of wisdom and willing to share it. Grandparents and older neighbors are good fits since they may be the last living holders of oral traditions that their children are uninterested in learning. Younger homesteaders can also offer great advice, but they're often very busy, so it may be hard to pin them down.

As you look beyond your own circle, consider places where possible mentors hang out. You'll have good luck finding gardening mentors at the farmer's market and will have quite a selection of elders with time on their hands at senior centers and hospitals. In our rural area, old-timers often pull up a chair and sit for hours at the hardware store and mechanic's shop—I'm sure at least some of them would be thrilled to teach you about DIY skills.

In the urban environment, people passionate about homesteading can be found by asking at the library and at churches and community centers. Newspapers may have notices about agricultural conferences, gardening or beekeeping clubs, county fairs, and history days, all of which attract enthusiasts who are often willing to talk your ear off about the topic in question. If you'd like to learn fabric arts, drop by a yarn or needlework shop. Finally, the 4-H program and Future Farmers of America can match your kids up with agricultural mentors.

If you've got one item on your skill list that you really want to focus on, you'll need to be more picky about choosing a mentor. "I'm looking for someone to teach me how to shear sheep," you might tell your friends and family. "Do you know anyone who fits the bill?" Chances are someone in your circle has just the right mentor in his or her address book. If not, try Craigslist.

This week's project simply involves finding someone willing to spend a few hours teaching, but if you have more time, why not look into a longer learning experience? The websites that follow below point you toward farmers willing to take on students for a few weeks or months at a time.

- WWOOF (www.wwoof.org) matches up people interested in learning about agriculture with organic farmers worldwide.
- ATTRA (www.attra.ncat.org/attra-pub/internships/) has a list of sustainable farming internships and apprenticeships in the United States.

## *How to be a good apprentice*

If you want the apprentice-mentor experience to be a win-win, follow these simple rules:

**Give as much as you get.** My husband I learned to slaughter chickens by "helping" friends process dozens of broilers they had grown as their cash crop. At the time, we were such raw beginners that I'm pretty sure we used up more of our friends' time than we saved by offering the extra sets of hands. Farmers are very busy people, so be aware that your unskilled labor might be more hindrance than help, and balance the scales in some other manner. Why not bring lunch or do an hour of grunt work to make up the difference? Maybe you can teach your mentor a skill he or she has been aching to learn, or you could even offer cold, hard cash (although barter tends to build more solid relationships). Finally, just be pleasant—a smile combined with a healthy dose of enthusiasm goes a long way.

**Be prepared.** Figure out how to reach your mentor's homestead in advance and allow a bit of wiggle room so that you're early (but not too early). Ask if there are any tools you should bring, and then wear work clothes, boots, and gloves. I hate to admit to being so critical, but if someone shows up on our farm wearing brand new, stylish jeans that have clearly never touched dirt, I assume he or she is not going to be putting in any real labor and probably don't invite him or her back in a work setting. Being prepared can also mean reading up on the subject a bit before coming so that you can ask informed questions.

**Listen more than you talk.** Remember, you're there to learn. Yes, you may have read three different books on the subject, but your mentor has put in hours of hands-on labor and probably has a reason to do things his way even if the books say he's wrong. I generally come with two or three questions I know I want to ask, but otherwise I keep my mouth shut and let my mentor tell me as much as he can. Meanwhile, I listen carefully and follow directions, requesting clarification if I don't understand what I'm being asked to do. Remember that your main goal is to soak up knowledge and you'll do just fine.

It's a bit daunting to ask a stranger—or even a friend—to take a day out of a busy schedule to teach you how to bake bread. But apprenticeships can be powerful tools that enable you to learn skills while building your homesteading community. You may even end your apprenticeship with a new friend.

# NOVEMBER

*(May Down Under)*

# Garden rotation

**GOAL**: Prevent disease and insect infestations by rotating plant families

**COST**: $0

**TIME**: 1 hour to 4 hours

**DIFFICULTY**: Medium

**KID-FRIENDLY**: Maybe

A couple of hours with pen and paper now will make next year's garden shine. Simply rotating plant families through your garden can keep diseases and pests at bay.

## *Why rotate?*

Early blight is one of the diseases that can be slowed or prevented by rotating your crops.

You've probably heard the term *garden rotation* before, but what does it mean and why do we do it?

242

Let's start with the example of early blight, a fungal disease that hits tomatoes in warm, damp weather. Once your tomatoes come down with early blight, fungal spores can survive in the soil for years. So if you plant tomatoes in the same ground next year, they're going to be infected with early blight nearly immediately, and you may get no crop at all.

Okay, you say, that's not too tough. I'll just move my tomatoes every year. But here's the thing—tomatoes and potatoes are in the same family, and they tend to share a lot of diseases.

Late blight is a fungal disease that's much more devastating than early blight, but luckily for us, late blight can only survive in living plant tissue. Since tomatoes shrivel up and die at the first sign of frost, you don't need to worry about late blight being carried over from one year to the next . . . unless you grow potatoes. Have you ever noticed that it's nearly impossible to harvest every tiny spud out of the soil and that "volunteer" potatoes tend to pop up in the spot where you grew potatoes last year? If you had late blight in last year's garden, those volunteer potatoes will spread the disastrous fungus to any tomatoes you plant nearby this year. So when you choose a spot for your tomatoes, you want to make sure neither tomatoes nor potatoes have grown there recently.

I could tell you dozens of interactions like this that you want to avoid, but garden rotation is really pretty simple. If you grow a vegetable in a spot that hasn't been home to any plants in the same family for at least three years, then you'll cut down on insects and diseases drastically. Wouldn't you rather spend an hour planning out your garden now rather than coddling sick plants all summer?

## Vegetable families

The first step in rotating your garden is to understand which vegetables share the same family. The list below covers all the vegetables you're likely to grow, and I've italicized the more common crops so they'll be easier to find.

**Amaranthaceae**—Amaranth

**Amaryllidaceae**—Chives, *garlic, leeks, onions*

**Basellaceae**—Malabar spinach

**Brassicaceae**—Asian greens, *broccoli*, broccoli rabe, *brussels sprouts, cabbage, cauliflower, collards*, cress, horseradish, *kale*, kohlrabi, *mustard, radishes*, rape, rocket, rutabaga, *turnips*, watercress

**Chenopodiaceae**—*Beet*, beetberry, Good King Henry, lamb's quarter, mangel, orach, quinoa, *spinach, Swiss chard*

**Compositae**—Artichoke, cardoon, celtuce, chicory, *endive, escarole*, gobo, Jerusalem artichoke, *lettuce*, salsify, shungiku, *sunflower*, yacon

**Convolvulaceae**—Water spinach, *sweet potatoes*

**Cucurbitaceae**—Balsam apples, balsam pears, cassabanana, chayote, *cucumbers*, gherkins, *gourds*, luffa, *melons, pumpkins, squash*

**Graminae**—*Corn*

**Labiatae**—*Basil, mint, oregano, thyme*

**Leguminosae**—*Beans*, lentils, peanuts, *peas*, pigeon peas, soybeans

**Liliaceae**—*Asparagus*

**Malvaceae**—*Okra*

**Polygonaceae**—*Rhubarb*, sorrel

**Portulaceae**—Miner's lettuce, purslane

**Solanaceae**—Cape gooseberry, *eggplant*, garden huckleberry, ground cherry, naranjilla, nightshade, pepino, *peppers, potatoes*, sunberry, tomatillo, *tomatoes*

**Tetragoniaceae**—New Zealand spinach

**Umbelliferae**—*Carrots*, celeriac, *celery*, chervil, *coriander, dill, fennel, parsley, parsnips*, skirret

**Valerianaceae**—Corn salad

Although this list seems overwhelming at first glance, a closer look will show that the majority of your garden vegetables fit into just a few families. Experienced gardeners have pet names for several of them, so you'll hear folks talking about "brassicas" when they mean broccoli, kale, and the like, "cucurbits" when they want to lump squash and cucumbers together, and "legumes" when referring to peas and beans.

# Rotating the diverse garden

Some gardeners keep rotation extremely simple by dividing their garden into four sections and growing different families in each section. For example, if the northeast quarter of your garden is home to the legume family, the southeast quarter to potatoes and tomatoes, the southwest quarter to cucurbits, and the northwest quarter to everything else, you can simple turn your map like a wheel to plan next year's garden. Now your legumes go in the southeast quadrant, the tomatoes in the southwest quadrant, and so forth.

Unfortunately, the method outlined above has several problems. Chances are your garden isn't entirely uniform, so the wheel rotation method would often require you to grow vegetables in spots they don't prefer from time to time. In my garden, a third of the growing area has deep, loamy soil that's good for root crops, and another third is very sunny and perfect for spring and fall crops. That means my brassicas are nearly always located in the sunny third, while carrots and potatoes dominate the loamy third.

Even if you are growing on a completely flat area with no shade and with the same soil type throughout, planting big blocks of the same type of vegetable together is asking for trouble. With the exception of corn (which requires a large planting in one spot to allow for wind pollination of the seeds), you'll have far less insect and disease pressure if you scatter each type of vegetable throughout the garden. A diverse garden with beans beside tomatoes beside parsley will make it tough for problematic insects to find the plants they prefer, while also tempting beneficial insects to spend time in every part of the garden.

To add one more complication to the mix, you should keep in mind that you can often grow two or more different vegetables in the same bed each year. For example, overwintering garlic is harvested in early June, just in time to plant sweet potatoes. Spring leaf lettuce takes about a month to bulk up, can be cut for a month, and then turns bitter, so I allot the lettuce two months out of the year before replacing it with a new crop, like bush beans. Your notes from last year will help you figure out how many months each crop will take, but there are always a few vegetables that are pulled out early or don't come up. As a result, I generally plan the location for my vegetables in stages, first figuring out where each variety will go for the spring planting (February to June) and only later planning my summer and fall gardens.

## Simplifying complex rotations

The problem with a diverse garden is that planning rotation can be a mind-bending exercise if you grow in a large space. Luckily, there are ways to simplify the process.

The legume family contains beans and peas.

The first step toward easy rotations is to figure out which families cover the most ground in your garden. These widespread families will vary depending on what you like to eat, of course, but I always struggle to find fresh ground for legumes, brassicas, cucurbits, the onion family, and the tomato family. Everything else is pretty easy since I don't grow enough okra, for example, to make it difficult to find the vegetable a home in next year's garden.

You could do worse than to start off your rotation by deciding on spots for the members of the five prolific families mentioned above. Make a list of all the vegetables you grow in each family and divide them up by planting date; then start finding homes for each crop from earliest planted to latest planted. Don't worry if you're stumped and can't find a good spot for the last few beds of vegetables—openings generally come up and let you squeeze them in.

The steps I use when deciding on a spot for each vegetable in next year's garden are as follows:

**Decide how many beds to devote to the crop.** I keep notes on how much I preserve of each type of vegetable and of the month when I ran out of those stored foods in the winter. If I had to buy tomatoes starting in February, that's a clue that I should plant more beds next year. On the other hand, if I ended up with peppers that I didn't want to eat when the time came to clean out the freezer in the spring, I might as well grow fewer this year. Don't get carried away, though—if this is your first or second year gardening, you'll want to keep your garden small and manageable. The chart below lists how many of my garden beds (each twenty square feet) I devote to various crops in my spring and summer garden.

| Vegetable | # beds |
|---|:---:|
| basil | 1 |
| broccoli | 8 |
| cabbage | 2 |
| carrots | 2 |
| cucumbers | 6 |
| green beans | 9 |
| greens | 4 |
| lettuce | 4 |
| okra | 2 |
| onions | 7 |
| parsley | 2 |
| peanuts | 2 |
| peas | 6 |
| peppers | 2 |
| poppies | 2 |
| potatoes | 10 |
| summer squash | 7 |
| sweet corn | 18 |
| sweet potatoes | 8 |
| tomatoes | 16 |
| watermelon | 4 |
| winter squash | 4 |

**Consider where the crop will grow best.** I like to save the sunniest spots for crops planted in the early spring or those that will survive late into the winter. The next sunniest spots go to tomatoes and cucurbits that succumb to fungal diseases during our hot, humid summers. Herbs can go anywhere, but you'll use more if they're close to your front door. Root crops require deep, well-drained soil, so keep them out of clayey or swampy spots. If you hand-water, you might want to keep moisture lovers like celery close to the hose.

**Hunt and check until you find a spot.** Now that I know I need ten potato beds and that the root crop needs to be located in the loamy third of my garden, I can start hunting through the garden until I find the appropriate number of beds that haven't grown tomatoes, potatoes, peppers, or eggplants for a few years. If you created a garden spreadsheet as I recommended in the "Plan your summer garden" chapter, you can simply search for the bed number (or sort by bed if you have all the information on the same sheet) and get a list of all the vegetables grown in each bed since you started taking notes. Although a bit time-consuming, this hunt-and-check method only takes me a couple of hours when deciding on spots for all the crops in our huge spring and early summer garden.

I repeat these three steps for each type of vegetable, working my way from the difficult-to-fit spring broccoli and summer tomatoes down to crops like poppies that are easy to slide into gaps. If you're feeling ambitious, you can add cover crops in any fallow periods to build your soil while waiting to plant those autumn carrots. (See the "Mulch" chapter for more information.)

If you need an incentive to make garden planning happen in a timely manner, you can use mine—once I know where each vegetable will go, I'm allowed to pore over seed catalogs. Garden porn!

# Roast a chicken

**GOAL**: Learn one of the easiest ways to cook a whole chicken
**COST**: $5–$10
**TIME**: 2 hours
**DIFFICULTY**: Medium
**KID-FRIENDLY**: Maybe

Understanding how to cook a whole chicken saves money on your grocery bill and also prepares you to process your own meat on the hoof.

## Meat and sustainability

Unless you're a vegan, animals died to make your dinner. Most of us are so divorced from the land that we don't realize that the hen that lays our eggs and the dairy cow that gives our milk each had a brother who was killed as soon as he entered this world.

Even if you don't eat animal products of any kind, thousands of animals, large and small, perished when your soybean field was plowed, sprayed, and harvested. And although the soybean industry will tell you that vegetarians use less land area, the truth is that a homesteader who follows intensive practices can grow more calories on her acre of land if she includes animals in the mix.

I'm not recommending that you make a habit of eating large quantities of factory-farmed meat, but in many cases, pastured animals are just as kind or kinder to the earth than plant products. The trouble is that even once I understood that fact, I was heartsick at the idea of slaughtering my own meat animals. In fact, I wasn't even comfortable working with raw meat in the kitchen. A boneless chicken breast or raw hamburger patty was okay, but if you handed me a whole, raw chicken five years ago, I would have handed it right back.

Only after learning to cook with real meat did I feel comfortable slaughtering my own chickens, butchering wild deer, and trying out the unusual cuts of meat that came with the whole pastured lamb we bought from a neighbor's farm. This week's exercise focuses on roasting a chicken because roast chicken was one of the first recipes that helped me gain meat-cooking confidence.

## How a roast chicken turns into meals for ten

Most American families will be stumbling through roasting a turkey this month, but I recommend that you experiment with something small enough to be consumed by the average modern household. A four-pound chicken will feed at least four people very well the first day; then you can pick enough meat off the bones for sandwiches for two tomorrow. Finally, you can simmer the carcass to make a delicious chicken stock.

It's hard to believe that an $8 chicken can provide the protein for ten meals, but that's the kind of value you can get used to as you start to cook with whole cuts of meat. If you grow most or all the vegetables to complement your chicken, you will be eating frugal, yet gourmet meals!

## How to roast a chicken

You'll need the following:

- 1 whole chicken (4–5 lb.), with the giblets and neck removed
- salt
- pepper
- 4 tbs. butter
- 4 tbs. olive oil
- 2 medium onions, diced
- 2 carrots, sliced into half-inch sections
- 2 potatoes, sliced into bite-size sections
- 1 sweet potato, sliced into bite-size sections
- 6 cloves of garlic, minced

Preheat the oven to 425°F.

Chop up the vegetables and put them in a large pan, then drizzle on olive oil and sprinkle on salt and pepper. Stir the vegetables until they're well coated with oil (adding more if necessary). You should feel free to substitute any other root vegetables you enjoy for some or all of the carrots, potatoes, and sweet potatoes.

Allowing vegetables to cook underneath your roasting chicken turns simple potatoes and onions into a gourmet side dish.

Place the chicken on top of the vegetables, breast up. If your chicken was frozen, it should be thoroughly thawed. Your chicken may have come with a pouch of giblets inside—if so, remove the pouch and save the contents to be stewed up with the bones tomorrow when you make stock.

Brush melted butter on the chicken to create a delicious, crispy skin.

Sprinkle salt and pepper on the chicken. Melt the butter and brush it over the skin of the chicken.

Now place the pan in the oven and allow the chicken to brown for five minutes. Take the pan out and quickly baste the chicken with butter.

Turn the bird onto one side. Brown for five minutes; then baste and turn the chicken onto the other side. Brown for five more minutes. This series of steps seals the skin of the chicken so that the juices stay inside to create the moistest meat possible.

Next, turn down the heat to 350°F and cook for half an hour, basting every ten minutes. Once you run out of butter, start basting the chicken with the juices collecting on the bottom of the pan, adding a bit more oil or butter if necessary.

Turn the chicken to the other side and baste every ten minutes for another half hour.

Check to make sure the chicken is cooked through by inserting a meat thermometer into the inside of one thigh.

Turn the chicken breast up and cook for fifteen minutes until the juices in the thickest part of the drumstick run clear. To be on the safe side, I recommend buying a meat thermometer and inserting it into the inner part of the chicken's thigh, close to the breast. A fully cooked chicken will register 165°F.

Once the chicken is done, remove it from the oven and let it cool for a few minutes before carving. If the vegetables in the pan aren't yet crispy, let them cook a little longer, then strain off any excess grease to be added to tomorrow's stock. The grease can also be used to make a delicious gravy.

Our heirloom chickens look a bit strange to people raised on plump-breasted, factory-farmed meat. However, the flavor is unparalleled.

You'll notice that the photos I've included don't look like an ordinary supermarket chicken. We now grow all our own chickens and choose to raise heritage breeds, which tend to have larger legs and narrower breasts while also weighing less than the average supermarket chicken. As long as you slaughter the birds when they are sixteen weeks old or younger, heritage chickens can be roasted using the recipe above, but since they are lighter weight, you'll need to shorten the cooking time accordingly. Figure on about twenty minutes per pound after the fifteen minutes of browning at higher heat, but use your meat thermometer to get the timing just right.

As a final step after you've enjoyed your delicious meal, put the carcass in a pot of water and simmer for about four hours, and then strain off the most wholesome and delicious chicken stock imaginable. Pour the contents of your pot through a colander to remove the bones; then pick yet more meat off the carcass until the bones are entirely clean. The "Soup" chapter gives you tips on turning the stock and meat bits from one chicken carcass into at least half a gallon of soup, or enough to feed four people as a main course.

# Garlic and thyme chicken legs

Garlic and thyme chicken legs are a quick and tasty way to cook leggy heirloom birds.

When you start cooking with heritage chickens, you'll soon need to figure out what to do with all that extra leg meat. You might have a similar dilemma if you're buying from the store on a budget, since drumsticks are often much cheaper per pound than breasts. This simple recipe is surprisingly delicious and takes just a few minutes of hands-on labor to prepare.

- 2 chicken legs
- 1 tbs. fresh thyme leaves
- 2 tbs. lemon juice
- salt
- pepper
- olive oil
- 1 clove of garlic, minced
- 3 tbs. water

If you're starting with a whole chicken, first cut off the legs. You'll be surprised how easy this is—just slice through the skin that connects each leg to the breast, bend the leg sideways until the bone snaps out of its socket, and then cut through the bit of meat holding the thigh to the rest of the chicken carcass.

*(continued)*

## Garlic and thyme chicken legs *(continued)*

Meanwhile, snip some thyme leaves out of your garden—about a tablespoonful is the goal if you're cooking two chicken legs. Dice the thyme and mix with two tablespoons of lemon juice and some salt and pepper in a bowl.

Heat a bit of olive oil over medium-high heat (being careful not to burn it). Then put your chicken legs in the pan, skin side down. Brush about half of your lemon juice and thyme mixture over top of the legs and cook for around five minutes until the skin turns brown.

Now turn down the heat to medium-low and flip the legs over. Brush on the rest of the lemon juice, leaving some thyme behind in the bowl. Cover the pan, and let cook for 20 or 30 minutes. You can tell the legs are getting done when the meat starts to pull away from the end of the bone (or you can use a meat thermometer).

Remove the legs from the pan once they're fully cooked, and add one clove of minced garlic, the remainder of the thyme, and three tablespoons of water to the pan. Cook over medium-high heat, scraping the drippings out of the pan and into the water. After a minute or two, the garlic will be cooked and the water should have evaporated enough to turn the drippings into a thick sauce to spoon over the legs.

This delicious and easy recipe serves two.

## *Beyond the basics*

I was quite happy depending solely on roast chickens for a couple of years, but if you're less timid, you might want to experiment with other cooking methods. Learning recipes for cooking chicken legs and old hens will stand you in good stead when you start managing your backyard flock. Even if you're eating out of the grocery store, you'll find that knowing how to cook with something other than boneless chicken breasts will save you a lot of cash.

Meanwhile, in the sphere of red meat, you probably won't be ready to cook a whole cow anytime soon. However, you might be able to find a local farmer (or 4-H member) who sells cows by the quarter or eighth and lambs by the whole or half. Although the meat will be more expensive than that found in the average grocery store, the increased taste and health benefits, as well as the boon to the environment, might be worth it. Plus, you'll be forced to learn to cook with cuts of beef other than steak and ground meat. Do plan to set aside a significant amount of freezer space if you follow this technique.

Once you discover how delicious and unique each part of a pastured animal tastes, you'll have a real incentive to grow or hunt your own. Hopefully, this week's exercise will help you see that the deer invading your garden is an opportunity, not a terror.

# Storing drinking water

**GOAL**: Store enough drinking water to keep your family from going thirsty during a power outage

**COST**: $0

**TIME**: 30 minutes to 1 hour

**DIFFICULTY**: Easy

**KID-FRIENDLY**: Yes

Filling clean milk jugs with drinking water is a cheap way to prepare for power outages.

During any type of emergency, the first thing you'll probably miss is being able to turn on the tap and fill up a cup with clean drinking water. Luckily, it's easy to store enough water to change a power outage from a disaster into an adventure.

## Why store water?

A few winters ago, heavy snows knocked down the power grid across several counties surrounding our farm. People living in small towns had their power back within the first few days, but our remote location was last on the electric company's list. During the ten days of frigid weather that followed, we learned the hard way that the bare necessities of life all seem to depend on electricity. Later chapters will walk you through other aspects of emergency preparedness, but for now we'll focus on the most important necessity—safe, clean drinking water.

Even if you live in an urban area, your faucet could stop working tomorrow. A power outage will prevent pumps in the city water system from pushing water to your sink, a line break could take out water in the whole neighborhood, and contamination of your municipal water reservoir might make the water that reaches your faucet unsafe to drink.

If you're a rural dweller, you should plan for regular and lengthy power outages that might keep your well pump from operating. And don't discount the weather—extended droughts could make your well or spring go dry.

Luckily, storing water will cost nothing except a little bit of your time. This week's exercise walks you through stocking up on water to keep your family from going thirsty.

## How much water do I need?

How much water to store depends entirely on your family's needs and on your situation. Now's a good time to consider the difference between potable water—safe to drink—and nonpotable water that's fine for flushing toilets, doing the dishes (with a bit of added bleach), and washing up. Many of you will probably have a source of nonpotable water (like the contents of the rain barrel you made in August), in which case you can focus solely on drinking water.

The average person needs about one gallon of potable water per day. You'll drink half of that or a bit more and use the rest for cooking, rinsing off vegetables, brushing your teeth, and so forth. If your nonpotable water is relatively clean, your pets will have no problem drinking from it, but some of you might choose to set aside a bit of water for your cat or dog as well. Either way, figure out how much drinking water your whole household needs in a day.

Next, you'll have to decide the duration of the emergency you want to prepare for. One option is to talk to your neighbors and find out the longest waterless period they remember for your region in the past. Three days should be your bare minimum, but I'd recommend storing enough water for two weeks to be on the safe side. So, if my two-person household was storing drinking water to last two weeks, we'd need twenty-eight gallons.

## How to store water

The great thing about water is that if you put potable water in an airtight container, it will last indefinitely. You can go out and buy gallon jugs of drinking water, but I highly recommend a cheaper route—bottling your own in cleaned-out milk jugs or soda bottles.

First, wash and sterilize a food-safe container. Milk jugs are best cleaned immediately after emptying; otherwise, the sour smell is very hard to dislodge. Rinse out the container well, and then add a squirt of dish soap and a cup or two of hot water. Put on the lid and shake the container for a few seconds until the soap has sudsed up the inside. Then pour out the soapy water and rinse with plain water repeatedly until the jug smells clean and all soap is gone. One easy way to get rid of the soap is to run water into the jug until all the suds float out the top.

Finally, put one tablespoon of bleach in the jug, fill it with water, and let the container sit for two minutes—this step kills any microorganisms that might have survived your previous cleaning. At this stage, you can store cleaned-out milk jugs to be filled later, as long as you dry them thoroughly first. Upending your jug into a small cup or jar will let it drain dry.

Most of you will want to fill your clean jugs immediately. Just pour out the bleachy water, fill the jug with clean drinking water, screw on the lid, and store in a cool, dark place. If there's any chance your water will freeze, leave a couple of inches of air space in the top of your jug so the container doesn't burst. And be aware that condensation will gather on the outside of your jugs and run down to the floor during temperature swings.

The biggest problem with storing water is that it takes up a lot of room. Here are some storage ideas:

- a bookshelf in the back of your closet
- under your kitchen sink
- on shelves in the garage or basement

You won't need to get to your water very often, so it's okay to put the jugs in that hard-to-reach corner. I have to admit that we've been known to store our extra drinking water in the barn, where it will freeze solid in the winter—this will sometimes crack the milk jugs open, but we have a lot of space there, so we can store extra containers to make up for any losses.

To be entirely safe, you should mark your calendar every six months with a note to refresh your drinking-water supply. That involves emptying the jugs (using the water to wash dishes or water your plants), sterilizing the containers, and refilling. To be honest, if you fill the jugs right, the water should last much longer than six months, and we've drunk water that's over a year old, but the water will taste nicer if it's a bit younger, and you're better safe than sorry. No matter how old the water is, never drink water that is cloudy or smells like anything other than bleach.

If you know you won't get around to rotating your drinking-water jugs, there are a few ways to make your supply last longer. Adding a quarter of a teaspoon of bleach to each jug as you fill it can help. Alternatively, you can buy gallon jugs of bottled water at the store—these usually have an expiration date at least a year away. If you have extra space in your freezer, you can put your drinking water inside and make the freezer more efficient while preserving your water longer.

Finally, you should plan ahead to the time when you'll be drinking that stored water. Even though it's still safe, stored water will sometimes taste stale. You can fix this problem to some extent by pouring a cup of water from glass to glass a few times to fill it back up with air. Alternatively, if you have picky drinkers, you might choose to store some tea bags or powdered lemonade mix with your water to make sure all stay hydrated even if they turn up their noses at plain water.

## Storing drinking water in canning jars

Kathleen Olsen wrote in with this water-storage tip:

> Every good homesteader has a hundred or so quart-size jars. Jars take up the same space whether they are full of beautiful fruits and veggies or empty.
>
> A great way to store water is in those jars once you use your precious preserves. Water and preserves need the same storage requirements—dark, cool, rotated often—so you can put those shelves to use in the off-season to store drinking water for emergency power outages.

## Other sources of drinking water

Storing water is a solution to short-term periods without drinking water, but what do you do if you only stocked up on enough water for three days and the power's out for a month? If your whole region hasn't lost power, you can head to the store and buy some drinking water or go to a friend's house to fill up your jugs. (I lived for years using the latter method, and it's not as laborious as it seems.) However, it's also worth finding some more dependable sources of water.

For short-term disasters, there are several hidden water reserves right in your home. Pour the water out of ice cube trays and drain your hot water heater for clean drinking water. If you are hooked into city water, you can sometimes shut the water off outside the house, turn on a faucet in an upstairs bathroom, and then collect water from the lowest faucet in the house. Finally, water beds can contain up to 400 gallons of water (but some will leach toxic chemicals into your water, so do your research before using this water internally). When draining water from any of these sources, treat the water using the methods explained in the next section before drinking.

Water collected off your roof or found in lakes, ponds, and rivers is usually moderately clean. In a pinch, you can drink this water if you purify it first, but you'll want to scope out your local area and find the water sources that are cleanest. Don't drink flood water, water containing floating materials, or water that smells bad or shows any coloration. In addition, most methods of purifying water won't remove heavy metals, so make sure your backup supply doesn't contain runoff from pesticides, herbicides, and other chemicals.

## Treating water before drinking

Clean water that is stored correctly in sterilized containers is safe to drink as is. However, if you need to drink from any of the sources of water outlined in the last section, you must treat the water before drinking.

If you can afford it, a small, hand-pumped, camping-type water purifier is my favorite purification option. You'll have to use a bit of elbow grease to push the water through the filter, but one filter can often last through several months of continual use. Water purifiers like this will get your water cleaner than boiling or treating with bleach. On the other hand, Brita-style filters don't take out the microorganisms that make you sick—these home water filters are simply meant to remove unpleasant flavors and shouldn't be considered a purification option.

Boiling your water is moderately effective, but some problematic germs can survive heat treatment. For best results, let water sit in a container until any sediment settles to the bottom, pour the clean water into a pan, and then boil for three to five minutes.

A less tasty (and not quite as effective) option is to add a quarter of a teaspoon of bleach to a gallon of water and let it stand for thirty minutes before use. Be sure to use plain bleach, not the fancy versions labeled "scented," "color-safe," or "with added cleaners." The water should smell a bit bleachy (like swimming-pool water) after standing—if not, add some more bleach and let stand again.

You can distill a small amount of water using a pot and a mug on a stove or over a fire.

The safest low-tech way of purifying uncertain water is to distill it. Find a pot that has a lid with a knob-type handle; then fill the pot part-way with nonpotable water. Turn the lid upside down and tie a cup below the handle, or simply place a mug in the pan below the knob of the lid. Either way, make sure the rim of the cup doesn't touch the water in the pot but does collect water that will come dripping off the center of the lid. Put the lid and cup contraption on top of the pot and heat the water until steam condenses on the lid, flows down to the knob, and then drips into the cup. Filling the lid with cold water or snow will speed up condensation. Water that collects in the cup has been distilled, meaning that all harmful materials have been removed.

No matter how simple or complex your backup water plan is, you'll sleep better knowing that your family will have safe drinking water during power outages. As long as you've stocked up on water, you can survive almost every other lack for days on end.

# Diversify your income

**GOAL**: Come up with one possible method of diversifying your income
**COST**: $0
**TIME**: 1 hour to 3 hours
**DIFFICULTY**: Medium
**KID-FRIENDLY**: Maybe

Is it possible to make a living without heading to the office five days a week? Dreaming up a small sideline business could help you figure out if self-employment is right for you.

## Incentives to diversify your income

I hope that calculating your real hourly wage got you thinking. Perhaps you decided that your paycheck isn't worth the 36 percent of your waking hours you spend behind a desk (plus all the extra time devoted to commuting, primping, and winding down at the end of a tough day at work). Or maybe you're just worried about what would happen if your job disappeared—after all, the average American will only work four years at his current job before being fired or quitting.

Do you dream of a job that gives you the recompense you really deserve, uses mental or physical muscles you enjoy flexing, will be there as long as you want it, and leaves you time to change the world and enjoy life? The only realistic solution is to work for yourself.

My husband and I make a living by selling POOP-free chicken waterers over the Internet, bringing in what amounts to an hourly wage of $64 apiece. Since we each work only about six or seven hours per week, we have plenty of time to pursue our homesteading dreams and to give back to the community. Although our specific niche product may not always be in demand, we've learned the skills that allow us to shift gears and create a new product if we need to. In essence, we've escaped the rat race.

The specifics of building an online business that pays all your bills in just a few hours per week is beyond the scope of this book. And most weekend homesteaders aren't ready or willing to put in the time required to leap to full-scale financial independence yet (or maybe ever). However, having a sideline income could be compared to storing water for a power outage or drying food for a rainy day. Your sideline will make life a little easier right now, and if you ever decide independence is right for you, you can scale all the way up to full self-employment.

## *Paying yourself more than minimum wage*

| Product | Hours per week | Profit per week | Hourly wage |
|---|---|---|---|
| Free-range eggs sold to friends (20 layers) | 7 | $10 | $1.43 |
| Honey sold twice a year at farmer's market (4 hives) | 2 | $7 | $3.50 |
| CSA (community supported agriculture) with two customers | 10 | $45 (about 20 weeks of the year) | $4.50 |
| Grapes sold twice a year at a farmer's market (50 established vines) | 2 | $10 | $5.00 |
| Our microbusiness | 13 | $827 | $64.00 |

"Egg money" used to be the sideline income of many farmers, but I can't recommend agricultural pursuits as a cash business for modern homesteaders. The table above outlines some of the money-making schemes we and our friends have tried over the years. What should jump out at you is the fact that each of the homesteading standbys—selling eggs, starting a small CSA—paid less than minimum wage!

In contrast, our chicken waterer brings in around $64 per hour for two reasons:

**We are selling a niche product.** Since no one else offers a chicken waterer that solves the problem of filthy water the way ours does, we can set the selling price high enough to make a living wage. In contrast, there are usually several people at the farmer's market selling free-range eggs, and customers will also remember the obscenely low prices stamped on egg cartons at the local grocery store. If you want to make more than minimum wage, it's essential that your product is unique, adds value, or otherwise distinguishes itself from the competition.

**We sell to an international audience using free or cheap Internet marketing.** The other reason we get a higher hourly wage is that our website does all the time-consuming work of selling our product to backyard chicken-keepers. We don't have to drive to the farmer's market, set up our table, and flag down passersby in hopes they'll make the endeavor worth our while. Instead, we pay about $100 per year to buy a domain name and rent hosting space; then our website does the work for us. If you're tech savvy, I highly recommend building an Internet presence (creating a blog on your own server, making a website, or even just starting a youtube account) since a well-maintained Internet presence will always pay off in the long run. Even if you're not tech savvy, now's the time to think about your method of advertising—it might be worth driving an hour to sell at a big city farmer's market where your wares will reach urban eyes rather than setting up shop at the tiny stand down the road.

Although you might be tempted to argue that you don't have to make a lot of cash from your sideline, I encourage you to think big right from the beginning. What's the point of creating a sideline that would require more time-consuming, backbreaking, and annoying labor than your current job, while bringing in less money? Instead, you should strive to create a small business that could one day turn into your dream job, even if right now it just pays the phone bill.

## Dreaming up a sideline

With the precautionary points from the last section fresh in your mind, now's a good time to think up a sideline you might like to explore. Some points to consider include the following:

**How much time do you have?** Be sure you don't bite off more than you can chew. If your week of vacation is coming up but you'll barely have any time to devote to a project after that, building a blog or writing an ebook might be a good choice. On the other hand, if you would like to devote your Saturdays to the project all year, you might consider a physical product that you can take to weekly farmer's markets.

**What do you love to do?** You'll have more fun if your sideline is in a field you are passionate about. Make a list of five or ten things you thoroughly enjoy doing and/or learning about, even if they seem to have no business potential.

**What are you good at?** If you're an excellent carpenter, you might consider making chicken tractors and selling them through Craigslist. Folks with green thumbs might instead start an assortment of heirloom tomatoes in the spring and peddle the unique seedlings online.

Your only assignment for this week's exercise is to come up with two or three business ideas that fit all the criteria above. Or maybe you already have a side business but realize that it could be tweaked to fit your needs better.

Building the business itself is beyond the scope of a weekend homesteader project, but I can't recommend the project highly enough. Making a living with a part-time job is one of the keys to success on any farm.

# DECEMBER
## *(June Down Under)*

# Plant a fruit tree

**GOAL**: Start your orcharding education by planting a fruit tree
**COST**: $10–$40
**TIME**: 2 hours to 3 hours
**DIFFICULTY**: Medium
**KID-FRIENDLY**: Yes

Peaches are one of the first fruit trees to bear in a young orchard.

Even if you haven't found your own patch of earth, planting a tree now will make bountiful harvests appear on your doorstep much sooner.

# Benefits of fruit trees

An orchard is the lazy man's garden. There's quite a learning curve involved in choosing, planting, and pruning fruit and nut trees, but once you've mastered the art, you can harvest bushels of food every year with very little input of time and money. An established fruit tree will require a couple of hours of pruning and adding compost and mulch in the early spring, another hour or so thinning after the tree blooms, and then a few more hours to pluck and process those bountiful fruits. In exchange, you could get fifteen bushels of apples from a single standard apple tree every year for the rest of your life.

Planting perennials is also better for the earth than our endless treadmill with the summer vegetable garden. Except for the hole you dig when planting the tree, you never disturb the soil and create the potential for erosion. Rather than returning carbon dioxide to the air when you till up the earth, you capture carbon by building humus in your no-till soil. And many farmers will tell you that you can grow more food per acre with tree crops than with annual crops, which allows you to leave more of the earth in its natural state.

I can just hear you saying: "Yes, yes, fruit trees are great. But I'm moving next year, so there's no point in planting a tree in my backyard." That's what I used to think too, so I put my orcharding dreams on hold until I finally bought my farm. What I didn't realize is that it takes several seasons of trial and error to learn the art of orcharding, so I lost another two years (and a couple of hundred dollars) when the first set of fruit trees I put in the ground died. That's why I recommend starting small and soon to learn the nuts and bolts of orcharding.

## Forest gardening

Traditionally, the ground beneath a fruit tree goes to waste since it is either mulched to protect the tree's roots or planted in grasses to keep down weeds. If you have a backyard homestead and don't want to commit a quarter of your yard to one plant, I recommend turning the area around and under your fruit tree into a forest garden island, allowing you to enjoy multiple yields from the same space.

*(continued)*

# Forest gardening *(continued)*

A forest garden island turns your fruit tree into the centerpiece of a complete ecosystem.

To create your island, lay down a kill mulch around your fruit trees and then plant a variety of flowers, herbs, fruits, and vegetables throughout the mulched area. Slow-growing herbs (like ramps and goldenseal) or early spring ephemeral flowers (like crocuses and hepatica) can handle the low-light conditions close to the trunk of your tree. The zone near the canopy edge

*(continued)*

## Forest gardening *(continued)*

gets moderate light, which is usually enough for perennial leafy greens like chicory and dandelions, or for dynamic accumulators like comfrey that pull nutrients from deep in the soil to feed your trees' most actively growing roots. Just beyond the tree's reach, you can plant any kind of light-loving annuals—consider letting a winter squash sprawl through this space, or install a variety of flowers to attract pollinators that keep your miniature ecosystem humming along.

Your forest garden island will change every year as the young tree grows, so you'll want to commit to laying down an additional circle of kill mulch every spring to expand the planting area for sunny annuals. At the same time, remember that last year's annual flower zone has become shady, so expand your edge species to that spot and let the forest interior species begin to take over last year's edge zone. If you think far enough ahead, one way to fill the soil of this expanding forest garden island with rich humus is to create a *hugelkultur* doughnut a year before planting, a method that was detailed in an earlier chapter.

I've had great luck with this type of forest garden island in the rich soil outside my kitchen window, but the eroded soil on the other side of the yard was more problematic. There, soil nutrients rather than sunlight were the limiting factor keeping plants from achieving their full potential, and comfrey competed so much with my peach tree that the latter had yellowing, unhappy leaves. If you're creating a forest garden island in poor soil or in an arid area, your tree might not grow fast enough to shade the understory, in which case I recommend keeping the root zone of your tree continuously mulched with no other plants mixed in, so the tree won't have to fight with faster growers.

If you'd like to learn more about forest gardening, *Edible Forest Gardens*, by Dave Jacke and Eric Toensmeier, is the most definitive reference guide. The first book in this two-volume set covers the ecological principles of forest gardening, while the second book delves deep into the nitty-gritty of designing your own forest garden. Read them both, and you'll be ready to create a flowering, fruiting orchard that is as healthy and productive as it is beautiful.

# Fruit tree types

Whatever you do, don't just head down to your local big box store, look at the pretty pictures on the labels of their six-foot-tall fruit trees, and bring one home. A fruit tree is a long-term investment that requires intensive research. Why wait three years for your pear tree to start fruiting only to discover you planted a variety you detest?

The first step in this week's exercise is to decide which type of fruit tree you want to plant—apple, pear, cherry, peach, plum, apricot, or nectarine. (You should also consider citrus trees if you live in the Deep South.) Chances are, you already like some fruits better than others, but you should also consider traits other than flavor for each fruit tree type.

| Fruit | Age of bearing (years) | Life span (years) | Yield (bushels) | Spacing (feet) | U.S. hardiness zones |
|---|---|---|---|---|---|
| apples | 4-8 | 25-40 | 8-18 | 25-35 | 3-9 |
| pears | 4-6 | 50-75 | 2-8 | 15-20 | 5-8 |
| cherries | 3-7 | 15-20 | 3 | 20-25 | 4-8 |
| peaches (nectarines, apricots) | 2-3 | 8-12 | 4-6 | 18-20 | 5-9 |
| plums | 4-6 | 20-25 | 2-6 | 18-20 | 4-9 |

All the information in the chart above is based on standard trees, as opposed to dwarfs or semidwarfs. Dwarf fruit trees have been grafted onto rootstocks that keep the tree smaller in stature, resulting in younger bearing, a shorter life span, lower yield, and less required space. Many people enjoy dwarf fruit trees, but dwarfs don't seem to do well for me, so I stick to the more vigorous standard trees.

The next factor to consider is diseases and insects, especially if you plan to grow your trees organically. Each part of the country has its own problems, so I recommend you look up your state's extension service website and consider their recommendations for fruit trees. The website will provide documentation about the potential problems you'll face when planting a certain type of tree as well as a list of varieties that do well in your area. In general, pears are the least susceptible of all commonplace fruit trees to insects and diseases, as long as you choose a variety resistant to fire blight. In my opinion, nectarines aren't worth growing organically, since they are simply a hairless variety of peach that is twice as susceptible to all the normal peach ailments. The other types of fruit trees fall somewhere in between those two extremes.

Before choosing a fruit variety, check with your local extension agent to discover which pests and diseases cause a problem in your area. In our humid climate, brown rot may ruin peaches before they ripen.

Third, consider pollination. In most cases, you'll need to plant at least two varieties of the same type of fruit tree—a Winesap and a Liberty apple, for example—if you want to get fruit. Lone sour cherry and peach trees can often set fruit by themselves, so those might be a good choice if you only have space for one tree. Some individual varieties of other species are self-fertile. If you're going to plant two varieties of the same species for pollination, do your research and make sure the varieties bloom at the same time and are compatible—most nurseries will provide this information for the selections they offer.

Time of fruiting is another important factor to consider when choosing fruit trees. Eventually, you'll probably want to plan your orchard so that you have fresh fruit available for as much of the year as possible, which is quite feasible if you plant a diverse array of types and varieties. Apples are especially helpful in this regard. We can eat fruits right off the tree from June through November and then enjoy storage apples straight through the winter. If you're just planting one fruit tree, though, why not choose a variety that ripens up during your usual vacation week? A bushel of peaches takes a few hours of work to put away for the winter, so you'll enjoy your tree more if you've got a bit of free time.

Finally, and most importantly, choose a species and variety that you enjoy. When looking at descriptions of varieties you've never tasted, the phrase "dessert quality" is key because it means the fruit tastes good enough to eat right off the tree without being doctored up in the kitchen. Don't plant a cherry tree if you hate cherries.

Using all that information, along with a bit more research on varieties that do well in your climate, you should be able to come up with one or two trees you want to try out. Despite their insect and disease problems, peaches would be my first choice if I had a limited space in town and didn't know how long I'd be living there—I could taste my first fruits in just two years. On the other hand, if I had the room and wanted a carefree tree that would last the rest of my life, I'd plant a pear.

## Chilling hours

If you live in a warm climate, you should consider chilling hours when choosing your fruit tree. Many temperate trees need a certain amount of winter cold before they will open flower buds in the spring, so it's important to select varieties with chilling-hour requirements that match your climate. Of the common fruit trees, most apple varieties have such high chilling requirements that they won't fruit in large parts of the South, while the hottest parts of the United States may not even provide enough chilling hours for peaches.

As you look through nursery websites and catalogs, you'll run across fruit tree varieties listed as "low chill." These trees—like Gala and Fuji apples—can be grown in areas with mild winters where other fruit trees would never bloom. On the other hand, don't choose a low-chill fruit tree if you live further north, or your tree will try to bloom in the middle of winter, nipping any potential fruits in the bud.

*(continued)*

## Chilling hours *(continued)*

How do you know whether to choose low-chill trees? Your state extension service website will list good varieties for your region, but consider your local microclimate as well. If your extension service suggests both low-chill and normal varieties, you should choose the former if your homestead is in a sunny spot beside a pond that mitigates winter cold, and the latter if you are farming on a windy ridgetop or on the shady side of a hill. You can also use the AgroClimate chill accumulation calculator (www. agroclimate.org/tools/ChillAccum/) to find average chilling hours for your area if you're in the southeastern United States, but be aware that listed chilling hours for fruit varieties may not be completely accurate. For no-risk variety selection, choose fruit types successfully grown by your neighbors or offered by a local nursery that raises its own stock.

## *Choosing a tree*

You'll notice that I've brought up the idea of fruit trees at a strange time of year—December. Most people plant trees in early spring, but you'll usually have better results planting between late fall and mid-winter, before the ground freezes up. Fall-planted trees spend all winter establishing their roots, so by the time hot, dry weather comes around, they're far less likely to be stressed and die. In fact, many experienced orchardists report that by planting a tree in the fall instead of spring, they gain a full year's extra growth.

While we're on the topic of beginner mistakes, I recommend buying the *smallest* tree offered. Intuitively, we think that a bigger tree will grow faster and fruit sooner, but just the opposite is often the case. A healthy tree will have just as much root area underground as leaf area above ground, but it's tough to dig up all those roots when transplanting a five-foot-tall tree. Instead, you end up with a top-heavy tree that has to struggle to support all its leaves with the few roots that made it to your backyard. A smaller but better-proportioned tree can thrive during the first year rather than spend all that time trying to stay alive.

The highest-quality trees come from small, local nurseries that raise their own stock.

Where should you look for your tree? Your best bet is a local nursery, but not the kind you'll find with one greenhouse and a lot of potted plants out front. If your area has a fruit tree enthusiast who grafts heirloom varieties on his back five acres, you've hit the holy grail—you can often stop by and dig up your tree and plant it in your garden that afternoon, preventing all kinds of stress to the plant while gaining a time-tested, locally adapted variety.

Second-best are mail-order nurseries. These large operations will generally take orders year-round, but they only dig up trees a few times per year. Place your order now, and you'll receive a bare-rooted tree in the mail when the nursery thinks the time is right for planting in your climate. I've had good luck with mail-order trees as long as I unpacked the tree immediately and soaked the roots in a bucket of water for a few hours before planting, to counteract the stress of spending several days out of the ground.

Always soak bare-root trees for a few hours before planting to rehydrate the roots.

Your worst option is the "nursery" at your local big-box store. Trees in these locations have probably been sitting around in tiny pots for months and aren't worth your time.

## Fruit cocktail tree

If you only have space for one small tree, you can have it all with a "fruit cocktail tree." Brian Cooper has filled his suburban yard with several multigrafted trees—the fruit cocktail tree shown here, a two-variety plum, a five-variety apple, and a two-variety pear.

You can buy multigrafted trees, or make your own by adding new varieties to trees already in your yard. You can't graft absolutely anything onto the same tree but can often graft closely related species together (like plum, peach, and apricot).

Although I've heard of an apple with ninety-two varieties on the same tree, you'll probably be happier if you keep your first fruit cocktail trees a little simpler. Brian reports that he has a bit of trouble pruning his fruit cocktail tree so that the more vigorous varieties don't take over. "The two-variety ones are much easier to keep balanced."

*(continued)*

# Fruit cocktail tree *(continued)*

This dwarf tree bears two kinds of peaches in addition to plums, apricots, and nectarines.

Photo credit: Brian Cooper

## Planting your tree

As with most aspects of orcharding, you should spend twice as much time *thinking* about where your tree will go as actually planting it. Most fruit trees require full sunlight and good soil, although you can work around the latter. Choosing a good spot for your tree is just as important as choosing a good tree.

A common mistake is to plant trees too close together, with the result that they'll compete with each other when they grow up. The spacing information listed in a previous section is the bare minimum, so if in doubt, give your trees a bit more room (especially if you plan to create a forest garden). If you're planting trees with two different spacing requirements—like an apple and a peach—add up the spacing for each tree and divide by two to find your new spacing requirement. So if you assume you need thirty feet between apples and twenty feet between peaches, you'd want to allow twenty-five feet between an apple tree and a peach tree. On the other hand, if you're planting a tree near your house, take the spacing information and divide it by two—a peach tree can be planted ten feet away from your house as long as you don't mind the limbs scratching on your windowpanes when the tree is fully grown. (Be sure to consider how the shade from your house will affect your tree.)

Tree roots may extend twice as far as the canopy of the tree, so don't plant your tree where the roots will be disturbed. Try to keep your fruit trees a considerable distance from heavily traveled driveways since they won't want to stretch their roots into that compacted soil.

In areas that have waterlogged soil or a hardpan layer close to the surface, your tree will do best if planted in a raised bed. See the section on *hugelkultur* in April's "Kill mulch" project to learn how to expand your mound as the tree grows.

Finally, try to plant into soil that would work well for a vegetable garden—a light loam full of organic matter that neither dries rock hard in the summer nor has standing water for long periods of time. If that prime soil is not available, you can plant your tree in a raised bed about four or five feet in diameter, expanding the mound each year as your tree grows. Since I have high groundwater, I plant all my trees in mounds, with the sole exception of pears, which are the one species very tolerant of bad soil.

Now that you've chosen your spot, dig a hole big enough to spread your tree's roots out well. Many sources recommend adding compost or other amendments to the hole, but studies have shown that amending the soil within a small hole does more harm than good since your tree won't want to spread its roots beyond the good dirt and will, in essence, become root-bound even though it is planted in the ground. Instead, you can add any amendments to the soil surface in a wide area around the tree itself.

After digging the hole, hold the tree upright with the graft union at least a few inches above the soil surface. The graft union is the scar left behind when the variety you chose was joined to a rootstock—it usually looks like a little bulge a few inches up the trunk. You want to make sure that the graft union always stays well above the soil so that the variety grafted on top (the scionwood) doesn't grow roots, which can change the mature size of your tree and some of its other characteristics.

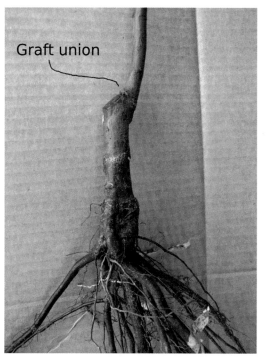

Graft union

The graft union is the junction between the roots and the scionwood. When planting, make sure your graft union stays at least a few inches above the soil surface.

Spread the tree's roots out evenly, then carefully shovel the soil back in. Once you've filled the hole, tamping down the soil with your foot ensures that no air pockets remain around the roots. A gallon or two of water poured over the surface also helps eliminate air pockets while getting your tree's roots off to a good start.

A thick layer of cardboard or several sections of newspaper form a kill mulch around the base of your tree. It's hard to go overboard on this step, so extend your kill mulch as far as you want from the base of the tree—at least two feet in every direction is adequate for a small tree. Then top it all off with mulch and spread over the cardboard without touching the tree trunk. I like using well-rotted wood chips or autumn leaves around my trees.

I know you're tired and happy, but don't head inside to drink hot chocolate in front of the fire yet. Take the tag off the tree so that it won't strangle your new plant, and add the variety, date planted, location, and source of the tree to your garden notes and map. Later, be sure to water your baby tree for the first year if you experience droughts (when there's less than an inch of rain per week), and keep deer and rabbits from eating your tree before it has a chance to grow.

# Potted trees

A few types of fruit trees, like persimmons, don't transplant well and should be purchased in pots.

Although I usually recommend bare-rooted trees, there are a few types that don't transplant well and should be purchased in pots. The traditional fruit trees listed in a previous section all do well bare-rooted, but if you choose to branch out—especially if you want persimmons or nut trees—you should find potted trees.

To remove a plant from a pot, place a finger on either side of the trunk, turn the pot upside down, and gently shake until the plant falls out into your hands.

Planting potted trees is very similar to planting bare-rooted trees, but you'll need to add a few extra steps. First, ease the tree out of the pot. If the tree is small enough, you can simply turn the pot

*(continued)*

## Potted trees *(continued)*

upside down, slipping your fingers around the trunk to hold the dirt in place as shown in the photo above. For larger trees, turn the pot on its side and gently pull the tree out.

If the roots have grown in circles around the inside of the pot, rough up the outside of the root ball with your fingers.

Next, check to see if the tree has become root-bound. Root-bound trees have been too long in a small pot, with the result that their roots have started to grow in a circle around the inside of the pot wall. Gently rough up the outer surface of the root ball to get the roots growing outward. Now you can simply plant your potted tree the way you would any other.

## *Pruning and training your tree*

Now that your tree is in the ground, your adventure with orcharding is just beginning. Over the next year, you'll need to learn to prune and train your tree, a topic that's beyond the scope of this book. However, the tips to follow should get you started.

**Decide on a final shape.** The purpose of shaping your tree is to create a well-balanced structure that allows as much light as possible to reach the eventual fruits while also building limbs strong enough to hold those apples or peaches without breaking. There are two common shapes often used for fruit trees: The central-leader system (like a Christmas tree) is appropriate for apples, cherries, and pears, while the open-center system (a vase-shaped tree) works well for peaches and nectarines. Plums respond well to both shapes.

**Train your tree.** Before you start cutting, you should try to guide your tree as close to its eventual form as possible with training techniques instead. You can tie young limbs to milk jugs full of water or to rocks on the ground to ensure a more spreading tree form, and you can add clothespins to the growing tips of small twigs for the same effect. Tools called spreaders slip into the notch where a small limb meets the main trunk to ensure that the branch exits the trunk at the optimal angle. The more you can mold your young tree with training instead of pruning, the faster it will grow, but be aware that training techniques generally require tweaking every few months to keep the tree on the right track.

**Prune in summer and winter.** Even if you're a pro at training, you'll still need to prune your tree twice a year. Summer pruning is best done before July, with the goal of snipping off the ends of upright growth (water sprouts) and channeling the tree's energy into flower buds for next year. Winter pruning is used to shape the tree but should be as minimal as possible since excessive pruning when the tree is dormant results in the growth of yet more water sprouts.

I find it very educational to take a photo of each fruit tree before and after a pruning or training session. The photos help me understand how my actions influence the shape of the tree, and the documentation keeps me on track from year to year. After about four years of this process, I started to get a feel for pruning, at which point I was rewarded by baskets full of beautiful fruit. In a few years, you'll be an orcharding pro as well.

# Soup

**GOAL**: Make a delicious soup using in-season produce
**COST**: $0 to $20
**TIME**: 2 hours to 4 hours
**DIFFICULTY**: Easy
**KID-FRIENDLY**: Yes

Soup is an economical and delicious way to use up vegetable odds and ends.

If you're new to cooking, soup should be on the top of your list. It's tough to mess up a pot of soup, and if you do, your errors can usually be fixed by throwing in some extra ingredients. Although soup takes a few hours to cook, your preparation time is minimal, and it's easy to double, triple, or quadruple the recipe, then store meal-sized servings in the freezer to take the place of fast food. In addition, soup can be extremely good for you, chock-full of vegetables and bone broth. All of that said, the real reason to make homemade soup is simple—taste.

## The anatomy of soup

There are hundreds of different kinds of soup to choose from, but they are all essentially the same. The first step when making soup is to brew

287

up a delicious stock, usually out of bone broth and vegetables that simmer together for an hour or more to create a complex flavor. Then you throw in the chunky bits and let them cook just as long as they would if boiled individually. If your soup is spiced, the spices go in at the stock stage. If it's creamed, the dairy goes in at the end. Finally, salt and pepper to taste when the soup is done.

For example, if I wanted to make a tomato-based vegetable soup with carrots, potatoes, onions, garlic, parsley, green beans, and sweet corn in it, I would first make a stock by simmering the tomatoes in chicken broth with the onions, garlic, and parsley for about three hours. I knew to throw in those vegetables early because they're seasonings, and I don't want to see distinguishable hunks of them in the finished soup. Next, I'd make a list of how long the other vegetables need to cook:

- potatoes: 40 minutes
- carrots: 30 minutes
- green beans: 10 minutes
- sweet corn: 1 minute

If I wanted supper to be served at 5 p.m., I'd start my stock at 3 p.m., throw in the potatoes at 4:20, the carrots at 4:30, the beans at 4:50, and the sweet corn just as I turned off the pot of soup and moved it to the table.

For your first soup-making exercise, think of a few of your favorite soups and jot down the ingredients you think are in each one. Once you have a sample recipe, google the name of your soup and "recipe," and look at a few online examples to see if you came close. I suspect that after just a few tries, you'll be making up meals from scratch!

## Chicken broth

For the carnivores among you, I highly recommend that most of your soups start with a homemade chicken broth. The real reason is that chicken broth turns a so-so soup into a gourmet meal, but it's also hard to argue with the health benefits of homemade stock. For the frugal-minded, there's yet another bonus—you're getting an extra meal or two out of that chicken carcass you were going to throw away.

Making chicken broth is so easy that after you try it, you won't be able to figure out why you ever bought the awful stuff from the store. Start out with a chicken carcass—what's left after you roast a bird and take off all the meat, or the remains when you've cut the raw meat off a whole chicken. Put about three quarts of water in a big pot with the carcass and bring it to a boil; then simmer for about three hours. In the winter, you can cook up chicken stock by putting the pot on top of your woodstove; just be sure to add water as necessary if some boils away. If you're stewing the carcass of a pastured chicken, your stock should turn yellow—some of that color is the high-quality fat that is quite good for you, so don't skim it off no matter what your recipe says.

Once your stock is yellow or tan (depending on the quality of your chicken), remove the bones by pouring the contents of your pot through a colander into a bowl. The stock can be frozen for later, or it can be used immediately to make soup. If you weren't very careful about taking the meat off the bones before making your stock, be sure to pick all the meat free now and add it to your soup for extra protein.

The most delicious chicken stock is made by stewing an old chicken in a covered pot at 325°F.

For the very tastiest broth, you'll have to head to the henhouse, not the store. As chickens age, their meat gets tougher, but the flavors increase dramatically, so "fowl" were traditionally saved to make chicken soup, chicken potpie, chicken salad, and for other recipes where the chicken's flavor was the centerpiece. Chickens older than a year can be baked at 325°F in a covered pot (like a Dutch oven) with a couple of inches of water in the bottom, creating a moist heat that cooks the bird without creating tough fibers. Bake for about an hour per pound; then cut off the meat to use later and simmer the carcass in the juices (and a bit more water) for a few more hours on top of the stove. I like to add onions, garlic, and parsley to the stock and simmer for another hour. Then add the chicken meat, potatoes, and carrots to create the most wholesome chicken soup imaginable.

## Substituting and cooking in season

Even in the dead of winter, I can pull root vegetables out of my larder and parsley from the garden.

Soups are a great place to stretch your culinary wings and start to experiment with substituting easy-to-grow vegetables for the more difficult ones you might find in your cookbook. For example, I've discovered that I can raise fresh parsley in my garden nearly year-round with very little work, but celery is only ready at a certain season and is much tougher to grow. Luckily, parsley and celery add similar flavors to soups, so I substitute a big handful of parsley leaves and stems for a couple of stalks of celery with great results. Your tastebuds will lead you to other substitutions, but here are some to consider:

**Sweet potatoes, carrots, and winter squash** are somewhat interchangeable, depending on the recipe. Carrots hold their shape better than the other two vegetables.

Many gourmet recipes call for **leeks,** which are tricky to grow and have a limited season. **Egyptian onions** are perennials that require nearly no care in the garden and can be used instead of leeks for ten months of the year (although Egyptian onions are a bit stronger tasting). You can also substitute the tops of Egyptian onions in any recipe that calls for green onions or chives.

**Zucchini and all the summer squashes (crookneck, pattypan, etc.)** are very similar.

The **winter squashes** are also easy to substitute for each other. We've found that **butternut** pies are tastier than **pumpkin** pies, which is a plus since butternuts are much easier to grow in our garden.

The real benefit of learning to substitute similarly flavored ingredients is that you can tweak your favorite recipes so that they're always in season. For example, fajitas classically contain meat, onions, garlic, summer squash, peppers, and mushrooms, making them a summer dish. But I've discovered that fajita vegetables can vary throughout the year—try snow peas in the spring and green beans in the summer. Getting creative with substitutions is the key to eating delicious, locally grown food year-round.

# Essential tools

**GOAL**: Make a list of basic homesteading tools
**COST**: $0
**TIME**: 1 hour
**DIFFICULTY**: Easy
**KID-FRIENDLY**: Maybe

Which tools do you really need to keep your homestead ticking along? Buying a few well-chosen tools will serve you better in the long run than picking up every tool you see at a yard sale.

## Tool acquisition strategy

Let's face it—homesteaders could go broke buying tools. You want to be a farmer, chef, mechanic, and builder, and each job requires its own set of tools. Meanwhile, you've probably realized that it's worth spending a bit extra to buy a quality hammer rather than getting a cheap version that will break in half after a few uses. How do you afford all those good tools?

This week's exercise is simple—you'll be making a list of the tools you need the most so you can avoid two pitfalls of tool acquisition. On the one hand, if you aren't sure what you need, you're more likely to spend too much money buying tools on impulse. On the other hand, you might get so overwhelmed by the tool selection out there that you don't hunt down any tools at all and end up using the wrong tool for the job, making your task more difficult. With a good selection of essential tools in hand, you can work smart, not hard.

## Tweaking your tool list

The tools you need will depend on which aspects of homesteading are most enticing to you. I'm assuming that you're going to be following the lead of *Weekend Homesteader*, focusing on growing your own food and preserving some for the winter, working on your DIY skills on medium-scale projects like building your own chicken tractor, and perhaps chopping a bit of firewood.

You should tweak this list to suit your own homesteading style, adding extra tools if you're going to be keeping an old tractor running, building your own house, or cutting all your own firewood. Tools like a chainsaw and table saw are extremely useful but are beyond the basics—not mandatory for a weekend homesteader.

The other factor to consider when deciding which tools make it on your list is how you feel about power tools versus hand tools. You'll notice that our list includes both—when building, we vastly prefer to use a power drill and screws over a hammer and nails, since the former makes it easy to take the screws out if we make a mistake and have to start over, but that hammer still comes in handy. Unless you're going to be living entirely off grid, I think it's good to have a combination of hand and power tools around.

## Basic tools

Five-gallon buckets, wheelbarrows, extension cords, and personal protective equipment come in handy for all kinds of projects.

Tools in this category are useful for many different projects. Most of these should be on every weekend homesteader's list.

*Gloves*  A good pair of leather gloves protects your hands from rough work while also giving you more power. I used to hate gloves because

I had only worn one-size-fits-all men's gloves, but when I realized that manufacturers make smaller work gloves for a woman's hands, I fell in love. Don't let your leather gloves get wet, or they'll turn stiff and ungainly. And do plan to replace them every year or two as you wear holes in the fingers.

*Eye protection and ear protection*   When using power tools, you should always wear eye protection. Ear protection comes in handy with loud motors like chainsaws.

*Wheelbarrow and/or wagon*   We work our wheelbarrows and garden wagon extremely hard, hauling mulch to the garden, weeds to the compost pile, firewood from the shed to the splitting area, and much more. You will too. That's why we recommend buying a very heavy duty version of one or the other (or both if you can afford it). If you're trying to choose, wheelbarrows are much easier to maneuver through tight spaces, but wagons sink into the ground less in mud. On pavement, a wagon is easier to pull, but homestead paths are rarely so regular, and I usually find it requires less strength for me to carry things in a wheelbarrow.

*Five-gallon buckets*   We use five-gallon buckets for everything from a stepladder to their intended use of hauling. If you have a small garden and no pickup truck, shoveling manure into five-gallon buckets allows you to take home manure from a neighbor's farm without dirtying up your car. And, of course, you'll use five-gallon buckets to carry water to the garden and to your animals. That's why I recommend having at least a dozen on hand, either bought new or picked up for free from bakeries and restaurants. Whatever you do, don't stack your buckets directly inside each other, or they'll form a suction and will be extremely difficult to pry apart. Instead, put a small stick or the handle of the top bucket between the two.

*Ladder*   You might not need a ladder very often, but when you do, you can't live without it. You can choose between an extension ladder, which always has to lean up against a support but which can be very long, or a folding stepladder, which can either lean against a support or hold itself up. Alternatively, some ladders are convertible, giving you both types of ladder in one package, with the downside that convertible ladders are heavy and expensive. And a word of caution—ladders can be the most dangerous tool on your homestead, so have someone steady the ladder as you climb, and never touch a ladder if you're alone on the farm.

*Tarp*   A couple of high-quality tarps are extremely useful for throwing over anything that needs to stay dry but doesn't have a home inside. You get what you pay for with tarps, so try to find one that is UV resistant.

*Extension cords*   Unless you completely eschew power tools, you'll need a few extension cords to get the job done at a distance from your house.

*Tow strap*   If you're starting from scratch in a rural area, your vehicles will definitely get stuck now and then (and old vehicles frequently need a tow when they won't start). That's why we consider a tow strap an essential item on our farm. A tow strap is simply a long cloth strap with metal hooks on each end.

*Come-along*   If you can't get another vehicle in place to pull your car loose, you can use a come-along, also known as a hand winch. Come-alongs come in handy when pulling down old chimneys, moving trees that fall in the wrong place (or tempting them to fall in the right place), and much more. They are also much less expensive than motorized winches, and even a cheap come-along will last a long time if you keep it dry.

*Ratchet straps*   If you don't want to spend a lot of time tying knots in rope, ratchet straps will make your life much easier. They help you attach ungainly loads to your vehicle or to anything else on the homestead quickly and easily.

## Garden

The no-till garden requires surprisingly few tools, and you can get away with using hand power only if you wish.

*Shovel*   More properly known as a spade, shovels with rounded ends that come to a point are perfect for digging. You'll use your shovel a lot, so spring for the contractor grade version, and have a spare on hand for working "guests." My husband loves the version with an expanded lip to give his foot more leverage.

The no-till gardener needs little more than a shovel, bow rake, pitchfork, hoe, and trowel.

*Hoe*   The type of hoe you choose should depend on your gardening style. In a conventional garden, hoes are used to cut young weeds and disturb the top of the soil, so they are square or looped in shape. In a no-till garden like the one I explain how to build in this book, you use mulch for weed control instead of a hoe but will still want a hoe to make trenches in the soil for planting rows of seeds. You can use an ordinary rectangular hoe tilted at an angle for the job, or you can find a diamond-shaped hoe like the one I currently use.

*Bow rake*   A bow rake (also known as a hard rake) is distinguished from leaf rakes by the shorter tines, which are stiff instead of flexible. If you till the soil, a hard rake is essential, since it is used to pull out weed roots and to flatten the soil. Even if you have a no-till garden, you'll use a rake to incorporate compost into the top inch of the soil.

*Clippers*   You'll need a pair of large and small clippers for pruning fruit trees and cutting back weeds. Small pruners are known as "bypass clippers" and are operated using one hand, a bit like you'd use scissors. Larger clippers (often known as "loppers") cut larger branches and generally are operated with one hand on each handle.

*Weed eater and/or scythe*   We waited until our fifth year on the farm to invest in a quality weed eater and wished we'd saved up the cash much sooner. If you're starting from scratch and trying to reclaim old farmland that has grown up in blackberry bushes and other weeds, you can either fence the whole thing off and put in a goat for a year or two or spend an afternoon with a good weed eater (complete with a metal blade). Weed eaters also help keep the uneven terrain of young forest gardens and *hugelkultur* mounds from turning into a weed jungle, while allowing you to quickly harvest patches of homegrown grains. Many homesteaders swear they use scythes in these types of settings, and if your homestead is already pretty manicured, you might get away with this hand-powered version of the motorized weed eater. Other weed cutting options include sickles and machetes, but these can be quite dangerous.

*Lawn mower*   I know that many of you probably think that lawns have no place on a homestead, but the truth is that a lawn mower comes in awfully handy. You can create permanent grassy aisles in your garden as long as you plan the paths to be wide enough for a mulching mower to pass through; you'll prevent erosion while growing high-nitrogen mulch for your vegetables. And if you're pasturing animals on a small scale, you need to run over the pastures with a mower a few times a year to cut down the less palatable plants that would otherwise take over. Lawn mowers don't have to be motorized—if you have a very small area, a properly sharpened push mower can require less work than trying to keep a gasoline engine running.

*Pitchfork*   A pitchfork is the easy way to move manure, partially composted materials, and animal bedding from point A to point B. Don't make the newbie mistake we did and try to use a shovel.

*Trowel*   In an established, no-till garden, a trowel is the only tool you really need. My favorite is the "trake," with a trowel on one end, a rake on the other, and solid metal in between.

## Cooking and preservation

Most households already have nearly everything they need to turn their kitchen into food preservation central. However, it's useful to add the equipment listed below.

Old fashioned cooking equipment like Dutch ovens and Foley mills come in handy on the homestead.

*Big pots*   The serious homestead cook should have at least one pot (or stainless steel pail) that's two or more gallons in capacity. You'll use this pot to make soup, to stew up your chicken bones into stock, and even to scald a chicken when it comes time to butcher your own. If you can afford it, one stainless steel pot is better than two aluminum pots.

*Canners*   If you tried out canning and decided you loved it, you should invest in a hot-water-bath canner. A high-quality pressure canner is definitely beyond the basics but is worth saving for if you want to can low-acid vegetables.

*Mason jars*   Even if you're not sure whether canning is your thing, I recommend picking up canning jars at yard sales and anywhere else you can find them cheap. Glass jars are the best reusable containers you can find, great for storing honey, dried foods, and leftovers. But be sure to check for cracks and imperfections on the rim, both of which make the jars useless for canning.

*Dutch oven*   A Dutch oven isn't exactly a necessity, but it makes cooking on a woodstove or open fire much easier. A Dutch oven is a cast iron pot with a lid that can be used on top of a stove or inside a fire or oven.

*Colander*   Colanders are useful for straining stock from bones, honey from comb, or just for rinsing off lettuce.

*Foley mill*   A hand-turned food mill is very handy for separating skins and seeds from the flesh of tomatoes and for making applesauce.

## DIY, building, and demolition

A combination of hand and power tools makes construction tasks easier.

*Hammer*   If you choose to avoid power tools, your hammer is going to be your best friend. Even if you buy a battery drill, you'll still use a hammer occasionally for pounding in or pulling out nails.

*Battery drill*   Our battery-operated drill is probably the most-used DIY tool on our homestead. By changing out the bits, you can drill holes or insert screws with the same tool, and a quick-change adapter makes it even easier to switch between the two applications. Be sure to find a good drill bit set as well, and to put your bits back each time you use them.

*Screwdrivers*   Don't forget to stock up on screwdrivers of a few different sizes, both Phillips and flathead.

*Tape measure*   A tape measure that's at least twenty-five feet long will come in handy during construction or when planning fruit tree locations. Be sure to keep the tape dry.

*Calculator*   If you're not fond of doing math in your head, a calculator will help you cut boards to the proper size.

*Tamping bar*   If you can lift it, a long iron bar with one flat end and one wedged end, known as a tamping bar or spud bar, has half a dozen or more uses. You'll use your tamping bar most often when digging holes, when the wedged end can make the walls of the hole straight and break up compacted soil or medium-sized rocks. Then when it's time to fill dirt back in around a wooden post, you use the flat end to compact the ground nearly as hard as concrete. Finally, a tamping bar also acts as a long and strong lever.

*Post-hole diggers*   If you want to dig a hole that's deeper than it is wide, you'll need post-hole diggers.

*Reciprocating saw*   Also known as a Sawzall, a reciprocating saw is a power tool that can do rough and fine sawing. Put in a metal blade, and your reciprocating saw will cut through old nails or pieces of rebar; then change over to the wood blade to cut your plywood into shape. If you don't have the cash to buy a miter saw, table saw, circular saw, and jigsaw, a reciprocating saw will serve in their place (although with slightly less pretty results).

*Hand saw*   We have several kinds of power saws, but we still use a simple hand saw quite regularly. It's often just not worth the hassle to pull out power tools for a bit of quick cutting, and if you choose a hand saw that cuts on both the push and pull strokes, you'll be surprised at how fast you can saw by hand.

*Hacksaw*   A hacksaw is the metal-cutting version of a hand saw. While not quite as essential on the homestead as a hand saw for cutting wood, you'll be glad to have a hacksaw in your toolbox.

*Pliers*   Pliers work like an extension of your hand, improving your ability to grip, turn, and squeeze. You'll use them to tighten and loosen nuts (if you don't have the right wrench on hand), to crimp wires, and to get into places you can't reach with your fingers. Needle-nose pliers also have a cutting edge behind the gripping section, so you can use your pliers to cut or strip wires. Put three types of pliers on your list—needle-nose, flat-nose, and channel locks.

*Adjustable wrench*  Wrenches (also known as spanners) are the best way to tighten and loosen nuts and bolts without stripping them. Amateur mechanics will want to invest in a set of wrenches of various sizes (including socket wrenches), but those of us with less mechanical know-how can get away with an adjustable wrench that converts to various widths using a dial.

*Sledgehammer*  A sledgehammer comes in handy for pounding in fence posts and demolishing old buildings, but be sure to choose one that suits your strength. My husband loves his full-size sledgehammer, while I prefer the mini sledge. Raw beginners (like me) should also be sure to choose a sledgehammer in which the head and shaft are all one piece. I often miss my target while using a sledgehammer, which eventually can cause the head to separate from a fiberglass handle, then go flying off wildly, breaking windows or bones.

*Maul*  If you're going to burn wood, you'll need to be able to split big chunks into smaller pieces. A maul is the preferred tool for the job since the wedge-shaped head forces two halves of a log apart with less work on your part. We've tried various types of mauls and fell in love with the Chopper 1, but any maul will do if you're not burning much wood.

*Crowbar and/or pry bar*  Crowbars (and their smaller siblings, the pry bars) come in various sizes and weights. Both crowbars and pry bars can be used to pull nails as well as to force boards apart. It's helpful to have a small pry bar combined with a hefty crowbar, especially if you're going to be doing serious demolition. However, if you're just puttering around with small DIY projects, a pry bar alone may suffice.

## Tool storage

We've learned the hard way that it's quite possible to have too many tools if you don't store them properly. Installing hangers for larger tools (or pegboard for smaller tools) and investing in a well-sized tool box will help you keep your tools organized so you can find the one you need when you need it. A useful rule for the toolaholic is: You can't bring home a tool unless you have a place to store it.

*(continued)*

## Tool storage *(continued)*

A tool in the hand is worth ten tools in a jumble somewhere over there.

## *Where to find tools*

Now that you know exactly what you want, you'll be surprised at how easily and cheaply your tools will materialize. Don't assume you need to run out and buy all the tools on your list right away; just keep your eyes open and wait until they come to you. A later project will help you find free or cheap tools, and since it's December, you might want to include a few on your holiday wish list as well.

# Stay warm without electricity

**GOAL**: Plan ahead so you won't freeze if the power goes off
**COST**: $0–$100
**TIME**: 1 hour to 2 hours
**DIFFICULTY**: Easy
**KID-FRIENDLY**: Yes

Winter power outages can be life-threatening, but you'll be snug and warm if you plan ahead. As an added bonus, many of the same strategies can be used to lower heating costs during an ordinary winter.

## Heat during power outages

Do you have a strategy for keeping warm if the electricity goes out during a winter snowstorm? Electric heaters clearly won't work, and gas furnaces require electricity to operate. Even wood heat might not be reliable if you depend on an electric fan to blow warm air where you want it.

A wood stove is the most reliable method of providing off-grid heat.

An energy-efficient woodstove in a central location within your home is the best choice for warmth (and cooking) during power outages, but the time and money required to install a woodstove is beyond the weekend homesteader level. This week's project helps you find other options for staying warm if snow knocks down the power lines.

## Heating one room

One strategy for keeping your family warm is to choose a small room and heat it using a backup option that doesn't require electricity. This is my least favorite method because it's awfully easy to spend a lot of money on a backup heater that seldom gets used and thus doesn't work when you need it. However, many Americans can't wrap their minds around heating themselves instead of the room (which I'll discuss in the later sections), so I'm including the room-heating option.

If you choose a one-room backup plan, your first step is to decide which room would be easiest to keep warm without electricity. Your whole family (and any cold-sensitive pets, like guinea pigs and parrots) should fit inside without getting on each other's nerves, but the room should also be as small as possible so that it's easier to heat. South-facing windows (or north-facing windows if you live in the southern hemisphere) will let in solar radiation that will warm the area considerably on a sunny day. The room should have space for everyone to sleep, so a master bedroom, den with a foldout couch, or area with lots of floor space is a good choice.

Once you choose your room, think about blocking off cold air that might want to flow in. That means having some heavy curtains (or blankets with a way of tacking them up) to keep heat from flowing out windows at night. The room should either close off from the rest of the house with a solid door (and a rolled up towel to fill the space underneath), or you should plan another large blanket or curtain to block off the entranceway.

Your room may already have a fireplace or woodstove. If so, you will just need to keep it stocked with plenty of dry wood, kindling, paper, and lighters or matches for getting the fire going. If not, you can install a stand-alone propane heater that doesn't need to be vented to the outdoors (around $200 for the low-end model). A cheaper alternative is a free-standing kerosene heater (around $120), but be aware that kerosene heaters create carbon monoxide, so you'll need to increase airflow through your room for safety. Kerosene heaters also tend to be a bit sooty and stinky, but that problem is lessened if you light the heaters and turn them off outdoors, carrying them inside only when they're already in use.

## Dressing for warmth

As I mentioned above, I don't really recommend planning to heat a whole room with a backup heating arrangement. If you don't use your backup equipment in your everyday life, it will take a long time for that equipment to pay for itself, and the heaters often won't work when you need them to. Instead, I recommend changing your habits so that you heat your body instead of the room, both during outages and to whatever extent you're comfortable with during your daily life. The great thing about learning to stay warm without electricity or fossil fuels is that you'll be prepared no matter how long the power outage lasts, and you will also enjoy a lower heating bill during normal winters.

Dressing in layers may not be the height of fashion, but the technique will keep you warm.

So how do you heat your body instead of the room? The first step is to invest in some winter clothes chosen for warmth and utility instead of style. A good winter coat, a hat that covers your ears, warm socks, sweaters, and long johns go a long way. On cold winter days, I wear fleece long johns under normal pants, two pairs of socks (if they fit in my boots), and on top am decked out in a T-shirt, a thin fleece shirt, a thicker fleece shirt, and then a winter coat. Throw a wool hat on my head and some good gloves on my hands, and I'm quite comfortable even sitting still at 40 or 50°F. If you head down to the local thrift store, you can probably find most of these items of clothing for just a few bucks apiece.

Three environmental conditions can make the outfit above useless, though: wind, precipitation, and constriction. I'll start with the last, which is the least intuitive. When you're building a house and adding insulation to the walls, you'll soon learn that you can't cram two layers of insulation into the space meant for one layer and get twice the protection from cold. Instead, that double layer of insulation will actually work *less* well than a single, properly installed layer would. Insulation—and that includes your winter clothes—works by creating pockets that trap air in place. So if you put on two pairs of socks and cram your feet into boots meant for one pair, your feet will be colder than if you'd only put on one pair, because the constricted clothing will push out all the insulating air pockets. Ditto if you try to wear long johns under close-fitting jeans. That's why, when planning your winter layers, you'll need to choose some clothes a bit bigger than normal to go on the outside.

You're probably more familiar with the way wind and rain can make you cold despite lots of insulative clothing. If you're going to be inside during cold weather, you probably won't have to worry much about these problems, but you should plan ahead in case you need to go out. A waterproof windbreaker on top of your other clothes goes a long way toward keeping both water and chilly winds from penetrating. This is especially important if you use synthetic fleece clothes, which wind cuts right through.

You also need to think about water that starts on the inside of your clothes—sweat. If you're outside chopping wood and notice that you're starting to heat up, take off layers until you're comfortable again. Otherwise, your sweat will quickly chill your body once you stop moving.

Finally, keep some plastic grocery bags on hand to deal with wet feet. Boots eventually spring a leak during slogs through the snow, and wet feet make even the most cheerful person cranky. If you can put on dry socks and slip each socked foot into a grocery bag before pulling on your boots, the plastic layer will keep water in your boots from seeping into your socks and coming in contact with your skin. You may look like a homeless person, but you'll be a *warm* homeless person.

## Sleeping bags

Once you've chosen your emergency winter wardrobe, I recommend you spend the majority of the cash you've set aside for this project on a good sleeping bag. If you snuggle down inside a sleeping bag rated at 0°F in all the clothes mentioned above (minus the boots), you'll be warm as toast no matter what happens.

When choosing sleeping bags for power outages, you don't need to buy the expensive, light-weight versions meant for backpacking. And as long as you keep your bag dry, the insulating material doesn't matter. Instead, make your choice based on two characteristics—temperature rating and style.

Sleeping bag temperature ratings should be taken with a grain of salt, since a 0-degree bag probably won't make you very happy in a tent on a windy mountaintop at 0°F. That said, lower ratings do mean warmer bags, so go as low as your wallet will allow.

There are two main types of sleeping bag styles—mummy bags and rectangular bags. Mummy bags are the warmest for one person sleeping alone since they follow the contour of your body when zipped up (and usually include a hood to keep your head warm). But don't buy a mummy bag if you can't sleep in a confined situation—a zipped-up rectangular bag will be warmer than an unzipped mummy bag. In addition, make sure you choose a bag that's big enough if you're especially tall or wide.

If you regularly sleep with someone, you might want to choose a right- and left-handed pair of sleeping bags. These bags can be used separately or can be zipped together to make a family-sized warm spot.

Finally, don't just toss your sleeping bags into the closet while waiting for a power outage. Rectangular bags can often be unzipped so they lie all the way flat and work as an extra comforter on your bed, allowing you to turn down the heat at night. I enjoy slipping my mummy bag inside the sheets to give me something to snuggle into when I first get into my cold bed at night—a sleeping bag heats up much faster than a traditional bed.

## Activity keeps you warm

One of the best things you can do to stay warm is to move around. This will also raise your spirits during an extended power outage. I've found that if I get up the courage to jump out of my toasty sleeping bag and into the cold air long enough to dress fully and give the dog a walk first thing in the morning, my blood has started pumping enough to keep me warm for an hour or more. Of course, if you have a woodstove, splitting wood is a time-proven method of warming you twice.

If you're a little less hard-core, warm foods and drinks will also wake your body and improve your mood. It's easy to heat a kettle of water on top of a woodstove to make tea or cocoa, and then you can make a pot of soup for lunch. You can even pull coals out of the stove to cook on top of, as I did during a ten-day power outage in 2009 when we had only an exterior wood furnace to keep us warm. A propane camp stove will do the job even better. If you use any kind of fire to heat up your food and drinks, be very careful, since synthetic fabrics are extremely flammable.

Finally, know the symptoms of hypothermia and keep an eye on young children or elderly family members who might not be self-aware enough to realize they're too cold. Early symptoms include constant shivering; pale or blue lips, ears, fingers, and toes; clumsiness; slurred speech; stumbling; trouble thinking; and poor decision making. You should be very concerned if you or someone in your family experiences blue and puffy skin; inability to walk; incoherent behavior; stupor; a weak pulse; and slow, shallow breathing. Don't risk it if you're experiencing even mild hypothermia—find a way to get warm and dry immediately.

# JANUARY
*(July Down Under)*

# Soil test

**GOAL**: Determine the quality of your garden soil
**COST**: $20–$50
**TIME**: 1 hour to 2 hours
**DIFFICULTY**: Easy
**KID-FRIENDLY**: Yes

The foundation of your homestead is soil. A paucity or overabundance of just one nutrient in the soil could result in insect infestations in your garden, sick milk goats, or even a deficiency in your own body. Over time, you'll start to see, feel, and smell the difference between high- and low-quality soil, but at least once every few years, you should send a sample off to a lab to test for more subtle changes.

## Soil structure

You won't need a laboratory for your first soil test—just a trowel and a mason jar. Head out into your garden and scoop up about a cupful of soil. Put the soil in the jar with another cup or two of water, shake vigorously until the soil dissolves, and then leave your container in a spot where it won't be disturbed for a day or two.

You can figure out the texture of your soil at home using a jar test.

Over time, the components of the soil will settle to the bottom, heaviest first—sand, silt, then clay. Even though the water may still be cloudy (meaning that all the clay hasn't settled out), you can go ahead and take measurements 24 hours after sampling.

Figure out the percentage of each type of soil particle by measuring how high the layer is, then dividing by the height of all the soil in the jar. My soil is 29 percent sand, 64 percent silt, and 7 percent clay.

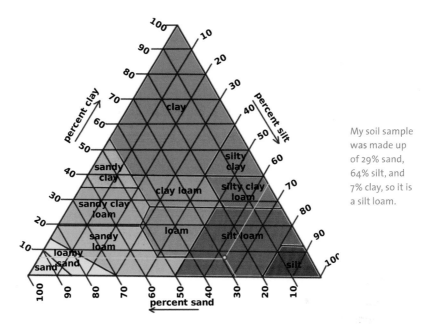

My soil sample was made up of 29% sand, 64% silt, and 7% clay, so it is a silt loam.

Next, use a soil triangle to figure out what kind of soil you have. In my example, I started at 29 percent sand on the bottom of the triangle, then followed that line up and to the left at an angle until I reached the lines for 64 percent silt and 7 percent clay. I put a dot at the result—a silt loam.

You can get this same information by looking at the soil survey for your area. The Web Soil Survey at http://websoilsurvey.nrcs.usda.gov/app/ allows you to find your soil type online, or you can ask for a paper copy at your local extension office.

## Where to send soil samples

Your jar test gives you an idea of the type of soil in your garden, but you'd need more sophisticated equipment to figure out nutrient levels.

There are dozens of options for soil testing laboratories, but the three below are my top choices.

**Your local extension service** (www.csrees.usda.gov/Extension)—I always recommend starting by checking with your state extension service since most offer free or cheap soil tests. However, extension service laboratories often skimp on testing micronutrients and heavy metals, so it's worth spending a bit more cash at least once during the life of your garden to get an idea of the bigger picture.

**A&L Eastern Laboratories** (www.aleastern.com)—This is the cheapest option I found, especially if you skip the interpretation. They don't test everything you might be interested in but will give you a good idea of the basic qualities of your soil for $8.50 per sample (in 2011).

**UMass Amherst** (www.umass.edu/soiltest)—I chose this slightly more expensive laboratory ($15 if you choose to add organic matter, which you should) since UMass tests just about everything a gardener will care about. This is also a good lab to use if you're growing food in the city and are concerned about heavy metals, since UMass includes several of the most common metals in their basic testing package.

Each laboratory has slightly different instructions, so you should read the website of the lab of your choice before heading to the next step in this week's project. For example, our state extension service requires soil tests to come in a box they provide, while other labs don't mind receiving samples in ziplock bags. Read instructions carefully to make sure you take the best samples.

## How to take soil samples

High-quality soil samples aren't just a shovelful of dirt tossed in a ziplock bag. Instead, you want to make sure to collect a representative sample (meaning you don't accidentally use a pocket of pure compost) from the area where your plants will concentrate their roots.

First, decide how many samples you're going to take. As you puttered around in the garden last year, you may have noticed that your garden contains different types of soil in different locations. The upper end of our garden is very loamy, while the lower end is dominated by clay—each of these areas should be a separate sample. In addition, previous owners of our land allowed one of our garden areas to erode down to the subsoil, so I wanted to test this plot separately. You might choose to test your lawn, your blueberry patch, or the mulched soil under your fruit trees as separate samples as well. Even as you are digging up patches of earth, if you notice differences in color between areas you had planned to include in the same sample, you should separate them. (But remember that each sample costs money and don't go nuts.)

Within each of your test areas, you'll want to take several subsamples (the more the better, but no fewer than ten). These subsamples should be scattered throughout the area—you'll mix them together to get an "average" soil for the whole site.

Pick a day when the soil isn't excessively wet or dry; then gather up a clean plastic bucket, a shovel, a trowel, a spoon, and your pen and notebook. Dig a small hole with your trowel or your shovel. Then slice a small amount of soil off one vertical wall of the hole. The spoon comes in handy to shave off the edges of this sample so that you have a similar amount of soil for all depths.

Your goal is to sample soil within the root zone, so you'll need to use a different sample depth for each type of garden area. In a lawn, pasture, or no-till garden, nutrients are concentrated near the soil surface, so you'll only want to gather the top two to four inches. Tilled gardens should be sampled as deep as you till or plow, usually around six to eight inches.

Put your sliver of soil of the proper depth in your plastic bucket, and then move to the next sampling spot. Repeat the steps above until you have at least ten soil subsamples from the same general area. All the subsamples should look about the same, since you've decided this area is all one type of soil. It's a good idea to take notes on where each subsample came from for future reference.

Now mix up your subsamples with the trowel and scoop out the proper amount to put in your labeled container—this is your soil sample. A few labs ask that you air-dry your soil by spreading it out on a sheet of paper for a day or two, but others simply tell you to put the sample directly into your sealed container. Dump any leftover soil from your bucket back into the garden and head to your next garden area to take sample 2.

Back inside, be sure to fill out the laboratory's form completely. And be careful not to lose your notes telling where each soil sample came from. Ten years from now, you might not know what "squash patch" means, so draw a soil-sampling map and add it your garden notebook.

## Cation exchange capacity and organic matter

When your test results show up in your mailbox or email inbox, the first soil characteristic you should look for is the cation exchange capacity (also known as CEC). Cation exchange capacity is closely tied to the amount of organic matter and clay you have in your soil, since both provide spots for positively charged ions—cations—to cling to the soil. In contrast, sandy soil without much organic matter will allow these nutrients to leach away during heavy rains. You're throwing away your money if you add soil supplements to raise your calcium, magnesium, or potassium levels without first increasing your CEC so that these essential nutrients will be held in place.

So what's a good CEC? CEC can range from 0 to 100 mEq/100 g, and your goal should be to reach or exceed 20 mEq/100 g. Although clay and any kind of organic matter will help you achieve this goal, humus is the most effective additive, since it provides many more cation binding sites per unit area. If you're not familiar with the distinction, humus is organic matter that has broken down to a stable point at which it may endure for hundreds or thousands of years. To make humus, add any kind of organic matter to your soil (compost, mulch, or cover crops) and promote soil conditions favorable for earthworms, bacteria, and fungi, which will turn that organic matter into high-quality humus.

Your soil test should also tell you the percent of organic matter in your soil, but I tend to ignore this number. More organic matter is usually good, but CEC is the true measure of soil quality. If your CEC is low but your organic-matter levels are high, that means you're doing something wrong, and your organic matter isn't being broken down into a stable humus. Maybe you've added too much high-carbon material all at once (for example, tilling wood chips into the soil) or have sprayed pesticides that killed off your soil microorganisms. If you work to increase your CEC, most other soil characteristics will naturally fall into place.

# pH

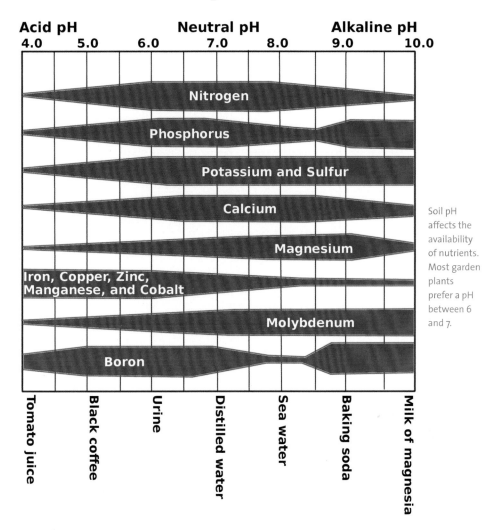

Acid pH 4.0 5.0 6.0 Neutral pH 7.0 8.0 Alkaline pH 9.0 10.0

Nitrogen

Phosphorus

Potassium and Sulfur

Calcium

Magnesium

Iron, Copper, Zinc, Manganese, and Cobalt

Molybdenum

Boron

Tomato juice · Black coffee · Urine · Distilled water · Sea water · Baking soda · Milk of magnesia

Soil pH affects the availability of nutrients. Most garden plants prefer a pH between 6 and 7.

After CEC, the next test result to consider is pH. A measure of the acidity or alkalinity of your soil, pH can range from 0 to 14. Neutral substances—like distilled water—have a pH of 7, while acidic substances have a lower pH, and alkaline substances have a higher pH.

Soil pH is extremely important because it determines the availability of many nutrients. Each type of plant has evolved to deal with specific micronutrient ranges, and a pH too high or too low can lead to deficiencies of some nutrients and to toxic overabundances of others.

The perfect pH for most garden plants is between 6 to 7 (although you'll want much more acidic soil for blueberries). The chart below shows the optimal pH levels for most of the common garden vegetables.

| | 5 | | 6 | | 7 | | 8 |
|---|---|---|---|---|---|---|---|
| asparagus | | | | █ | █ | █ | █ |
| beets | | | | █ | █ | █ | |
| cabbage | | | | █ | █ | | |
| canteloupe | | | | █ | █ | | |
| carrots | | █ | | █ | █ | | |
| cauliflower | | | █ | █ | █ | | |
| cucumbers | | █ | █ | █ | | | |
| eggplants | | █ | █ | | █ | | |
| green beans | | █ | █ | █ | | | |
| lettuce | | █ | █ | █ | | | |
| parsnips | | █ | █ | █ | | | |
| peas | | | | █ | █ | █ | |
| peppers | | █ | █ | █ | █ | | |
| potatoes | █ | █ | █ | | | | |
| pumpkins | | █ | █ | █ | █ | | |
| radishes | | | | █ | █ | | |
| spinach | | | | █ | █ | █ | |
| sweet corn | | █ | █ | █ | █ | | |
| tomatoes | | █ | █ | █ | █ | | |
| watermelon | | █ | █ | | | | |
| winter squash | | █ | █ | █ | | | |

Take a look at the pH value in your soil test report. If the number is below 6 or above 7, you might have trouble growing some vegetables, and you should definitely be concerned if your pH is below 5 or above 8.

If you're worried about the pH of your soil, your first step should be to determine why the pH is outside the recommended garden range. The culprit could be as simple as your bedrock—our soil is derived from limestone, so it is naturally alkaline. However, if one part of your garden has a vastly different pH from other areas, you should consider supplements you added to the soil. Wood ashes and biochar will raise the soil's pH, while certain mulches and composts will lower the pH.

Now flip back and take a look at your CEC. Although a high CEC is generally a good thing, the extra cation binding sites also mean that the soil is very resistant to changes in pH. If you've already built up your CEC and your pH is out of whack, you'll probably want to combine short-term fixes (like adding sulfur to acidify the soil or lime to "sweeten" the soil) with longer-term fixes (like adding peat moss or pine mulch for slow-release acidity).

Use extreme caution when changing the pH of your soil. For best results, apply any soil amendments in the fall, and test your soil again in the spring to see how effective your pH alteration was. Apply less than the recommended amount and plan to change your soil quality over a few years rather than all at once.

## N-P-K: The macronutrients

Now that you understand the structure and pH of your soil, you can flip to the easier-to-understand parts of your soil test. Nitrogen (N) is perhaps the most important nutrient used by plants, but this is the number I recommend you pay the least attention to on your soil test report. Your annual applications of compost are meant to increase the nitrogen content of your soil, and nitrogen doesn't stick around when it's not in use. So low nitrogen levels simply mean you haven't added compost recently. High nitrogen levels in a winter soil test are more worrisome, since they mean you've been overfertilizing, and nitrogen might be running off to pollute nearby streams.

Phosphorus (P) and potassium (K) levels should be considered with a more critical eye. These are the other two nutrients used in large quantities by plants, and they tend to be longer lived in soil than nitrogen is (especially if you've built up your CEC). Excessively high or low levels of phosphorus or potassium in your soil probably represent an imbalance in your fertilizing campaign. You can boost levels of each using organic supplements like greensand (for potassium) or bonemeal (for phosphorus). Wood ashes increase your potassium levels but should be used with care unless you have very acidic soil, since the ashes will also raise your pH. In addition to supplements, though, you should consider changing your fertilizing campaign—for example, if your soil is excessively high in phosphorus, maybe you need to stop adding so much chicken manure to the garden.

## Micronutrients

There are eight main micronutrients that affect your plants' growth—boron (B), chlorine (Cl), cobalt (Co), copper (Cu), iron (Fe), manganese (Mn), molybdenum (Mo), and zinc (Zn). However, scientists are still learning about plant micronutrients, and most think that your plants also need doses of sodium (Na), iodine (I), fluorine (F), silicon (Si), sulfur (S), magnesium (Mg), and calcium (Ca). I wouldn't be at all surprised if we added another half-dozen plant micronutrients to this list as we delve deeper into plant biology.

The amount of each micronutrient available to your plants depends not only on the absolute amount in the soil but also on the soil's pH. In addition, some types of plants need more of certain micronutrients than others do. It can be a mind-bending exercise to figure out just how much of each type of micronutrient you need in your soil, so it's a good thing most labs will do the math for you. As long as you tell the lab how your soil is used, they will usually report the actual amount of each micronutrient in the soil and also whether the levels are low, sufficient, or high for your crops.

Luckily for the backyard gardener, micronutrients generally take care of themselves if you follow an organic fertilizing campaign using high-quality compost. I recommend getting a very comprehensive soil test that covers most or all of the micronutrients early in your gardening career, and then relying on simpler soil tests for several years before worrying about micronutrients again. If you do need to increase values of a certain micronutrient, take a look at the chart of dynamic accumulators in the "Mulch" chapter to find out which plant you can grow to soak up hard-to-find micronutrients.

## Heavy metals

Most problems with garden soil can be remedied with judicious application of organic matter or other supplements, but heavy metals are more troubling. Although humans, plants, and soil microorganisms need small amounts of many heavy metals, high concentrations can be toxic. To decide whether you should be concerned, look for these possible sources of contamination near your garden:

- lead paint on old buildings
- chemical fertilizers or pesticides
- gas stations and mechanics' shops
- landfills
- industrial factories
- runoff from streets and parking lots
- treated lumber

The table below gives information on the seven heavy metals found in soil that are regulated by the EPA. Of these, lead is the most likely to be found in your soil and is the one about which you should be most concerned.

| Heavy metal | Natural levels (ppm) | Unsafe for vegetable gardening (ppm) | Unsafe for children to play (ppm) |
|---|---|---|---|
| Arsenic (As) | 3–12 | more than 50 | more than 200 |
| Cadmium (Cd) | 0.1–1.0 | more than 10 | more than 50 |
| Copper (Cu) | 1–50 | more than 200 | more than 500 |
| Lead (Pb) | 10–70 | more than 500 | more than 1,000 |
| Nickel (Ni) | 0.5–50 | more than 200 | more than 500 |
| Selenium (Se) | 0.1–3.9 | more than 50 | more than 200 |
| Zinc (Zn) | 9–125 | more than 200 | more than 500 |

You have to ingest heavy metals to get sick, which generally means eating plants that have sucked those heavy metals up out of the soil. Luckily, plants don't tend to accumulate lead the way they do some other heavy metals, so you can garden in soil with moderately elevated lead levels as long as you don't eat much dirt. At a lead concentration of 100 ppm, you'd need to have eaten two teaspoons of soil per week to create any problem; at 300 ppm, you'd need to have eaten 3/4 of a teaspoonful per week.

Like micronutrients, heavy metals are worth testing at least once in your gardening career, if only to set your mind at ease. Maybe you'll learn that even the zone you thought would be polluted between your porch and the street has low levels of heavy metals. Then you'll have more space to grow vegetables!

# Baking bread

**GOAL**: Learn a simple bread recipe
**COST**: $1 or less
**TIME**: 3 hours
**DIFFICULTY**: Medium
**KID-FRIENDLY**: Yes

Once you know how to make bread, you can easily bake your own rolls, buns, and loaves.

If you eat bread, you should know how to bake it. Once you understand the technique, making your own bread turns into a therapeutic ritual that fills your house with a delightful scent while putting preservative-free bread on the table. You can easily tweak bread recipes to suit your fancy, creating whole-grain bread that would cost a bundle in the grocery store, or splitting your dough down the middle to make a loaf for sandwiches along with half a dozen hamburger buns. The smart home chef doubles the recipe and freezes some dough for a quick and easy meal in the middle of the week, perhaps pizza or dinner rolls. And, all of that flexibility aside, everyone knows that nothing you buy in the store can compete with the flavor of fresh-baked bread.

## The science of bread

I'll be honest with you—your first attempt might not be perfect. You need to get the hang of rising and kneading if you want perfect, fluffy rolls. And you have to understand the chemistry behind each ingredient before you can start mixing and matching to create your own recipes. In this section, I'll walk you through making a fluffy white bread from scratch so you'll understand the basics.

First, find your ingredients:

- 1 1/3 c. water
- 2 tbs. sugar
- 1 tbs. yeast
- 2 tbs. olive oil
- 2 tsp. salt
- 3 c. bread flour

I usually skip the next step—proofing—but I do recommend you try it once just to understand the yeast organism. Heat your water to "baby-bottle temperature" (just warm enough so that it feels neither hot nor cold when you put a drop on the inside of your wrist); then mix in the sugar and yeast. Wander away for about ten minutes. Then see whether your yeast has woken up and created a foamy mass on top of the water.

*Yeast is a fungus with one job—making your bread rise. When fed sugar and flour, the yeast excretes ethanol and carbon dioxide. The ethanol gives a yeasty flavor to the bread, while the carbon dioxide puffs the bread up. Proofing yeast shows whether your yeast is young enough to do its job. If your water doesn't turn foamy in* ten or fifteen minutes, you've either started with too hot or cold water or your yeast is too old to work.

Whether you gave your yeast time to proof or not, the next step is to make your dough. To the warm water, yeast, and sugar, add the rest of your ingredients, which in the case of this recipe are oil, salt, and bread flour. You'll want to mix all the ingredients other than the flour first, because the last cup of flour is going to take some heavy stirring to incorporate it into the dough.

*Each of the ingredients in this basic recipe has a job. As you saw in your proofing step, yeast makes the bread rise, and sugar feeds the yeast. Oil makes the bread tender and keeps it from going stale as quickly. Salt not only enhances flavors the way it does in all cooking, but it also slows down the yeast so that the microorganisms don't work too fast. Finally, bread flour is higher in protein than other flours, so it causes the bread to rise better (for reasons I'll explain later).*

Kneading creates strands of gluten that help your bread rise and give texture to the finished product.

When all the ingredients are in the bowl and the dough is getting hard to stir, clean off a table or countertop, toss down a handful of flour to keep the dough from sticking, and pour the contents of your bowl onto the counter. Knead the bread by stretching it out, then folding it in half, turning ninety degrees after each stretch and fold. You may have to add a bit more flour to keep the dough from sticking to your hands and the counter, but try not to add too much—a slightly sticky dough will produce fluffier bread.

*Kneading your bread is kitchen alchemy. Proteins in the flour combine with water to create gluten, and your kneading lets the gluten form long strands. Have you ever noticed that well-made bread tears along lines, while muffins simply crumble? That's the difference between a dough in which gluten did or didn't form.*

*Gluten isn't only important for the texture of the bread—it helps dough rise as well. When yeast excretes carbon dioxide, strands of gluten trap that gas within the dough. Without gluten, your bread would rise a bit, then fall.*

*The amount of gluten in your bread will depend on two factors. First is the length of your kneading time. Bread products that don't need much gluten (like pizza crusts) don't have to be kneaded very long, but if you want fluffy whole wheat bread, you might have to knead for as much as half an hour.*

*Type of flour is just as important as length of kneading. If you use a low-protein flour like all-purpose wheat flour, there simply won't be enough protein present to create sufficient gluten fibers. Flours made from grains other than wheat can be high in protein but lack the specific proteins that create gluten. Finally, whole-wheat flour has another problem—the tough bran particles cut through the gluten, fragmenting the fibers even as you knead. That's why it's often helpful to add some gluten to your recipe if you want fluffy bread made with flours other than wheat bread flour.*

For a white bread like this one, ten minutes of kneading is sufficient. It's not mandatory, but you'll find it easier to knead your dough if you stop after the first five minutes and give your dough five or ten minutes to relax before finishing the kneading process.

*Relaxing your dough in the middle of the knead allows water to work its way into the flour. As a result, your dough feels less sticky, and you add less flour, so your bread's texture comes out perfectly.*

Let your bread rise until it has doubled in bulk.

Once you're done kneading, return the dough to the bowl and cover it with a damp dish towel to rise. In a modern home, you can just let the bread sit on the counter, but if you're a more serious homesteader who heats with wood and doesn't maintain an even temperature inside during the winter, you'll want to find a warm spot for your dough to rise. Many wood cookstoves have a warming oven just high enough above the fire to keep the dough warm without cooking it. In a pinch, you can turn your electric or gas oven to "warm" and put your bread inside. Depending on the model, you may also need to crack the door open to keep the dough from getting too hot. No matter how you do it, your bread should have risen to the point where it has achieved twice its original size ("doubled in bulk") after about an hour.

*Rising gives your yeast time to do its job. As I mentioned before, the dough rises because the yeast excretes carbon dioxide, which gets trapped by the gluten fibers and held in the dough. If you skip or shorten the rising steps, you'll end up with rock-hard bread.*

After it has risen, punch down your dough, shape it, and let it rise again. If you want to save some of the dough for later, put it in a plastic bag after the first rise and stick it in the freezer. Otherwise, shape the dough however you want—into rolls, buns, or loaves. You can even form long strands of dough to make braided loaves or add cheese or herbs to make flavored buns.

*If you're a raw beginner, I recommend keeping it simple and making buns. It can be difficult to know when your bread is fully baked in a loaf pan, but dough in the shape of a hamburger bun cooks perfectly in very little time. Simply tear off a hunk of dough about half the size of your fist and flatten it, placing each bun on a greased cookie sheet. If you want to get fancy, brush on an egg yolk and sprinkle poppy or sesame seeds on top. The yolk will make the seeds stick and give the bread a beautiful shine.*

Now it's time to let the dough rise until it doubles in bulk again. Pay more attention this time to ensure you don't ignore the dough too long and let it over-rise: After a certain point, the gluten can't hold the carbon dioxide any longer, and your buns will flatten out. But don't try to rush this rise either—you want your dough to be as high as possible so you get fluffy bread.

Preheat your oven to 350°F, then bake your bread on the top rack until the top and bottom of each bun are very lightly brown, about fifteen minutes. Don't worry, the living yeast will be killed by heat, so all you're left with is a delightful texture and flavor.

## Simplifying (or complicating) bread-making

If you find yourself picking up loaves from the store because you just don't have time to make your own bread, you might consider some bread-making shortcuts. There are kneadless bread recipes that replace fifteen minutes of kneading with a day sitting in the fridge, or you can get a machine to do the work for you. I've found that bread machines do a pretty good job of kneading but aren't so great at baking. Instead, my favorite labor-saver is the bread hook on my mixer (I use a KitchenAid). I let the mixer do the kneading, and I monitor the rising and baking myself.

Others of you might have the opposite reaction to this week's project—you may love bread-making so much that you want to try out whole grain breads or your own pizza dough. The latter is the easiest next step since the recipe I've included above works perfectly as a pizza dough. You'll just have to learn how to stretch the dough into a round shape. Even if you don't want to toss the dough over your head, I recommend doing this step in the air with your hands rather than on the counter with a rolling pin.

You can use the same bread dough recipe to make delicious pizza.

As with other types of cooking, once you learn the basics of bread-baking, the sky's the limit. Soon, you'll be baking artisanal breads so beautiful you'll turn up your nose at the loaves in the grocery store.

# Media consciousness

**GOAL**: Figure out how the media affects you
**COST**: $0
**TIME**: 1 hour
**DIFFICULTY**: Easy to hard
**KID-FRIENDLY**: Yes

My husband and I raise all our vegetables and some of our fruit and meat using hand tools. The question I hear most often is "How do you find time?!" In part, the answer is that we have created jobs that allow us to work from home during just a few hours per week, but we've also deleted another huge time-drain from our lives—mainstream media. One study suggests that the average American spends twenty hours per week in front of the television, which is equivalent to *twice* the time I spend tending our garden during the growing season.

Television isn't the only form of media we lose ourselves in, nor is time loss the only result. Modern Americans can choose between the Internet, radio, movies, books, magazines, computer games, and other forms of media that I probably haven't even heard of. Each one affects us both positively and negatively in ways far beyond the simple entertainment value we think we're getting. This week's exercise helps you figure out which types of media leave you feeling energized, educated, and ready to take on the world . . . and which ones result in you gorging on chips in the den to alleviate your depression.

## Keeping track of your consumption

One easy way to pay attention to how you are affected by the media is to keep a diary of your consumption, jotting down a bit of information every time you pick up a magazine or turn on the computer. For best results, try to maintain your media journal for at least a week, but if you're extremely busy, one weekend might suffice.

| Type of media | Date and time | Hours spent | Mood before | Mood after | Value |
|---|---|---|---|---|---|
| Television (baseball watching party) | April 5, afternoon | 4 | excited | energized | Met new people, had fun with old friends |
| Television (random shows after work) | April 6, evening | 3 | tired | cranky | None. (What did I watch?) |
| Computer (read blogs) | April 7, morning | 0.5 | sleepy | alert | Found out about a technique I want to try in my garden |
| Radio (drive home from work) | April 7, afternoon | 0.5 | tired | depressed | Caught up on the news but can't remember any of it |
| Computer (multiplayer game) | April 7, evening | 2 | excited | wired | Fun figuring out how to work with other play-ers (but couldn't sleep afterward) |

Jane Doe filled out the chart above and started noticing trends right away. She realized that whenever she tuned in to the media while tired, she ended up in a worse mood afterward than when she started. On the other hand, when Jane combined media exposure with real people (during her baseball party and multiplayer computer game), she went into the event excited and enjoyed thinking and talking about the experience long after it ended.

Jane was surprised to realize that television and radio shows that she thought were educational didn't actually serve their purpose. After watching three cooking shows, she was less likely to make meals from scratch because she knew she could never achieve the perfection shown on the screen. She also couldn't remember any of the news she'd heard on the radio, so she questioned the program's educational value.

Hopefully, your journal will be just as illuminating, helping you figure out which forms of media serve their purpose in your life. Personally, I choose to tune into types of media that are either truly educational (meaning that they positively impact the way I live my life), help me socialize in meaningful ways, or entertain me and calm my mind so I find it easy to fall asleep. Which items on your chart make the cut?

## Voluntary simplicity and the media

One of the most troublesome aspects of mainstream media is its tendency to change the way we feel about ourselves and our possessions. Psychologists report that we relate to television characters as if they are our friends, mourning when a fictional character "dies." Even if you ignore the ads scattered amid your favorite shows, chances are you're unconsciously comparing your own possessions to those of your "friends" on-screen. Since most of those "friends" drive new cars, have huge wardrobes, and live in fancy houses, you feel obliged to follow suit.

No wonder homesteaders who tune in to the mainstream media find it difficult to live up to the homesteading tenet of voluntary simplicity. Followers of the simple living movement strive to minimize their purchases so that they can spend more time with friends and family (rather than in a cubicle), but I know from experience that it can be depressing to do without a gadget that you really want. Rather than being an ascetic who steers clear of luxuries to elevate the spirit, I instead advocate changing your mindset and practicing cheerful self-sufficiency. After removing the peer pressure exerted by glossy magazines and upscale television characters, I very rarely feel like I want to buy anything.

## Trial separation

A second way to discover how the media is affecting your life is to turn off your radio, television, and computer for a day or weekend. Many of us use the media as white noise to fill up our minds while we perform tasks we consider boring or distasteful. I can see the appeal—I used to pipe NPR out into the garden to keep my brain occupied while I weeded. However, when I stopped tuning in and spent my garden time watching the natural world and letting my mind wander, I began to think deeper thoughts and to channel that creativity into writing.

An early reader of this book wrote in with a similar reaction to turning off the television:

> *"I didn't realize how much I was addicted to TV until I read your book. I've tried to quit cold turkey but watch the weather guy when there is bad weather. I have a lot more time to do things now, I'm getting caught up on all the things I've wanted to do that I usually saved for the weekend, and I feel like I am able to spend more quality time with my wife. Thanks for the motivation."*

In the end, this week's project is all about using your most valuable possessions—your time and attention—in pursuit of what matters most. I urge you to strive for mindful consumption of media that enhances your life and helps you achieve your dreams.

# Turning trash into treasures

**GOAL**: Stock up on homesteading essentials for free or cheap
**COST**: $0
**TIME**: 1 hour to 4 hours
**DIFFICULTY**: Easy
**KID-FRIENDLY**: Maybe

Planned obsolescence is the bane of the environment and of consumers who want quality products that will last the rest of their lives. But the cloud has a silver lining—scads and scads of free stuff. If you're willing to put in a little legwork and repair a chipped edge here and there, you can find many items on your shopping list for little or no cash.

## Know what you want

Before you delve into the sea of free stuff, you need to be realistic about what you really want. Using the tool exercise as an example, make a list of other items you'd like to own without paying for them. Be as specific as possible—you don't just want a power drill; you want a drill from a good manufacturer with batteries that work.

While you're deciding what you want, spend some time thinking about what you don't want. One factor to be aware of is understanding your limitations and knowing what you can and can't (or will and won't) fix. If you find an iPod just like the one you've been dreaming of, but the headphone jack is broken and you aren't skilled with electronics, don't get it. If you're willing to sand off ugly paint and refinish furniture, you'll have a wider assortment of tables to choose from, but be realistic about how long repairs take and whether you're really interested in adding that hobby to your limited free time.

Next, ask your spouse, family members, or housemates how they feel about your new passion for dumpster-diving. They'll probably be much happier with your hobby if you are realistic about storage locations for all this newfound wealth. Keeping free supplies in your own space and getting rid of any you don't fix or use within a reasonable amount of time will prevent your spouse from feeling like he or she is living in a thrift store. But don't let your spouse's nay-saying discourage you. If you understand which items are high quality and easily repairable, you might be able to fix up "junk" and sell it for a premium on eBay or Etsy, diversifying your income.

## Sources of free supplies

The list below is far from an exhaustive overview of places I've found quality free stuff in the past.

**On the curb on trash day**—If you live in a city with garbage pickup, it's worth taking a spin through the neighborhood on trash day. You'll often find slightly damaged furniture and building supplies sitting beside the trash cans, just waiting for a new home. And don't forget those bags of autumn leaves for your garden.

**Freecycle**—Visit this organization's website at www.freecycle.org and sign up to be on their email list for your area. When people have an item too valuable to throw away but which they don't want to bother selling, they send out an email, and you have an opportunity to snatch it up. Although most Freecycle users are extremely nice, to be on the safe side it's best to met people in a public place, preferably with a friend along for the ride.

**College towns**—If you live in or near a college town, keep an eye on bulletin boards and email lists at the end of the school year. Students often have lots of stuff to give away because they just don't want to haul it home, so items like dorm fridges and futons can be available for free or cheap.

**Dump and dumpsters**—Rural homesteaders can often find extremely useful items at the county dump or leaning up against dumpsters along the side of the road. In our area, courtesy dictates that you leave potentially useful items outside the dumpsters so that they're easy for your neighbors to notice and take home. But be careful—these spots often also host homeless cats and you might end up with a new pet.

## Sources of cheap supplies

If you're willing to spend a bit of cash but don't want to pay full price, check these out:

**Craigslist**—Craigslist (www.craigslist.org) is like Freecycle, but most items are offered for sale instead of free. If you know exactly what you want and how much the item is worth—and are willing to kiss a few frogs before finding your prince—you can find good deals on Craigslist.

**Auctions**—You won't find anything for free at an auction, but it is possible to get good deals on quality tools, furniture, and more. As with Craigslist, it's essential that you do your homework and know exactly what you're willing to spend, and don't get carried away with the auction mentality that can often cause you to bid more than an item is worth.

**Junkyards**—The era of finding cheap, used car parts at junkyards is rapidly coming to an end, but you might get lucky and find a nearby junkyard that hasn't started selling its parts online yet. If so, be prepared with all the tools you'll need to take the part out of the junked car, and know which parts aren't worth buying used.

**Thrift stores**—Depending on the economic status of your neighborhood, your thrift store will either be full of junk or of quality goods sold at a low price. Clothes are the primary reason to head to a thrift store, since it's quite possible to find stylish clothes for pennies on the dollar if you search until you discover one of the more posh establishments. If you don't care about style, any thrift store will do.

**Yard sales**—Yard sales are extremely hit or miss, but if you see similar items to those on your wish list as you cruise by, it's worth stopping.

**Bulletin boards**—Churches, community centers, and many other gathering places often have bulletin boards littered with advertisements for free pets and cheap supplies.

## Turning trash into a way of life

The sources of free and cheap stuff outlined above will turn up tools, supplies, furniture, clothing, and more. However, some people take the hunt a step further. They find food for free—either by dumpster-diving or by hunting nuts, berries, and deer out of the woods. They heat their homes with firewood cut for a small price in a nearby National Forest or for no cost from a neighbor's fallen shade tree. They build entire houses out of materials laboriously ripped from decaying structures whose owners want the buildings gone. And they find all the organic matter for their gardens using the methods outlined in the "Scavenging biomass" chapter.

How far you take the pursuit of trash is up to you, but do try out one of the simpler options as this week's exercise. If nothing else, sign up with your local Freecycle and read the emails showing what kind of free stuff your community has to offer. You may make new friends as you fill your pantry with reusable canning jars, or you may decide it's just not worth your time to hunt down free stuff.

# FEBRUARY
## *(August Down Under)*

# Planting berries

**GOAL**: Put in a berry patch for fast and easy homegrown fruit
**COST**: $5–$25
**TIME**: 1 hour to 2 hours
**DIFFICULTY**: Medium
**KID-FRIENDLY**: Yes

One year after planting, your strawberry patch will overwhelm you with delicious fruit.

In the long run, an orchard provides the most fruit per hour of maintenance, but berries fill in the gap while you're waiting for your apple trees to produce. Luckily, easy berry plants like strawberries and raspberries will start producing in a year or less. Better yet, they're so easy to propagate that you'll soon have filled up every nook and cranny of your yard with edibles and will be begging neighbors to take extra plants off your hands.

# Choosing your berries

The primary purpose of this exercise is to be harvesting your own fruit in a year or less. As a result, I'm going to focus on the quickest-bearing berries—blackberries, raspberries, and strawberries. Each of these plants requires only minimal to moderate care, with their differences detailed in the chart below.

| | USDA hardiness zones | pH | Spacing (feet) | Notes |
|---|---|---|---|---|
| blackberries | 5–10 | 5.5–7.0 | 3–10 | Best in southern climates and for people with lots of space |
| raspberries, red | 3–8 | 6.0–6.8 | 1–2 | Best in northern climates; can fit into smaller spaces than other brambles |
| raspberries, black | 5–8 | 6.0-6.8 | 2-3 | A good southern berry for those with less space, but not as productive as other brambles |
| strawberries | 3–8 | 6.5–6.8 | 1–2 | You can tuck a few strawberry plants into even the smallest garden, but they take more care than the brambles. |

If you're feeling patient, you might want to select additional small fruits from the second chart on the next page. Although you may get a grape or blueberry the first or second year, these "advanced" species all require four or five years to reach their full potential. I consider a blueberry patch a long-term investment—on par with planting a fruit tree—while strawberries and raspberries can be sneaked into the yard of a rental property.

| | USDA hardiness zones | pH | Spacing (feet) | Notes |
|---|---|---|---|---|
| blueberries, highbush | 3–8 | 4.5–5.5 | 6–8 | Best in northern climates; must have acidic soil; needs more than one variety for pollination |
| blueberries, rabbiteye | 7–9 | 4.5–5.5 | 6–8 | Best in southern climates; must have acidic soil; needs more than one variety for pollination |
| currants | 3–6 | 6.2–6.5 | 4 | Best in northern climates; some states don't allow you to plant certain varieties because of the white-pine blister rust |
| gooseberries | 3–7 | 6.2–6.5 | 4 | Best in northern climates but can be planted a bit further south than currants; if you live in the south, try to find a cool microclimate |
| grapes | 3–8 | 6.0–7.5 | 8–10 | Bunch grapes hate hot, humid summers, so consider muscadines in the Deep South |
| kiwis | 5–8 | 5.0–6.5 | 10 | Kiwis come in male and female varieties—be sure to plant at least one male for every eight females; only hardy kiwis can survive below zone 7 |

For the rest of this chapter, I'll be focusing on care of the simplest berry varieties. If you decide to plant any of the more "advanced" small fruits from the second chart, you'll need to do a bit of extra research on pruning and trellising. But don't let that discourage you—all these small fruits are well within the reach of the weekend homesteader.

## Strawberries

Be forewarned—once you taste a homegrown strawberry, you'll never be able to eat another berry from the grocery store. Even ripe fruits plucked fresh from a you-pick operation don't hold a candle to the explosion of flavor from a strawberry grown in the humus-rich, no-till garden. Luckily, strawberries are pretty simple to grow in your backyard, so you'll be able to feed your new addiction.

*Choosing and planting strawberries*   Your first step when planting strawberries is variety selection. Although everbearing strawberries look good on paper, I find June bearers to be less work with higher returns, so I recommend the beginning homesteader start there. Even if you stick with June bearers, you can count on a full month of strawberries if you plant early, midseason, and late varieties (and be aware that "June bearers" actually fruit in April and May in the South and middle of the country—the name simply refers to the single annual crop). Your extension service is the best source for recommendations of varieties that do well in your area.

Strawberries can be planted in the early spring or in the fall. I tend to plant in the fall when expanding my own strawberry patch but in the spring when buying in fresh plants—that way, I don't lose my expensive new stock to drought.

You'll get the most value for your money if you buy bare-rooted strawberries in sets of 25 from an online nursery. The strawberries will come with few or no leaves and will look quite dead, but when planted with the roots spread out just below the soil surface and the growing crown peeking up slightly above the ground, new leaves will soon appear.

There are several different methods of growing strawberries, and your initial plant spacing will depend on which technique you plan to follow. I put in a bit more work to get tastier fruits, spacing my plants 12 inches apart and removing all the runners—this is called the hill system. If you're more of a laissez-faire gardener, you might prefer the matted row system, in which plants are spaced much further apart and allowed to fill up the gaps with runners. The benefit of the matted row system is that it's less work in year one and you don't have to buy as many plants; the downside is that you'll spend more time next year picking lots of small fruits that often aren't quite as tasty as the fewer big fruits you get from the hill system.

No matter which spacing method you choose, be aware that strawberries can handle a little bit more shade than most vegetables but will give you the sweetest fruits in full sun. Strawberries can also become quickly overwhelmed by weeds, so mulch them carefully and repeatedly and hand weed as necessary. If you're planting into weedy ground, you might choose to lay down a kill mulch and plant your strawberries into small holes cut in the cardboard.

*Care of your first-year plants*   Your new plants will try to bloom their first spring. For best results, carefully pick every flower off the plants so they'll put their energy into growing healthy roots and leaves instead. Yes, that means you won't get to taste your first berry until next year—it will be worth the wait. Using my growing system, this first year is the only time you'll have to pick off flower buds, since you'll plant new strawberries in the fall from here on out. (Fall-planted berries have generally established themselves enough that you can let them fruit their first spring.)

After trying to bloom, the strawberry plants will send out lots of runners. Those of you following the hill system will want to snip back runners during your usual weeding sessions. You don't need any fancy equipment as long as you catch the runners when they're young and tender—just pinch them off between your thumb and forefinger.

Strawberry plants often keep green leaves through most or all of the winter, but you'll want to put some mulch over the plants once the rest of your garden has died back. Freezing and thawing can otherwise push your berries' shallow roots up out of the ground and kill the plants. Be sure to rake the mulch back from the tender new leaves in early spring and top-dress the bed with a healthy coating of compost, topped off with the old mulch plus a new layer of straw.

A strawberry flower with a blackened center has been damaged by frost and won't turn into a fruit. But the same plant will put out several more blooms that may miss later freezes.

*Flowering and fruiting*   After patiently waiting twelve months, you're ready for your strawberry harvest. This time, leave all the blooms and keep an eye on the weather. Late-spring freezes can damage strawberry flowers, so I toss row cover fabric over the plants if lows are expected to drop below 30 degrees once flower buds have opened. You'll know your flowers were damaged if the centers change from yellow to black. All is not lost, though—strawberry flowers tend to open a few at a time over the course of a week or two, so losing the earliest flowers will just allow the plant to put more energy into later fruits.

Topping off a dark chocolate brownie with strawberries and cream puts a gourmet twist on the classic strawberry shortcake.

While watering is important throughout the growing season, the time between flowering and harvest is a critical period. Strawberries need an inch of water per week, and if the weather isn't cooperating, you have to irrigate. Otherwise, just watch and wait, picking your strawberries when they are bright red on the outside and at least slightly red clear through. You'll need to set aside time to harvest strawberries at least every other day, but daily harvesting is better. Berries are sweetest in the afternoon and are least tasty if picked right after a rain (or watering session).

*Renovating and expanding the strawberries*   After gorging on strawberries in May or June, it's time to start plucking runners again. This year, you don't need to be quite as careful about removing every single runner, because you'll want to expand your patch. By the middle of summer, missed runners will have rooted and turned into new strawberry plants. When the weather forecast promises three or more rainy days in a row, head out into the garden with your trowel and carefully dig up all these baby strawberry plants. Then start a second patch in a new garden bed. This is another time when irrigation is critical, since summer-planted strawberries can easily wither up and die before they get their feet under them.

By late summer, your strawberry bed will have formed a solid mass of plants.

Thin the bed until each plant has about a foot of breathing room in all directions.

If you use my method of expanding the patch in the late summer, you can skip this step, but if not, you'll need to renovate your bed in the fall. Many sources recommend mowing off the strawberry leaves, but I find that step unnecessary. Instead, I simply rip out plants that have gotten too close together, leaving at least one foot of mulched soil between plants.

I've found that flavor and vigor begin to diminish after a strawberry patch has fruited once, twice, or three times. (How many seasons you can eke out of the plants depends on the quality of your soil.) I generally eat two years' worth of strawberries from a bed, then rip the plants out and rotate the bed back into the general vegetable garden. As long as I transplanted runners the previous year, I'll have a fresh bed ready to produce more berries the following spring.

## Brambles

There are only two potentially complicated parts of growing blackberries and raspberries—variety selection and pruning. Otherwise, care is simply a matter of annual fertilizing, mulching, and (most important) eating all those fruits.

*Choosing your brambles*   As I mentioned previously, blackberries and black raspberries do better in the South, while red raspberries like areas with cooler summers. Over large parts of the United States, you can easily grow all three types of brambles, but your life will be a bit easier if you begin your experiment with ones that are well suited to your climate.

Once you decide which type of brambles you want to grow, your next step is to settle on which additional characteristics you're looking for. Thornless blackberries are easier to work with, but I've noticed they don't seem to be as cold hardy as the thorny varieties, so northerners should bear with thorns. Among raspberries, you'll need to decide whether you're interested in a spring or everbearing variety—unlike with strawberries, I have had very good luck with everbearing raspberries and recommend them highly.

Bramble plants tend to be more expensive than strawberries, often costing several dollars apiece, but you don't need to start with many. In my garden, one everbearing raspberry plant became a clump large enough to provide lots of fruit that fall, and by the next spring I was able to transplant yet more new raspberries to fill up a whole row. The third spring, I gave away gobs of raspberry starts, and by the fourth year after planting, all my friends stopped answering the phone when raspberry-planting season came around. So—choose your variety wisely, but don't be concerned about starting small.

*Planting and training brambles*   Blackberries and raspberries have a tendency to try to take over the world, so plan ahead when selecting their location. I find it helpful to plant brambles in mulched rows about eighteen inches wide; then I mow anything that tries to grow beyond the mulch boundary. Unlike most other garden plants, brambles can handle tough clay soil and even some degree of waterlogging, so feel free to put them in that spot where nothing else will grow.

If you're turning lawn or weeds into a berry patch, lay down a thick kill mulch and plant your brambles into holes in the cardboard. The best time to plant is in early spring, which means you'll probably be putting in dormant, bare-rooted stock. The young brambles will have a dead-looking cane poking up out of the roots—the cane is indeed dead, but the plant will send up a new cane once warm weather rolls around. Mulch the patch well, preferably with something a bit more carbon-rich than you used for your strawberries. (See the chapter on mulch for more information, or just use well-rotted wood chips.)

Twist ties make it easy to pin canes to your trellis and then to take them back down when pruning time comes.

Brambles don't need an extremely sturdy trellis, but it is helpful to find a way to tie the plants so they don't bend down over the path. I use lightweight metal fence posts about five feet apart with two strands of thin wire running between them. Twist ties are a simple way of attaching canes to the wire temporarily—you'll need to be able to unhook them when you prune out dead canes next winter.

*Bramble growth*   Unless you planted everbearing raspberries, you'll spend your first year watching your berries grow and learning to prune them. That gives you a chance to get a handle on the unique aspects of bramble biology so that you'll understand which canes to cut and which to leave in place.

The first factor to consider is how each type of bramble spreads vegetatively. Blackberries and black raspberries grow long, arching canes that bend down and then root at the tip. If you cut the tip loose and dig it up, you can transplant that youngster into a new part of the garden and expand your patch. Red raspberries, on the other hand, send out horizontal roots just beneath the soil surface; then new plants pop up along those roots. If you want to prevent your berry patch from turning into an impenetrable thicket, you'll need to understand which type of reproductive strategy your berries favor and prune accordingly.

The next thing you'll notice is that most blackberries and raspberries fruit only on second-year wood. The first shoots that come up are known as primocanes and will only be vegetative, making leaves but no blossoms. Next year, those primocanes will have matured into floricanes and will flower and make berries; at the same time, the roots are sending up new primocanes to prepare for the third year's berries. After fruiting, floricanes die and must be removed if you don't want your berry patch to turn into a thicket. But don't remove the primocanes or you won't get any fruits next year!

*Bramble pruning*    Now that you understand how the three types of brambles grow, pruning them should seem less complex.

The first type of pruning you'll need to do is summer tip pruning and is only necessary on blackberries and black raspberries. Once your primocanes get about three or four feet tall, simply walk by and pinch off the top of each cane. Tip pruning prevents the plants from forming long arching canes, so the brambles instead put their energy into branching out into a bush that will have more room for flowers and fruits next year. The three photos above show a black raspberry being tip-pruned—first the top is pinched off, then side shoots form, then the next year the bushy plant is loaded with fruits.

Summer tip pruning tells your brambles to put their energy into lots of short branches that will bear bountiful fruit next year. Start by pinching off the top of the cane once it is three or four feet tall.

The topped cane will begin to branch out within a couple of weeks.

Next year, the summer-pruned bramble will produce fruit close to the main stem.

The second type of pruning is winter pruning. In early spring, go into your patch and cut out any dead canes—you'll be able to tell which ones are dead because they'll be brown on the outside, often with peeling bark. If in doubt, cut the top off the cane and take a peek inside. Living canes will have a ring of green just under the bark. They also tend to have plumper buds.

After taking out all the dead canes, winter pruning is different for each type of bramble. If you didn't summer prune carefully or often enough, blackberries and black raspberries will have reached out beyond the edges of the row. Prune each plant until the side branches are one to two feet long. While you're at it, use your twist ties to attach these new canes to the trellis wires. If any canes got away from you and rooted at the tips, dig up those extra plants and give them away or expand your patch.

In the winter, bramble canes may look dead, but living canes will always have a ring of green inside if you make a test cut.

Cut out dead canes and then thin the patch until red raspberries stand about six inches apart.

You'll recall that red raspberries grow differently, sending up new shoots from their roots rather than making long, trailing canes. As a result, you only need to prune spring-bearing varieties once a year in the winter. First, cut out any dead canes, then thin until canes are about six inches apart.

Everbearing raspberries have two fruiting periods each year—one in the spring and one in the fall. If you only want a fall harvest, pruning is absurdly simple—just mow down the whole row of raspberries in the winter. However, if you want to enjoy raspberries in both the spring and the fall, you'll need to follow the advice above for spring-bearing red raspberries and also cut the tops off the canes that fruited the previous summer. Most people admonish you to remove the top third of these canes, but the truth is that you're cutting off the dead part. After snipping off a few tops, you'll start getting an eye for the point at which the plump, live cane turns into the more shriveled, dead cane.

## Annual care

All berries taste best if picked when the afternoon sun has filled them chock full of sugars.

Except for the complexities of pruning, your bramble patch will mostly take care of itself. Each spring, you'll want to top-dress your plants with compost and then smother any potential weeds with mulch. The brambles will flower and then fruit, generally bearing between late June and August.

Bramble fruits tend to be more resilient than strawberries, so you can probably get away with picking the berries only twice a week. Red raspberries, though, have a tendency to mold in hot, humid climates, so harvest more often.

A well-tended patch of blackberries or raspberries can last a very long time. Keep pruning and mulching and you'll be eating from your row of brambles a decade or more after planting. Now that's a good return on your investment!

# Stocking up on dried goods

**GOAL**: Buy and store nonperishable foods
**COST**: As much or as little as you like
**TIME**: 1 hour to 2 hours
**DIFFICULTY**: Easy
**KID-FRIENDLY**: Maybe

Buying grains, dried beans, sugar, and cocoa in bulk can lower your grocery bills and ensure you have a stash of food to eat during emergencies.

## Why buy in bulk?

Purchasing nonperishable staples in bulk is a boon to the wallet, to the environment, and to your emergency preparedness. I've found that I can save as much as 50 percent when I buy certain foods in bulk, and even if I only save 10 percent on other items, bulk buying still lowers my food bill with no coupon cutting.

One of my favorite parts of bulk buying is decreasing my waste stream. One big bag of cocoa replaces a dozen of those plastic tins from the grocery store, which means less packaging to be reprocessed at the recycling plant or to use up space in the landfill.

As long as you rotate your stored food—eating last year's savings while you buy more for next year—you won't even be consuming food that's less fresh than the offerings in the grocery store. After all, corn gets ripe only once a year, so the kernels have to be stored somewhere, whether that's in your larder or in a grain silo.

Of course, the most obvious reason to buy in bulk is to be prepared for short- or long-term emergencies. The emergency could be personal (you lose your job and need to tighten your belt for a few months) or environmental (a heavy snowstorm prevents your local grocery store from filling their shelves). Either way, wouldn't you like to be the smug homemaker whose pantry is full of six months worth of pasta and flour?

All of that said, there are also reasons *not* to buy in bulk. If you stock up on food you don't normally eat, chances are it'll go to waste, and you will be losing—not saving—money. And if you aren't careful about storage conditions, your "nonperishables" can be ruined by damp, mice, pantry moths, and other problems. So make sure you only buy as much food as you can store safely and eat within six months.

## Good and bad foods to buy in bulk

If you wander around the Internet looking for bulk food, you'll probably stumble across emergency preparedness sites that would love to sell you sealed containers of food to nourish your family for six months or more. In most cases, these kits are chock-full of processed items like pancake mix and dehydrated potatoes that are neither good for you nor tasty. In my opinion, you're wasting your money if you fall for these packages, since they're liable to go bad before they get eaten. And if a true emergency prompts you to break into your stash, won't you be even more unhappy if you're forced to subsist on canned evaporated milk and sugary cereal?

Sharon Astyk is a well-known blogger and author who explains emergency preparedness as an "Anyway Project." The idea is to make changes in your life that not only prepare you for an uncertain future but are also good things to do *anyway*. So, rather than stocking up on a few emergency food kits and forgetting about them, she recommends learning to buy your staples in bulk and then using more of these basics in your everyday life. If you'd be buying fifty pounds of spaghetti over the course of the year *anyway*, why not purchase it all at once, filling your emergency larder at the same time you do the year's shopping? Why not learn to bake your own cakes from big bags of flour, sugar, and cocoa rather than spending far too much for the same ingredients labeled as "cake mix" in the grocery store?

Using Sharon Astyk's *anyway* principle means going back to the basics with your bulk purchases. After all—unless you buy foods in individual packages that are sealed for freshness—the less processed your food, the longer it will last. Processed whole grains (like rolled oats, whole wheat flour, and even brown rice) will only last about six months in the average pantry, but unprocessed grains will last at least a decade (if they have a hard coating like wheat and corn) or at least six years (if they have a soft coating like barley and oats). In between those two shelf lives are processed grains that have had the germ removed, so white rice, white pasta, and white flour last about a year, twice as long as their more wholesome counterparts.

If you want to turn this week's project into a real learning experience and you have the cash to buy a grain mill, you might choose to purchase fifty pounds of wheat and learn to grind your own flour. However, it's also important to be realistic. If you're going to keep buying flour from the store because that grain is too hard to deal with, just stock up on items you use frequently with at least a year shelf life. Top contenders in that category include white flour, white rice, dried beans, unsweetened cocoa (if you're a chocoholic like me), pasta, and sugar. Even though ingredients like salt will last for years, I recommend against bulk-buying items you only use a pinch at a time—who has the space for fifty pounds of salt under his or her bed?

## Grinding your own flour

If you choose to grind your own flour, your first step is to choose a grain mill. Hand grinders can be extremely inexpensive, but they require quite a bit of labor. I recommend hand mills for families who have energetic and helpful children willing to turn the handle for half an hour every other day. The rest of us will probably make much more flour if we splurge on an electric mill.

Among electric grain mills, micronizers explode the grain rather than grind it. As a result, you can't sift out bran to make white flour, and you have to get a bit more creative when making homemade bread. Mills that use stones are more expensive but might be worth the price tag if you're serious about baking from scratch.

Once you select your mill, you'll need to make some choices about wheat as well. There are many varieties of wheat, which are usually distinguished as hard or soft, spring or winter, and white or red (plus durum wheat, which is used to make pasta). Of these, hard red spring wheat is most commonly used as bread flour, while soft red winter wheat and soft white wheat make all-purpose and cake flours for pastries and biscuits. Hard white wheat is preferred by many bakers who like the taste of white bread but the nutritional profile of whole wheat bread.

## Making your bulk purchases

Once you've decided which foods you're going to buy in bulk, the next step is to calculate how much of each item your family uses in six months or a year. The FDA estimates that the average American eats about 250 pounds of flour per year, but that figure also includes flour-based items like pasta, breakfast cereal, cake mix, and so forth. Instead of looking for a one-size-fits-all figure, I instead recommend that you save your grocery store receipts for a month or so and estimate annual usage from there.

While you're crunching those numbers, start looking for storage locations around your house. It's essential that bulk foods be stored in sealed containers if you want to keep out critters who will ruin your food in short order. Food grade five-gallon buckets with lids are a good choice as long as the grain comes weevil-free. In addition, your food needs to be maintained in cool and dry conditions. The USDA notes that dropping the temperature of your stored goods by 10°F will double its storage life, and you can work that correlation in reverse too—if you keep your bulk goods in a stuffy attic that reaches 90 degrees in the summer, your flour may only last a few months. Basements can be useful storage locations because they often stay cool, but only if you're able to seal your food well enough that it won't get damp. If you only have room to store three months' worth of food in optimal storage conditions, you should scale back your purchases accordingly.

Now it's time to head to the store—but which store? Online bulk food companies abound, but once you add in their shipping costs, you might as well pick up your flour in five-pound bags at the local grocery store. Here's where you'll need to do some legwork and look for sources of bulk food near you. Possibilities include co-ops where you and other community members pool your resources to buy a whole truckload of bulk goodies; health food stores (although check the prices—they can sometimes be higher than in a grocery store even if you buy in bulk); and mainstream stores like Aldi, Sam's Club, and Costco. I've had good luck buying from Mennonite stores, and I've read that you might be able to buy bulk food very cheaply from Latter-day Saints (aka Mormon) warehouses (www.providentliving.org/location/map/0,12566,2026-1-4,00.html), although I've heard mixed reports about whether you need to be a member of the church to buy from the latter.

If you're able to grind whole grains, you've got a few additional options. The cheapest grains can be found at your feed store, but ask lots of questions to make sure the kernels haven't been treated with chemicals, then plan to pick through the food in search of stones before grinding. Alternatively, if you're buying straw from a local farmer to mulch your garden, why not ask him what he does with the grain that grew on those plants? Maybe you can buy your wheat and mulch from the same source.

## Using bulk food

The final step in this week's exercise is to figure out a rotation system so that you're always eating the oldest food first and know when to refresh your stash. This system can be as simple as keeping three buckets of wheat on hand and buying a new bucket to go in the back once you use up the contents of the bucket in the front. Marking purchase date on all bulk food will also simplify rotation.

Keeping out insects like weevils and pantry moths can be more difficult. If you have a chest freezer that's halfway empty by spring, why not wait to make your bulk purchases then and rotate each item through the freezer for a week apiece? The cold should kill any pesky insects, and if you keep the containers sealed afterward, there's no chance of new pests getting in.

Despite all your care, though, eventually something will go bad. If you've bought brown rice or whole wheat flour, it may start to smell rancid in the summer heat. Or those weevils might get into your grain after all. Don't force yourself to eat food that's neither tasty nor good for you, but don't throw it away either. Chickens will consume just about any human food (but do dole it out a bit at a time), or you can soak the food and mix it with bedding to add to your worm bin. Then learn from your mistakes and buy less next year while improving your storage conditions. Remember, buying in bulk only makes financial sense if you use what you buy!

# Backup lighting

**GOAL**: Prepare off-grid light sources so you won't be stuck in the dark if the power goes out
**COST**: $5–$100
**TIME**: 1 hour to 2 hours
**DIFFICULTY**: Easy
**KID-FRIENDLY**: Yes

Winter nights can feel very long when the power goes out.

A simple and cheap backup light source will keep your spirits up during an extended power outage.

## *Let there be light*

A short summer power outage is often no big deal, but a winter week without electricity would send most of us spinning into dangerous territory. In previous chapters, you learned to store drinking water and to keep your family warm during extended power outages. Assuming you add a bit of food that doesn't require much preparation, you'll be all set physically.

But not emotionally. I love camping and adventures, but I have to admit that our experience of spending ten winter days without power was psychologically difficult. During the darkest days of the year, the sun provides less than ten hours of daylight in our neck of the woods. That's nine hours of sleeping and then five more hours of darkness when I would usually be reading blogs and books or writing on the computer. None of those activities are possible without some sort of backup lighting or electricity.

This week's exercise will help you prepare so you're not stuck in the dark if the power goes out. Backup lighting solutions range from extremely simple (a candle) to expensive and complex (a generator), with lots of options in between. I'll run through the pros and cons of the most obvious solutions next.

## Types of backup lighting

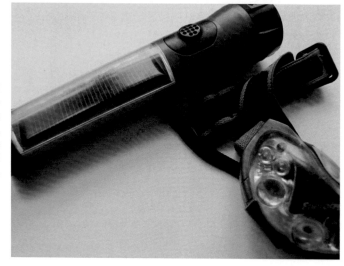

Solar-powered flashlights are always ready when you need them, while headlamps make it easy to read in the dark.

You won't need to shell out much cash if all you want is some sort of lighting so that you're not sitting in the dark twiddling your thumbs for five hours on a winter evening. The lowest tech and least costly light source is candles, which are quite easy to make if you have excess wax from your beehive and a bit of braided string. However, I suspect you'll get sick of candles pretty quickly and will want to invest in one of the more powerful solutions listed below.

My favorite off-grid light source is a solar-powered LED flashlight, available for $10 to $20. Solar flashlights have come a long way in recent years, and if you make a habit of storing your flashlight in a sunny window, it will always be ready when you need it. Turn your solar flashlight into your primary tool for night-time chores, and you'll repay your start-up costs in no time since you won't have to keep buying batteries.

Some of you might want a more ergonomic light source than a hand-held flashlight, though. I spent a lot of time in tents as a kid and learned just the right way to prop my flashlight on my shoulder so I could read by its light, but my husband rolled his eyes during our power outage and went out to buy a headlamp. I've yet to see any solar-powered headlamps, so if you go this route, you'll need to stock up on batteries, which add an ongoing cost and chance of failure to the project. But the bright, focused light will definitely raise your spirits during a lengthy power outage, making a headlamp worth the extra effort.

Another option is to ditch electricity altogether and invest in a propane or kerosene lantern. After buying the lantern, a few extra mantles (since they break easily), and some fuel, you will probably be out $50 to $100. The beauty of these lanterns is that they light up a whole room, so you can eat dinner or play games together rather than each being isolated in your own circle of light. On the other hand, both types of lanterns are a fire hazard, and you need to stock up on fuel, so lanterns aren't nearly as low-work as solar flashlights.

If you're feeling ambitious, why not change some of the lights in your home over to solar power for use even when the grid is up and running? Lighting makes up 9 percent of the average American's electric bill, so rigging up a solar-powered reading lamp could be a money-saving project. My inventive husband is pretty sure you could convert a solar yard light (often available for $5 or less) into an indoor reading light by extending the cord, then mounting the panel outside and the light inside. We haven't tried it out yet—maybe you'll experiment and report back?

## Generators

The other option for lighting during a power outage is to buy a generator and just get on with your life. Generators have a place, but I wouldn't recommend them for the average weekend homesteader because . . .

**They're expensive.** Even the cheapest generator is over $100, and you'll have to pay even more for a better model.

**Generators don't always play nice with electronics.** Don't just buy any old generator and think you'll be able to hook up your computer for hours of entertainment. You'll need to pony up more cash for a generator that produces clean current and won't fry your electronics.

**Generator power is expensive.** I estimate that fuel alone costs about a dollar per hour when running a 3,000-watt generator in 2009, and gas prices are still going up. Depending on how long your generator lasts, total cost per hour could be considerably higher.

**Generators need maintenance.** Like any other internal combustion engine, generators don't like to be ignored for years and then expected to run smoothly. You'll need to invest in some fuel stabilizer so your gas isn't too old to use and will also want to give your generator regular tune-ups.

**Generators can be hard to start.** We have a generator, and if the power went off when my husband wasn't home to tinker with it, I wouldn't even try to get it going. (But maybe that's just me—I can make any plant grow and any internal combustion engine fail.)

**Generators are loud.** It's a lot more fun to read by solar flashlight than to try to relax with the generator roaring outside.

All of that said, generators can be a good backup option if you have the time and technical know-how to keep them humming along. If you freeze a lot of food, you can keep your freezer in good shape by running the generator for just an hour or so per day, and it's nice not to lose all the perishables in your fridge during an extended power outage. Just know what you're getting into before you take the plunge.

## Having fun in the dark

While you're thinking of backup lighting options, you might as well figure out how your family is going to stay entertained during long, dark evenings without juice. If you're used to watching TV every day after work, I guarantee you'll be cranky without your favorite shows, and kids can require a lot more TLC if their gaming system is down.

Cultivating an interest in activities that don't require electricity is a useful life skill. Reading and board games are my favorite nonpowered entertainment options, but you might take up knitting, whittling, or some other pursuit. If you do nothing else as the hands-on portion of this week's exercise, try spending an evening entertaining yourself and your family at home without electricity. Maybe you'll discover the experience is so much fun that you'd rather play games together in the evening than watch TV alone in your room.

My final piece of advice for dealing with power outage psychology is to figure out how you'll stay in touch with the outside world. Do you usually check in with friends and family using a cell phone or cordless house phone? Investing in a corded landline that doesn't require house electricity will make it much easier to report power outages to your electric company so the juice comes back on sooner, and you'll also be able to keep your extended family from worrying when you go incommunicado. You might even dig up a battery-operated, solar-powered, or hand-cranked radio so you can listen to the news and stay up-to-date with the outside world.

Remember—power outages can be fun bonding experiences, or they can be painful endurance tests. The difference lies in your state of mind and level of preparedness.

# Setting homestead goals

**GOAL**: Stay on the right track—and keep your dreams from overwhelming you
**COST**: $0
**TIME**: 2 hours
**DIFFICULTY**: Medium
**KID-FRIENDLY**: Maybe

When you expand beyond the weekend homesteader level, focusing on the most important projects on the farm becomes challenging. This week's exercise will help you figure out what you really want to do, then set a realistic time frame for each task.

## Long-term goals

Are you overwhelmed by the nitty-gritty of realizing your dreams? Or perhaps you're annoyed with yourself for not being able to remember the truly important tasks when your homesteading afternoon rolls around. Either way, the first step is to draw up a list of long-term goals.

Long-term goals should be embraced as group projects, so try to get the whole family involved in the planning process. For some of you, that might be as easy as asking each family member to brainstorm projects they'd really like to have on the table. In other cases, you might need to trick recalcitrant teenagers (or spouses) into taking part in this exercise by chatting about homesteading during a family dinner. Or maybe you're a visual thinker and would like to draw a diagram of what you want your homestead to look like in ten or twenty years. Either way, make sure everyone dreams as big as he or she wants to; then jot down a list of everyone's great (and not so great) ideas.

Right now, focus on big-picture projects. These are often expensive or time-consuming tasks that make me twitch when I gaze out over our

364

homestead and realize we haven't even begun to work on them. Big-picture goals might include growing your own meat, becoming energy independent, or quitting your job. Be sure to jot down everything that keeps you up at night and also the things you daydream about while you're weeding the garden.

I find it helpful to break big-picture goals down into categories like buildings, garden, livestock, and energy. If you're less fixated on one aspect of homesteading, you can skip this step and just type up all the goals your family has brainstormed onto one list. Whether your list has subheadings or not, print out a copy for each member of your family and sit folks down with a pen and strict instructions to number the projects from most important to least important (repeating the numbering exercise within each category if you've split your goals up by type).

In past years, I've simply averaged my husband's and my numbers for each potential project to come up with a group ranking, but recently I've decided it's more fair to make sure that everyone's top choice happens soon. Chances are, you'll only nibble away at your long-term goal list this year, so focusing on the most important item on each family member's list will keep you all feeling like a team. Either way, make a new list with your big-picture goals ranked from most to least important, and move on to the next section.

## *Bite-size goals*

Once a year, we make a new big-picture goal list, but if we worked from that list on a day-to-day basis, I'd drive myself nuts. Instead, I spend a bit of time at the beginning of each year, month, and week developing to-do lists in bite-size segments.

(The astute reader will notice that "we" suddenly became "I" in that last paragraph. Although I think it's essential for each family member to be consulted when planning big-picture projects, I've found that my husband is quite happy not to be involved in more day-to-day list-making. As long as you're fair and true to the big-picture list, there doesn't seem to be a problem with the more anal retentive member of the family finishing the rest of this week's exercise solo.)

Your first step is to figure out how much of your long-term goal list you want to chew on this year. I urge you to be realistic and think about how much time you really have to work on homesteading projects each year. My husband and I homestead full time, and we've yet to finish ten big-picture projects in a given year—one of these days I'll learn to put few enough tasks on the annual list that we feel accomplished rather than inept come next year's list-making day. If you're a true weekend homesteader with a full-time job and a bunch of other commitments, one or two big-picture projects may be all you can handle.

After deciding on your annual goals, break that list up into monthly sections. If you already homestead, you probably know that there are times of the year when you won't be able to fit any extra projects into the cracks between weeding the garden, canning tomatoes, and falling into an exhausted heap at the end of the day. I like to go through my planner, writing down the major projects for each month of the year before trying to slide in any additional long-term goals—generally, the main months for big-picture projects in our household are December, January, February, and April.

Those of you with weekend homesteads can probably stop your list-making at the month level, but if you spend all day every day homesteading, you might want to make weekly and even daily lists. I've found that spending the last fifteen minutes of my "workday" on Friday penning next week's projects then summing up all our accomplishments from the past week allows me to play during the weekend without worrying about all those zucchinis that need to be dried for the winter.

Another list-making technique that has saved my sanity is what I call "catch and release goals." As soon as I put a project on a list, I know I won't forget it, so I simply let the urge to complete the task go. My method means that anything on our ten-year plan that didn't make it into this year's goals simply flies out of my head until next year. Again, anything from our annual list that isn't on the monthly list doesn't need to keep me awake at night. It sure feels nice to delegate all my angst to a sheet of paper.

# Cutting your goals in half

It's important to realize that life on a farm takes a lot of work just to stay afloat. During the growing season, we fill our days with weeding, harvesting, mowing, killing chickens, and so forth, with barely a lick of time left for working on long-term goals. Even in the winter, splitting wood and cooking from scratch use up a considerable amount of time.

That's why one of my biggest pieces of advice for ambitious homesteaders is—put only half as many projects on any list as you think you can complete in the slated period of time. You'll feel really, really good if you complete everything on your list and can work ahead, while you'll feel just as terrible if you only get a third of your list done. Why not prime the pump of happiness rather than despair?

It also helps to lower your standards a bit and realize that it's not essential for your farm to look like the pictures in the glossy magazines, at least not at first. The most fun part of farming is figuring it all out, so why rush through the early days in search of an elusive goal when you could be enjoying every minute of your journey into self-sufficiency?

# MARCH
## (September Down Under)

# Spring planting

**GOAL**: Sow cold-tolerant vegetables for meals in April, May, and June
**COST**: $5–$30
**TIME**: 1 hour to 4 hours
**DIFFICULTY**: Medium
**KID-FRIENDLY**: Yes

Those of you who have worked your way through the weekend homesteader projects since last spring will notice that you've come nearly full circle. You planted a simple summer garden and learned how season extension can make the fall garden produce deep into the winter months. Now it's time to begin round two, starting the garden year a bit sooner so that you can taste homegrown produce as early as April.

Before diving into this week's project, you may want to refresh your memory by perusing the chapters "Plan your summer garden," "Quick hoops," and "Garden rotation." But don't get bogged down if you're just starting out. Your spring garden can be as simple as a lettuce bed, thrown together in a few minutes and enjoyed just as thoroughly.

## *Preheating the soil*

Quick hoops help the soil warm up faster in the spring, so you can eat new lettuce even sooner.

The main difference between planting in early spring and after the frost-free date is soil temperature—cold ground makes seeds rot before they sprout. Luckily, there are several methods of heating up the soil, ranging from the simple to the complex.

**Rake back the mulch.** I'm assuming you're working with a no-till garden, mulched heavily for the winter to keep weeds from taking over. (If not, you're going to have trouble planting early in the spring, since your ground will probably be too wet to till, sometimes until June.) While mulch is extremely handy during most of the year, the coating of organic matter acts like a layer of insulation in early spring, preventing the lengthening days from warming the ground. The solution is simple—rake back the mulch. I usually pull my spring mulch to the sides of the beds a week or two before planting each one. That way, weeds don't have time to grow, but the soil gets a chance to warm up. Once the seedlings are a few inches tall, you can push the same mulch back up around their ankles, preventing competitive weeds from outgrowing your vegetables.

**Add dark organic matter.** You've probably noticed how wearing a black shirt in the sun heats your body up quickly. You can put the same science to work in the garden by top-dressing your beds with a layer of dark-colored organic matter like good compost, well-rotted manure, or biochar. For more extreme soil preheating, you can lay down a dark sheet of plastic, but be aware that this technique can kill soil microorganisms.

**Erect a quick hoop.** The quick hoops you built in October are easy to move to a fresh plot of land to create minigreenhouses on top of your spring beds. Putting up a quick hoop a week or two before planting can warm the soil by several degrees.

You probably noticed that each of these techniques share two factors—sun and time. Your soil will naturally warm up as spring advances; you're just trying to expedite the process so you can jump-start the garden year. To eat from your garden as soon as possible, combine all three methods and plant seeds as much as three months before your frost-free date.

# What to plant

Many cool-season crops—like carrots—taste much sweeter during cold weather.

Even under quick hoops, you won't want to plant frost-sensitive vegetables, like tomatoes and cucumbers, anytime soon. However, there is still a wide selection of crops to choose from for your spring garden (the easiest of which I've highlighted in the chart below).

| Vegetable | Start from | Notes |
|---|---|---|
| beets | seeds | Beet seeds can sometimes be difficult to germinate. As with other root crops, beets need loose, loamy soil. |
| broccoli | transplants | The more advanced gardener can start her own seedlings either inside or in a quick hoop. Otherwise, buy sets from the local feed store when night temperatures have risen into the high 20s to low 30s Fahrenheit. |

| Vegetable | Start from | Notes |
|---|---|---|
| brussels sprouts | transplants | The more advanced gardener can start her own seedlings either inside or in a quick hoop. Otherwise, buy sets from the local feed store when night temperatures have risen into the high 20s to low 30s Fahrenheit. |
| cabbage | transplants | The more advanced gardener can start her own seedlings either inside or in a quick hoop. Otherwise, buy sets from the local feed store when night temperatures have risen into the high 20s to low 30s Fahrenheit. |
| carrots | seeds | Well-drained, loamy soil is mandatory. Carrots are slow-growers, so weed carefully to give the seedlings breathing room. |
| cauliflower | transplants | The more advanced gardener can start her own seedlings either inside or in a quick hoop. Otherwise, buy sets from the local feed store when night temperatures have risen into the high 20s to low 30s Fahrenheit. |
| collards | seeds | Spring greens are some of the easiest vegetables to grow. In addition to collards, spinach, and Swiss chard, consider trying some Asian greens for variety. |
| leeks | seeds | Leeks take a long time to grow, so I generally prefer the perennial Egyptian onions instead. As with other root crops, leeks need loose, loamy soil. |

| Vegetable | Start from | Notes |
| --- | --- | --- |
| lettuce | seeds | Leaf lettuce is my earliest harvest of the year because I always plant it under quick hoops. You can cut leaves within a month of planting, but be sure to seed a second bed as soon as you start eating the first—lettuce becomes bitter within a few weeks of first harvest. |
| onions | seeds, sets, or transplants | Getting your onions to germinate out in the cold can be a bit tricky, so you may choose to start them inside or under quick hoops to ensure they have time to grow before summer heat stunts them. Select a variety appropriate for your day length (short day in the South and long day in the North). Many gardeners simplify planting by buying sets (tiny bulbs) from the local feed store, but onions grown from sets usually don't store well. |
| parsley | seeds | Parsley is grown very similarly to carrots, but you pick the leaves a few at a time rather than digging up the root. |
| peas | seeds | Soak your seeds overnight before planting to ensure they sprout quickly. Erect a trellis for your peas to grow on. |

| Vegetable | Start from | Notes |
|---|---|---|
| potatoes | cut up pieces of potato, each with two eyes | Hill up your potatoes by adding soil or mulch extending a few inches up the growing stem once the plant is about eight inches tall. This prevents the new tubers from being exposed to sunlight and turning green. If you're planting early into cold soil, consider cutting your seed potatoes a few weeks in advance and laying them out in a bright spot so they'll presprout. |
| radishes | seeds | Some gardeners plant radish seeds in their carrot rows. The radishes come up quickly and mature before they compete with the slower-growing carrots. |
| spinach | seeds | I find that spinach plants usually bolt in the spring, so I generally focus on other varieties of leafy greens. |
| Swiss chard | seeds | Swiss chard seeds can sometimes be difficult to germinate, but otherwise Swiss chard is perhaps the easiest green to grow and will keep producing all summer. |
| turnips | seeds | Like other root crops, turnips prefer loamy, well-drained soil. |

The raw beginner should start out with collards, lettuce, peas, potatoes, radishes, and Swiss chard. Second-year gardeners might add broccoli, carrots, and parsley. But ignore my advice if you love beets and hate lettuce—plant what you like to eat!

# When to plant

Every winter is a little different, so I use a soil thermometer to keep an eye on the temperature of the soil and plant accordingly. The thermometer pictured above is actually a meat thermometer, bought for less than $10, but it works just as well as the more expensive soil thermometers you'll find in gardening stores.

A soil thermometer is the most accurate way of determining when to plant spring crops.

To check the soil temperature, get up early—before the sun has hit the ground—and insert the thermometer into the ground. Wait a few minutes, then take a reading. If you have garden areas that are more sunny than others, you'll want to test the soil temperature at several places—I usually find that our soil is two to five degrees colder in the shade of our hillside than in the sunnier parts of the garden.

The table below lists the germination temperatures for common spring crops.

| Vegetable | Minimum temperature (°F) | Optimum temperature (°F) |
|---|---|---|
| beets | 40 | 50–85 |
| broccoli | 40 | 45–85 |
| brussels sprouts | 40 | 45–85 |

| Vegetable | Minimum temperature (°F) | Optimum temperature (°F) |
|---|---|---|
| cabbage | 40 | 45–95 |
| carrots | 40 | 45–85 |
| cauliflower | 40 | 45–85 |
| collards | 45 | 70–75 |
| leeks | 40 | 70–75 |
| lettuce | 35 | 40–80 |
| onions | 35 | 50–95 |
| parsley | 40 | 50–85 |
| peas | 40 | 40–75 |
| potatoes | 45 | 60–70 |
| radishes | 40 | 45–90 |
| spinach | 35 | 45–75 |
| Swiss chard | 40 | 50–85 |
| turnips | 40 | 60–105 |

In most cases, you can get away with planting once the soil has reached the minimum germination temperature, but don't plant your seeds if a cold spell is going to set in within a couple of days. You should also be aware that some vegetables will give you spotty germination until the ground was warmed up closer to the optimum temperature—you might want to double your seeding rate to ensure a good stand if planting near the minimum. Once a seed has sprouted, it's less sensitive to cold soil, so expediting germination by soaking your seeds overnight before planting can also help.

To plant earlier than cold soil will allow, many gardeners are tempted to start seedlings indoors. However, unless you have grow lights or a heated greenhouse, I recommend that beginners stick to growing their plants entirely in the earth for the first year. A quick hoop might be enough to let you plant a couple of weeks earlier than you otherwise could have; then you can transfer the same protection to a new bed in April to jump-start your summer garden.

## How to plant

Planting spring crops is extremely easy in a no-till garden. If you haven't already done so, rake back the mulch and add half an inch to an inch of high-quality compost to feed your vegetables. For best results, you'll want to work the compost into the top inch or two of your soil with a bow rake, but don't disturb the soil profile further down.

Small seeds can be scattered directly on the soil surface in damp spring weather. Larger seeds (like peas) and seed potatoes should be planted in a trench made by dragging your hoe in a line down the length of the bed. Add your seeds, then fill the trench back in, lightly tamping the soil with the flat part of your hoe to remove air pockets. Your seed packet will tell you how deep to plant your seeds, but a good rule of thumb is that depth should be proportional to the size of the seed—miniscule seeds can go on the soil surface, medium-sized seeds might sit a quarter of an inch below, while large seeds can be planted an inch or more deep.

As long as you pay attention to soil temperature, germination shouldn't be a problem in the spring. Once your seedlings are up and running, weed carefully and then mulch to prevent further weeds from growing. Now all you have to do is watch and wait for April, May, and June vegetables.

# Growing edible mushrooms

**GOAL**: Raise oyster or shiitake mushrooms on logs
**COST**: $20–$50
**TIME**: 2 hours to 3 hours
**DIFFICULTY**: Medium
**KID-FRIENDLY**: Maybe

Edible mushrooms are one of the easiest foods to grow, enabling you to turn tree trunks into dinner.

## "Will I poison myself?"

For many of us, the excitement of growing our own mushrooms is tempered by the fear that we'll accidentally poison our families. Let me set your mind at rest. While I don't gather mushrooms other than oysters and morels from the wild, growing mushrooms on logs is very safe.

Turkey tails are a common weed fungus that grow on oyster and shiitake mushroom logs.

*(continued)*

## "Will I poison myself?" *(continued)*

The danger with eating your own mushrooms is that you might misidentify the fungus and accidentally imbibe something poisonous. Luckily for us, there are no poisonous mushrooms growing on logs in the United States that look anything like shiitakes or oyster mushrooms. The turkey tail mushroom, shown above, is the most likely "weed fungus" you'll see on your logs, and even though it's not very tasty, the mushroom is edible (and is actually reputed to cure a variety of ills, including cancer).

The truth is that once you start growing oysters or shiitakes, you'll soon know exactly what these edibles look, smell, and taste like. The concept of accidentally eating a weed mushroom will start to seem as far-fetched as a farmer going out into her garden to pluck a tomato and instead chowing down on poison nightshade berries. In fact, growing your own mushrooms might help you work through enough of your mycophobia that you'll want to join a local mushroom club and forage for wild edibles. Even more mushrooms for even less work!

## *Choosing your mushroom variety*

If you're like me, the only mushrooms you've eaten may have been button mushrooms from the grocery store. Although I usually tell you to grow foods you're familiar with, in the mushroom world I instead recommend expanding your palate. Button mushrooms need to be raised on specially sterilized, manure-rich compost, which makes them tough to cultivate on a small scale. Oyster and shiitake mushrooms, in contrast, can be grown on newly cut logs—and they taste better than button mushrooms too!

Oyster mushrooms are my favorite species of edible fungus because they can grow on "weed" trees like box elder, sycamore, and just about anything else except conifers. If you decide to become a self-sufficient mycologist, oyster mushrooms can even be reproduced at home using corrugated cardboard. Oysters are also native to the United States, so once you grow your own and are familiar with their fruiting structures, you will probably start finding wild food as you walk through the woods.

Oyster mushrooms are one of the easiest types of edible mushrooms to raise at home.

On the other hand, shiitake mushrooms have a reputation for being a bit more gourmet. (We find that oyster mushrooms taste just as good if picked at the peak of perfection, but your taste buds may be more discerning.) Shiitake mushrooms also come in more strains, allowing you to harvest mushrooms throughout the summer rather than just in the cool weather of spring and fall. On the downside, shiitake mushrooms require hardwoods (preferably oaks) to grow on, and they can't be reproduced without sterile laboratory conditions.

Shiitake mushrooms have a reputation for being the most gourmet mushroom you can grow in your backyard.

My favorite sources for buying mushroom spawn are Field and Forest Products (www.fieldforest.net), Fungi Perfecti (www.fungi.com), and Mushroom Mountain (www.shop.mushroommountain.com). You'll notice that all three companies offer several varieties of mushrooms beyond the ones mentioned here; most of the other types of edible mushrooms are tougher to grow and should be avoided until you have more experience. In addition, you may be tempted by the ready-to-go nature of kits, but I recommend steering clear, since these kits aren't very productive. Instead, look for plug spawn, which consists of small sections of wooden dowels impregnated with mycelium (the vegetative part of the fungus).

## Mushroom biology

Most of us understand the basic reproductive cycle of plants and animals, but mushrooms may be a mystery. When you see a red-capped toadstool on the forest floor, do you assume it just sprouted like a sunflower out of the dirt? Actually, the mushrooms we're familiar with are simply the fruiting structures of a much larger fungal mass—a bit like the apple on a tree.

You can often find large masses of mycelium in wood chip mulch. The white strands of fungus will hold the chips together into a solid ball.

The main body of a fungus is the mycelial network, which may be too small to see or which may look like a network of white roots. If you've been growing a no-till garden, you've probably seen mycelium in or just below the mulch. Fungi are quite happy to grow in this vegetative state until they are shocked by reaching the end of their substrate

*(continued)*

## Mushroom biology *(continued)*

(what they're growing on) or by a change in temperature or moisture. Once shocked, the mycelium sends up a mushroom to create spores, which you can think of as a bit like seeds.

Mushrooms are usually at their peak tastiness just before they release spores, but if you wait a bit longer, you can see the spores as a white or colored powder that falls out of the gills when tapped. Spores are much smaller than seeds, so they are easily carried through the air to a new log or patch of mulch. There, spores may sit dormant for months or years until the right environmental conditions tempt them to sprout and grow.

Here's where mushroom biology gets a bit complicated. The spores don't just grow into mycelium. Instead, each spore turns into a structure known as a hypha, which has to mate with a slightly different hypha to create mycelium. This step is why most backyard mushroom-growers choose to buy mushroom spawn (aka mycelium) rather than starting with spores.

Luckily for us, fungi don't have to go through their complex sexual reproductive cycle in order to produce fruit. Like potatoes, fungi can also be reproduced vegetatively by simply cutting the mycelial network into sections and using each chunk of fungus to start a new mushroom log. When you buy plug spawn, you're getting clones of one mycelial body that has grown into the wooden dowels.

## *Selecting logs*

Once you understand what you're working with, growing mushrooms is pretty easy. First, you need to find and prepare your substrate, which in the case of this exercise is logs cut from a living tree. Shiitakes can be grown on oak, sugar maple, ironwood, sweet gum, or sycamore, while oyster mushrooms love softwoods like poplar, willow, elm, alder, tulip tree, and box elder. If you heat your house with a wood-stove, think of the trees you'd use as kindling when you're looking for oyster substrates; then save the trees you'd use to make a hot fire to grow shiitakes. Just as coniferous trees like pines and cedar make bad firewood, the species should also be avoided when you're hunting down mushroom logs.

The perfect log will come from a healthy tree cut after sap begins to flow up into the limbs but before the buds burst open. During this period (usually in March in our area), the tree is full of sugars that will allow your mushrooms to grow quickly, and it's also quite damp, which will keep your mycelium from drying out. You can cut a tree during the optimal period and then let it sit for a few weeks until your spawn arrives, but don't cut the tree into logs until the last minute. Otherwise, wild fungi may colonize the logs before you insert your spawn and act like weeds do in your vegetable garden, outcompeting your oysters or shiitakes.

Log size depends on how strong you are, how soon you want mushrooms, and how long you want the log to last. As a rule of thumb, cut the tree into logs thirty-six to forty inches long and use only logs that are between three and eight inches in diameter. The shorter and skinnier your log, the sooner you'll get your first fruit, but also the sooner the log will run out of food and your fungi will die. You'll need to soak the logs in water later to get them to fruit, so pretend the logs weigh twice as much as they do at this moment—will you still be able to lift them?

## Supplies

Now it's time to order your spawn and gather your supplies.

The well-stocked toolbox will have most of your mushroom inoculation supplies, but you'll need to track down plug spawn, beeswax, and a spade drill bit.

**Plug spawn.** Count up how many plugs you need to purchase, keeping in mind that a three-inch-diameter log will need about twenty plugs, while a seven-inch-diameter log will need forty-five plugs. Spawn is the one item you'll probably need to buy through the mail; everything else will be cheaper locally. If you buy more than one variety of mushroom spawn, be aware that each log should host only one mushroom variety—companion planting doesn't work with mushroom logs.

**Portable drill with a 5/16-inch spade drill bit.**

**Electrical tape.** Use a small piece of electrical tape to mark a spot two inches down your drill bit. This will help you drill holes of the proper depth.

**Hammer.**

**Tape measure.**

**Marker that will write on wood.**

**Beeswax.** Your beekeeping friend is the best source for wax.

**An old pot that you don't mind ruining to melt the wax in.** For safest wax melting, this pot should fit into another pot partially filled with water to make a double boiler. As you can see in the photo above, an old can makes a good, disposable, wax-melting pot. Another option is to melt your wax over a hot plate.

A pot partially full of water and an old tin can make a passable double boiler to melt your wax.

**A paintbrush about one inch in diameter.** Choose a brush with natural rather than synthetic bristles so that the brush doesn't melt in your hot wax.

Labeling your logs makes it easy to manage them in future years.

**Labels for the logs.** I like to use small pieces of metal flashing with a number scratched in each. The flashing is easy to screw into the end of my logs.

## Inoculating the logs

Inserting spawn into logs is known as inoculation. The process is a bit like planting seeds in your garden—the plugs need to be spaced properly and "planted" at just the right depth. Then you use melted beeswax to cover up each plug so that the mycelium doesn't dry out and so that wild fungi can't invade the log.

Although an assembly line—drill all the holes, pound in all the plugs, then cover them all with wax—is most efficient, I recommend dealing with one log from start to finish before moving on to the next. Unlike seeds, the fungus in your plug spawn is active rather than dormant, and it can be stunted by being left out in the sun for even a few minutes. So, keep the bag of spawn closed when not in use and make sure you can cover spawn up with wax soon after it goes into the log.

Here are the steps I use to inoculate a log. Keep in mind that all this goes much faster if there are two to three people involved in the project.

**Melt your beeswax.** If you have a double boiler, you can set it on medium heat and let your wax melt as you prepare the log. Another option is to use an extension cord and plug in an electric hot plate near where you're working, so you'll have wax on hand at all times.

**Mark where you plan to drill the first holes in your log.** Plugs should be spaced two to four inches apart all around the circumference of the log. The easiest way to begin this pattern is to set your log flat on the ground (perpendicular to how it grew as a tree), then mark plug locations every four inches in a straight line.

A battery-powered drill allows you to drill your holes out in the woods rather than hauling the logs back to your house to be inoculated. But a corded drill has more power and doesn't need its batteries refreshed at intervals.

**Drill two-inch-deep holes at each location.** You can use a piece of electrical tape on your spade drill bit as a guide so you'll know how deep to drill each hole. Drill all the holes in the line you marked.

Be sure to pound in each plug so that it lies flush with the log surface.

**Pound in plug spawn.** As the first person drills, the second person can come along behind and pound a plug into each hole. This is a bit like driving a nail—once you get good at it, you should be able to drive in the plug with one or two blows. Be sure to line up the plug as straight as possible so that it ends up flush with or slightly below the log surface. Try not to nick the bark of the tree while pounding in the plug.

Our dog came along behind and gnawed the honey-scented beeswax off our logs. If your pets are similarly inclined, be sure to keep the logs out of their reach for a few days until the sweet scent disperses.

**Brush melted wax over the top of each plug.** The first person has finished drilling and can now come along behind and dab hot wax on top of each plug. If you don't have a hot plate, you may want to save the wax step until you've got the whole log inoculated so that you don't have to run into the house so often. In that case, be sure to stop dabbing on wax once it starts to harden back up—if your wax isn't completely liquid, it will flake off the log once dried.

**Move on to the next row of plugs.** Rotate the log a few inches and start a second line of holes parallel to the first. Offset each plug so you create a diamond pattern. Once you've marked and drilled another line of plug locations, pound in the plugs and coat them with wax. Repeat until you've gone all the way around the log back to the beginning.

**Label your logs.** Labeling each log is useful for record-keeping purposes. Even if you're only growing one kind of mushroom from a single source, I still recommend labeling logs so you can easily write down which ones are still producing next year and the year after that. Logs that stop producing or that get colonized by weed fungi should be removed from the mushroom area.

We set our logs on a pair of old metal pipes, just high enough off the ground that wild fungi won't invade but low enough to remain damp.

**Set the logs off the ground, in the shade.** Depending on the size of your logs and on which species of mushroom you chose to grow, you will need to wait 6 to 18 months before seeing any fruit. Large scale producers will water their logs and make sure they stay at just the right moisture level for this colonization period, but if you're like me, you'll inoculate your logs and then forget about them. So it's essential that you put them in a conducive environment from the beginning. The best mushroom log location is damp and out of direct sunlight, perhaps under a large shade tree. You want the logs to be close to the ground so they stay moist, but not touching the earth (since that can make it easy for weed fungi to invade). There's no single right way to stack your logs—you can see our current method above, which simply involves laying the logs on two metal pipes to keep them slightly elevated above the ground.

# Homegrown oyster mushroom spawn

You can propagate your own oyster mushroom spawn on corrugated cardboard.

After a few years, your mushroom logs will peter out and you'll need to create new ones. Do you have to keep buying spawn?

If you're growing oyster mushrooms, you can propagate your own mycelium in the kitchen without any fancy equipment. Just rustle up some used corrugated cardboard, a big cooking pot, a medium-sized, clean plastic flowerpot, and some freshly picked oyster mushrooms. If you're propagating more than one type of oyster mushroom, keep the varieties separate and plan to fill multiple flowerpots.

Fill the cooking pot with water and bring it to a boil as you cut the cardboard into sections small enough to layer horizontally within the flowerpot. Meanwhile, clean out your sink or dishpan and fill it up with your cut cardboard, then with the boiling water. You will probably need to weigh the cardboard down with something to keep it from floating to the surface, since you're trying to completely saturate the cardboard with hot water.

As the water cools, cook up some oyster mushrooms for supper. Carefully cut off the stem butts—the base of the mushroom that looks a bit fuzzy with mycelium—and save them; then eat the rest of the mushroom however you like.

After an hour or two, your corrugated cardboard should be falling apart into three pieces, since the hot water has loosened the glue. The flat, outer layers aren't a good mushroom-growing substrate, so separate them from the corrugated central portion. Crumple up a few of the outer layers to put in the bottom of the flowerpot. This crumpled cardboard will allow air to move through the pot

*(continued)*

## Homegrown oyster mushroom spawn *(continued)*

and will keep your spawn from sitting in water as the cardboard drips out excess moisture.

Now fill up the rest of the flowerpot as if you're making lasagna. (The corrugated cardboard is the noodles, and the stem butts are the sauce.) Lay down a sheet or two of corrugated cardboard; then place a stem butt or two on top. Add another layer of corrugated cardboard, another stem butt or two, and so forth until you run out of cardboard, stem butts, or pot space.

Finally, top the pot off with a few more layers of the outer cardboard pieces, flat rather than crumpled. The purpose of the topping is to hold in moisture, so if you notice the top cardboard starting to curl up later, water it lightly to keep the contents of the pot moist.

The glue and air space in corrugated cardboard make it a perfect environment for oyster mushroom mycelium to grow. If you keep your flowerpot at room temperature and out of direct sunlight, you should see white spawn starting to spread across the cardboard a week later if you gently pry the layers apart. After a couple more weeks, the mycelium will have taken over all the cardboard, gluing it together as you can see in the photo. (The green moss came along with a stem butt—don't expect to see it in your pot.)

Now you're ready to inoculate new logs using the method outlined elsewhere in this chapter. If you find it difficult to push pieces of mycelium-laden cardboard into holes in logs, you can simply create long gashes down the logs' length with a chainsaw and inoculate the logs that way. As you work, be sure to cover up your spawn with wax to hold in moisture.

The only tricky part about growing your own oyster mushroom spawn is timing. Your oyster mushroom logs may not fruit until March, which would mean you won't have spawn ready to inoculate into logs until April. If you've got space, maybe you should find a way to soak one log and bring it inside to fruit in February so that you'll have spawn ready to go at the right time of year.

To learn how to propagate mushrooms using sterile, laboratory conditions, check out Paul Stamets's *Growing Gourmet and Medicinal Mushrooms*. Or read his *Mycelium Running* to become inspired about adding fungi to your permaculture homestead.

## Harvesting mushrooms

Soaking your mushroom logs tempts them to fruit.

The first fall after inoculating oyster mushroom logs or the next spring after inoculating shiitake logs, you should test whether your fungi are ready to fruit. The best way to do this is to take two or three logs and soak them overnight (for no more than twelve hours) in cool water. We have a cheap plastic kiddie pool that we fill up with water in the spring and rotate our logs through, using cinder blocks to hold the logs underwater.

After soaking the logs, stack them as before, slightly off the ground, but this time make sure to allow at least three or four inches between logs. Within a week, you should see small mushrooms popping out of the log. The mushrooms grow very fast, so check them at least once a day and break them off, stem and all, when most of the mushrooms are fully grown, but the edges of the caps are still slightly rolled under.

If you can't use the mushrooms right away, store them in the fridge for later. Before eating, tap each mushroom on your hand to knock small beetles out from between the gills, but don't bother to wash them unless they're covered in dirt. Pull off the stems of shiitake mushrooms, and cut off the bottom inch of oyster mushrooms. Then tear the mushroom caps into strips with your fingers and cook them in omelets, soups, or alone.

Mushroom logs need at least a month after being soaked before they will fruit a second time. If you inoculated a dozen logs, you can soak three logs every week and have homegrown mushrooms to pluck throughout the fruiting season. Here's where labeling the logs comes in handy—you could soak logs 1, 2, and 3 the first week, 4, 5, and 6 the next week, and so forth, using the labels to make sure each log gets its month of rest before being asked to fruit again.

Oyster and shiitake mushrooms have seasons just like garden vegetables do, and you can't force them to fruit if it's too hot or too cold. Oyster mushrooms prefer the cool, damp weather of spring and fall, and you can buy shiitake mushroom strains that like cold weather or warm weather. If you play your cards right, you could eat homegrown mushrooms from March to December.

## Lower-work mushroom harvests

If it seems too complex to rotate your mushrooms through a kiddie pool each week, you might decide to try out mushroom totems. "Plant" your mushroom log with about a third of its length underground and the log will soak up water from the soil when it rains. You'll get a lot of mushrooms all at once rather than spaced through the year, but mushrooms are easy to freeze or dry for later.

Totems in a damp spot are a lower-work option for those who don't mind seasonal harvests.

Mushroom totems can be a bit problematic in dry weather since the logs will often fruit right above the ground, meaning you end up with dirty mushrooms. To counteract this, you might want to "plant" your totems where your gray-water system overflows and wets the soil, or under the overhang of a gutterless roof. It may help to lay down mulch around the base of your totems to prevent dirty water from splashing up onto the mushrooms.

## Mycoremediation

Fungi help fruit trees grow, expedite decomposition of woody organic matter, and taste great in omelets, but their benefits don't stop there. Scientists have also discovered that mushrooms are capable of cleaning up our messes, a process known as mycoremediation. If you have a contamination issue on your homestead, you might want to use mushrooms to solve the problem.

Mycologists like Tradd Cotter and Paul Stamets have found fungal species that can chow down on *Escherichia coli* and *Salmonella*, suck up lead, mercury, arsenic, and other heavy metals, and break down chemicals into nontoxic compounds. The trick to using mushrooms to deal with these contaminants is to find the right species for your problem. For example, morels and puffballs are great at absorbing heavy metals, but they won't touch coliform bacteria with a ten-foot pole. Luckily, King Stropharia and turkey tails fill that niche. Oyster mushrooms can break down 80 percent of DDT in twenty-eight days, and the aptly named "Train Wrecker" fungus can eat through railroad ties impregnated with CCA (copper-chromium-arsenic).

You have to think a little differently to grow mycoremediators compared to raising edible mushrooms for the dinner plate. Fungi won't be breaking down much DDT while the mycelium is putting its energy into producing mushrooms, so you want to keep your mycoremediators actively growing rather than changing over to fruiting mode. That means you want to keep adding more substrate so that the fungus doesn't hit a wall and figure it's time to sent its kids off to explore a larger environment.

In general, you can eat the mushrooms that grow as part of the mycoremediation process, since fungi break most contaminants down into nontoxic byproducts. However, heavy metals accumulate in fungi, so you won't want to consume mushrooms grown on colored paper or similarly polluted organic matter.

# Bees

**GOAL**: Provide habitat for native bees, encouraging pollination
**COST**: $0–$30
**TIME**: 1 hour to 3 hours
**DIFFICULTY**: Easy
**KID-FRIENDLY**: Yes

The greater bee fly is a common pollinator in diverse orchards.

The majority of our fruits and vegetables depend on insects to pollinate their flowers. This week's project will make your homestead a conducive spot for native bees so that your garden grows beautiful, copious fruits.

# Pollinator 101

Bumblebees are important early spring pollinators since they can fly during cold, wet weather that keeps other bees at home. Bumblebees are also big and strong enough to force their way into legume flowers, reaching pollen that smaller bees can't access.

Grains like corn spread their pollen from flower to flower on the wind, but most fruits and vegetables instead depend on bees, butterflies, wasps, moths, beetles, and flies to ensure the pollen gets where it's needed. We often take the work of these inconspicuous garden helpers for granted, but the results of poor pollination are all around us. Have you ever picked blackberries in which only a few of the juicy kernels were developed? Does your garden produce cucumbers with a stunted, pointy end, or does your apple tree grow lopsided fruit? All three of these problems are the result of flowers that didn't get pollinated all the way.

Most farmers turn to honeybees to ensure optimal pollination of their crops, and I'll include a section at the end of this chapter for those of you who want to start your own hive. However, honeybees are a long-term commitment and can be difficult to raise organically in this modern era of varroa mites and colony collapse disorder.

Instead, gardeners interested in boosting their populations of pollinators will do well to focus on native bees, since these fuzzy pollinators actively gather pollen and are the most efficient pollinators for most crops. Some fruits and vegetables are more picky—for example, carrots are only pollinated by flies—but the tricks you'll use to make sure wild bees thrive in your yard will also give other types of native pollinators food and shelter. The flowers you plant can feed honeybees as well if you decide to become a keeper of cultivated bees, and a healthy pollinator population tends to keep pest insects at bay. Finally, your family and neighbors are bound to enjoy the beautiful flowers in your pollinator garden.

## Choosing flowers for bees

Echinacea, also known as purple coneflower, attracts butterflies and other pollinators.

Bees and other types of native pollinators need a copious supply of nectar- and pollen-rich flowers that bloom from early spring until late fall. While your fruits and vegetables provide flowers for some of this time, native pollinator populations will plummet if there are major lulls between blooming periods. A simple way to make sure there are bees around when you need them is to plant flowerbeds near your garden to fill in any months when garden plants aren't blooming.

Your first step is to figure out which flowers your bees already enjoy and when those plants bloom. As you pay attention over the course of the next year, you'll probably start to notice that your most ornamental selections—like modern roses—don't attract many pollinators, while less conspicuous flowers (often in the rose, carrot, or mint families) are swarming with life. Some common garden plants that native bees love include the following:

| Spring | Summer | Fall |
|---|---|---|
| • almonds | • alfalfa | • asters |
| • blueberries | • coneflowers | • boneset |
| • borage (continues to bloom in the summer) | • basil | • goldenrod |
| • cherries | • bee balm (if you're adding new bee plants to your garden, the related wild bergamot and spotted beebalm are even more attractive to bees than the red variety commonly grown in gardens) | • ironweed |
| • clover (continues to bloom in the summer) | | • Joe Pye weed |
| • mustard (continues to bloom in the summer) | | • mountain mint |
| • peaches | | • sneezeweed |
| • plums | | • wingstem |
| • radishes (continue to bloom in the summer) | • buckwheat | |
| • roses (continue to bloom in the summer) | • cosmos (continues to bloom in the fall) | |
| • rosemary | • lavender | |
| • squill | • Mexican sunflowers | |
| • vetch (continues to bloom in the summer) | • mint (spearmint and native wild mint are two of the best species) | |
| | • oregano | |
| | • partridge peas | |
| | • Russian sage | |
| | • stonecrop (continues to bloom in the fall) | |
| | • sunflowers (continue to bloom in the fall) | |
| | • sweet marjoram | |

For best results, make sure you have at least three types of plants blooming in your garden for each of the three bee seasons—spring, summer, and fall. You'll notice that none of the garden plants is a major fall bloomer, but weedy edges often contain the fall-blooming species listed above.

## Expanding your bee flowers

In addition to filling in any temporal gaps in your bee garden, you should look at the spatial design of your homestead from a bee's point of view. Large bees (like bumblebees) can fly a mile or more in search of food, but tiny sweat bees will travel 600 feet or less. For best results, you'll want to scatter your bee flowers throughout the garden, preferably growing clumps of the same species of flower that are at least three feet in diameter to make these snacks more visible from the air. Connecting large patches with smaller corridors or floral "stepping stones" will help draw native pollinators into the center of your garden.

Although the project is beyond the scope of the average weekend homesteader, some of you might choose to plant an entire pollinator meadow. The first step is to lay down a heavy kill mulch and leave it in place for twelve months to kill off all perennials. Then seed wildflowers that bloom from spring until fall, mixing in at least one native warm-season bunch grass. The meadow will need a bit of TLC as the plants get established, but then maintenance can be as simple as mowing at a height of 12 to 16 inches once or twice a year to make sure trees and weeds don't invade. Wildflower meadows can often be slipped into otherwise "unusable land," such as the ground on top of your septic field or along fence lines.

## Nesting habitat for bees

In addition to growing food for wild pollinators, you can help them out by providing spots for bees to nest and overwinter. Leaving wild, weedy areas alone can do a lot of this work for you, but it's also fun to create a few nest sites to draw bees closer to your kitchen window where you can enjoy their bright colors and interesting behavior.

Many wild bees nest in the ground, digging tunnels into bare patches of earth in dry, sunny spots. Bee enthusiasts usually let ground-nesting bees fend for themselves, since it's tough to create optimal habitat for ground nesters to move into. However, if you notice little bees flying up out of the ground during the spring or summer, you should mark the spot and leave it alone, making sure you don't lay down a mulch or till up the soil in that area.

Bumblebees like to nest in dry cavities about the size of a shoe-box on or under the ground. You can build bumblebee boxes, but an easier way to give these cute pollinators a home is to allow grass to grow up high in one area. During the fall and winter, the tall grass will naturally bend over and create cavities which mice and voles will move into; then bumblebees will reuse the rodent nests in the spring.

Finally, about a third of our native bee species nest in small tunnels bored out by beetles in dead or dying trees, branches, or twigs. These bees are the easiest to provide habitat for using one of the methods outlined below:

A piece of scrap two-by-four can be turned into a nesting site for wild bees.

**Wooden block.** Take a scrap piece of two-by-four, approximately 8 inches long, and drill four to six holes in one end. The holes should range between 3/32 and 5/8 of an inch in diameter, with the smaller holes extending 3 to 5 inches into the wood and the larger holes extending 5 to 6 inches deep. Make sure that the holes don't go all the way through your block of wood, since bees will only nest in dead-end tunnels. For best results, use a sharp drill bit that leaves the insides of the holes as smooth as possible; then blacken the entrance either by charring the wood lightly with a propane torch (or in your woodstove) or by spraying on black paint. Attach the nest block to the east side of a visible landmark (like your house, a fence post, etc.), and if you want, add a small awning to prevent rain from flowing in the holes. A simpler alternative to this method is to simply drill holes in an existing stump or snag in your yard, or you can use a big chunk of firewood instead of store-bought lumber. If you make more than one nest block, space them at least 25 feet apart around your garden.

Drill a hole most of the way through a six-inch piece of twig to invite bees to lay their eggs inside.

**Stem bundle.** Cut bamboo or hollow weeds with the same dimensions listed above (3/32 to 5/8 of an inch interior diameter, 3 to 6 inches long). If possible, cut right below a node, so the end of each stem is plugged on one side; if there's no node, you can close up the end with mud. Another alternative is to use sections of elderberry, sumac, or chinaberry twigs and drill out the pith for most of the length. Tie four to six stems together into a bundle and hang them horizontally in your garden.

You can build (or buy) larger nest blocks, but doing so congregates bees in one spot and risks spreading diseases and pests through the native bee populations. If you choose this route, read *Attracting Native Pollinators* by the Xerces Society to learn management techniques that will ensure these larger nest blocks help your pollinator populations rather than harm them.

# Honeybees

Raising a hive of honeybees will ensure your crops get pollinated and that your meals are sweet.

When native bees are managed well, they are just as effective pollinators as honeybees, and sometimes give even better results. However, honeybees produce delicious honey vastly superior to any you can find in the store, so you might choose to nurture a hive for the same reason you'd keep a milk cow. The specifics of raising honeybees are beyond the scope of this book, but here are some tips for beginners:

**Finding free bees.** Getting started with a hive of bees will cost around $200 if you buy all the equipment and bees. Some state extension services have grants available that will pay part or all of these start-up costs. Another alternative is to learn how to catch a swarm and then build a top-bar hive to house them—if you're handy, this method of raising bees can cost little or nothing.

**Learning about bee biology.** Honeybees live in complex colonies with a single queen, thousands of workers, and a variable number of drones (males). Understanding how the hive works is essential to raising healthy bees, so you'll want to read a beginning beekeeper book or take a class. Many areas have local beekeeping groups, and if you're lucky, you might find a mentor to take you under his wing and teach you the ropes.

**Raising healthy bees.** You've probably heard of colony collapse disorder, but did you know that your bees can also die from varroa mites, foulbrood, and a range of other illnesses? Modern methods of keeping bees in Langstroth hives (the tall, rectangular boxes you most often see in apiaries) and of trucking large colonies of bees from field to field have promoted the spread of these diseases. In addition, pesticides on farms up to eight miles away can negatively affect your hive. If you want to raise healthy bees without regularly dosing the hive with chemicals of your own, a good place to start is by researching Warre and top-bar hives and by talking your neighbors into excluding the pesticides from their repertoire.

No matter which steps you take to boost your pollinator population, don't forget to keep your eyes open as the spring flowers unfurl. Maybe you'll see metallic green sweat bees and hummingbirdlike sphinx moths and fall in love with native pollinators for their own sake.

# Learn to enjoy
# what you've got

**GOAL**: Find joy in the journey of homesteading
**COST**: $0
**TIME**: 2 hours
**DIFFICULTY**: Hard
**KID-FRIENDLY**: Yes

When you look out your kitchen window, do you notice a beautiful peach tree in full bloom, or do you fixate on the area that you never got around to weeding and mulching? Can you enjoy time spent with your family, or do you wish your spouse would go back to work and get out of your hair? The goal of this week's exercise is to find beauty in your daily life and to remember that the best part of homesteading is the journey, not the destination.

## *Taking yourself with you*

A decade ago, I spent an entire year backpacking through the wild areas of the United Kingdom, Australia, and Costa Rica. My explorations were funded by a generous fellowship that asked nearly nothing from me—just a one-page report every three months and an accounting of how I'd spent their money at the end of the year. I got to camp out under the stars, see howler monkeys and Tasmanian devils up close, and learn about new cultures.

When I tell people about my experience, they tend to get starry-eyed. "How can I get a fellowship like that?" they ask. "You must have had the time of your life!"

The sad truth is that as much as I enjoyed parts of my adventure, I also spent quite a few nights crying myself to sleep. I was a shy 21-year-old, and it hurt to be cut off from my family and friends. It was also tough to spend so much time with myself—with no job to sidetrack me, I did a lot of soul-searching and was often melancholy.

Homesteading is a lot like my previous adventure. When you spend all afternoon weeding the garden, any problems you have are eventually going to float up to the top of your mind and leave you in emotional pain. Meanwhile, working on a project together is the surest way to bring those issues with your spouse out into the open. In the end, you take yourself with you on the homesteading adventure, and if you're not happy with who you are, you really might be better off working a full-time job and sedating yourself with television in the evenings.

But if you're willing to find joy in yourself and in your daily life, homesteading can be one of the most amazing experiences you've ever lived through. After five years on the farm, my husband and I have become a nearly seamless team, and an afternoon spent working by his side feels like the best date ever. I looked up one day in the middle of year four and realized that I was content at a depth I'd not felt since leaving grade school. You can achieve bliss on your homestead too.

## *Enjoying the adventure*

So, how do you make sure your homesteading adventure is a gift rather than a drag? The answer depends on your homesteading Achilles' heel.

My problem was my overachieving nature that never allowed me to relax if there was any work left to be done. Let me break it to you—on a homestead, there's always work left to be done. Folks with my Achilles' heel tend to get off to a great start, build a gorgeous homestead within a few years, and then burn out and move back to the city. If you're a homesteading overachiever, your homework this week is to review last month's goal-making exercise and remind yourself how to take time off. Make yourself a cup of hot cocoa and go out and walk through your homestead, pet the goats, take two hundred photos of your apple tree, or find some other way to have fun without getting a lick of work done.

Another common complaint by ex-homesteaders is that the experience was extremely isolating. It's true that the further you delve into self-sufficiency, the more you set yourself apart from the consumerism of mainstream society. You may find it hard to figure out what to talk about with folks who spend their spare time playing Farmville instead of growing real carrots. Or maybe you just don't see people much anymore—after all, if you make your living on the farm and don't buy groceries, why would you need to head to town more than once or twice a month? Luckily, technology makes it easy to connect with folks down the road or across the world—websites like Meetup.com help people who share an interest get together, and several forums exist on homesteading-related topics if you'd rather chat online.

There are probably dozens of other reasons homesteaders give up on the lifestyle and start buying frozen dinners again. The trick is to find out what's holding you back, then think of a solution so that you can maintain your enthusiasm with growing your own food and simplifying your life.

This final exercise is probably the hardest one in the entire book but also the most essential to your success. So spend a couple of hours now reveling in the antics of your chickens or relaxing in the shade of your apple tree, then spend the rest of your life enjoying the fruits of your labor.

# Index

407